Ways of Sensing

Ways of Sensing is a stimulating exploration of the cultural, historical and political dimensions of the world of the senses. The book spans a wide range of settings and makes comparisons between different cultures and epochs, revealing the power and diversity of sensory expressions across time and space. The chapters reflect on topics such as the tactile appeal of medieval art, the healing power of Navajo sand paintings, the aesthetic blight of the modern hospital, the role of the senses in the courtroom and the branding of sensations in the marketplace. Howes and Classen consider how political issues such as nationalism, gender equality and the treatment of minority groups are shaped by sensory practices and metaphors. They also reveal how the phenomenon of synaesthesia, or mingling of the senses, can be seen as not simply a neurological condition but a vital cultural mode of creating social and cosmic interconnections. Written by leading scholars in the field, *Ways of Sensing* provides readers with a valuable and engaging introduction to the life of the senses in society.

David Howes is Professor of Anthropology and Director of the Centre for Sensory Studies at Concordia University, Montreal. His books include *The Varieties of Sensory Experience* (1991), *Cross-Cultural Consumption* (1996) and *Empire of the Senses* (2005).

Constance Classen is a cultural historian specializing in the body and the senses, and the director of an interdisciplinary research project on the senses in art and the museum. Her books include *Worlds of Sense* (1993), *The Color of Angels* (1998) and *The Deepest Sense* (2012).

Ways of Sensing

Understanding the senses in society

David Howes and Constance Classen

Routledge
Taylor & Francis Group

LONDON AND NEW YORK

For our mothers

First published 2014
by Routledge
2 Park Square, Milton Park, Abingdon, Oxon OX14 4RN

and by Routledge
711 Third Avenue, New York, NY 10017

Routledge is an imprint of the Taylor & Francis Group, an informa business

British Library Cataloguing in Publication Data
A catalogue record for this book is available from the British Library

Library of Congress Cataloguing in Publication Data
Howes, David, 1957–
Ways of sensing : understanding the senses in society/David Howes,
Constance Classen.
    pages cm
1. Senses and sensation–Social aspects. 2. Senses and sensation–History. 3.
Human body–Social aspects. I. Classen, Constance, 1957- II. Title.
BF233.H65 2013
152.1–dc23 2013024488

ISBN: 978-0-415-69714-9 (hbk)
ISBN: 978-0-415-69715-6 (pbk)
ISBN: 978-1-315-85603-2 (ebk)

Typeset in Bembo
by Taylor & Francis Books

Printed and bound in Great Britain by
CPI Group (UK) Ltd, Croydon, CR0 4YY

Contents

Acknowledgments

This book is the outcome of a quarter-century of research into the anthropology and history of the senses, which began in 1988 with 'The Varieties of Sensory Experience' project. Many people have assisted us along the way with their insights, advice and support. We are indebted to the members of the Centre for Sensory Studies, including our long-standing friend and collaborator Anthony Synnott, Bianca Grohmann, Chris Salter, Marc LaFrance, Aaron Johnson, Andra McCartney and Jordan LeBel, who together brought a stimulating range of disciplinary perspectives and a lively enthusiasm to the project of exploring the social life of the senses.

Other colleagues active in the field of sensory studies whose support for and commentaries on our work we deeply appreciate include Michael Bull, Fiona Candlin, Alain Corbin, Elizabeth Edwards, Kathryn Geurts, Michael Herzfeld, Laurence Kirmayer, Carolyn Korsmeyer, Richard Newhauser, Sally Promey, Herman Roodenburg, Mark Smith, Charles Spence, David Sutton and Mirko Zardini. Constance would also like to thank all the people who worked with her on the 'Cultural History of the Senses' book series (Classen forthcoming) and made abundantly evident the value of an historical approach to the senses. David appreciates the support of Fran Shaver, as well as of Nicholas Kasirer, Daniel Jutras and his colleagues in the Faculty of Law at McGill University. We both wish to thank the many people who have invited us to speak at their institutions and conferences and afforded us an opportunity to get the word out about sensory studies and to hear about diverse research initiatives in the field. Most recently these include Heather Tilley at Birkbeck, Alexandre Vincent at the Institut française de Rome, Dan Bender at the University of Toronto, Keizo Miyasaka at Keio University and Stefan Helmreich and Heather Paxson at MIT.

Ways of Sensing has also benefitted immensely from fieldwork trips to northwestern Argentina, the southwestern United States, British Columbia and Papua New Guinea. Our respective research in these sites enabled us to see sensory difference 'in action' and thus better understand it as a lived experience. We are very grateful to everyone who assisted us abroad, in particular Elsa Núñez de Battich and Viky Battich in Tucumán. At home our families supported our work with their interest, assistance and advice. Special thanks are due to Jonathan, Emma and George, and to our mothers, to whom this book is gratefully dedicated.

Our research into the different social domains – from art to medicine to marketing – covered in this book was funded in part by major grants from the Social Sciences and Humanities Research Council of Canada and the Fonds de recherché du Québéc – Société et Culture over the years, as well as by Concordia University, in particular the Office of the Vice-President Research and Graduate Studies, the Office of the Dean of Arts and Science and CUPFA. We would further like to thank our editors at Routledge, Lesley Riddle and Katherine Ong, for their strong support of this project, as well as the four anonymous reviewers who signalled its potential for consolidating and expanding the field of sensory studies. While this book is indeed the fruit of many years of research, we hope that it may also provide the seeds for much future research in the field.

Introduction

Ways and meanings

The ways we use our senses, and the ways we create and understand the sensory world, are shaped by culture. Perception is informed not only by the personal meaning a particular sensation has for us, but also by the social values it carries. We are perhaps best able to recognize this in the case of sight. Along with its physiological and practical importance, sight has a high cultural value in Western society. It has been exalted as a 'noble' sense and associated with both spiritual and intellectual enlightenment. The traditional link between vision and knowledge was enhanced when books and paintings became more commonplace after the Renaissance, and by the invention of photography and film in the nineteenth century. With the advent of televisions and personal computers in the twentieth century even more of our information about the world came to us through our eyes.

It is not only how, and how much, we see that is shaped by culture, however, it is also what we see. The subject matter of paintings reflects not only the preferences of artists and patrons, and not only the reigning artistic conventions, but also particular ideologies that support – or sometimes challenge – the social values and hierarchies of the day. In *Ways of Seeing*, John Berger argued that the convention of perspective, developed during the Renaissance, contributed to the growth of individualism in the West by centring everything on the eye of the observer. 'The visible world is arranged for the spectator as the universe was once thought to be arranged for God' (Berger 1972: 16). The viewer becomes the unique centre, pried loose, as it were, from the hierarchized, communal structure of the medieval social order.

Photographs, while appearing more value-neutral than paintings, also carry cultural messages by capturing certain scenes and leaving others unrecorded, or by portraying subjects so as to convey notions of power or weakness, amity or aggressivity, attractiveness or repulsion. Studies on bias in media photography have shown, for example, that in *The New York Times* foreign perpetrators of violence are consistently represented as more explicitly violent than US perpetrators. This fosters perceptions of foreigners being aggressive and dangerous (Fishman and Marvin 2003). In 1990 the Royal Ontario Museum came under attack by community groups for displaying colonial photographs that showed Africans as subservient to and dominated by Westerners without sufficient critical commentary or contrasting imagery. The assumption of some visitors was that the museum was upholding the racist values of the colonial era (Butler 2007). There are many instances of the apparent objectivity of photography being used to advantage by propagandists to influence the perception of events (Sturken and Cartwright 2009).

What is true of sight is also true of hearing. Like sight, hearing has a strong association with the intellect. This is due to the importance of speech as a means of communication. In fact, for many centuries the ability to hear and to speak was taken to be the prime indicator of an ability to reason. For this reason, the deaf were long treated as mentally incompetent in Western law and society.

Even aside from speech, sounds have meanings that can only be fully understood within their particular cultural context. Music is perhaps the best example of this. Certain themes will evoke particular concepts and emotions due to their cultural associations. To give a basic example from the modern West, Mendelssohn's Wedding March instantly conjures up images of marriage for most hearers while Chopin's Funeral March evokes funereal thoughts, even among those who are unaware of the titles of these pieces. (This ability of music to evoke old associations and create new ones is, of course, central to cinematic scoring.) A non-Westerner, however, could listen to these pieces without any such associations. Similarly, a Westerner listening to, for example, the music produced by the Desana people of the Colombian rainforest would have no cultural associations beyond, perhaps, 'exotic' or 'tribal'. However, for the Desana, different musical sounds and melodies carry definite meanings. In the case of one type of flute music: 'The melody is said to be of a merry kind and is associated with the image of a multitude of fish running upriver to the spawning beds. The vibrations produced by the sounds are said to trigger a message which refers to child-rearing' (Reichel-Dolmatoff 1981: 91). These are instances of sounds being invested with cultural significance, of 'ways of hearing'.

During a recent seminar on the History of the Senses at the University of Toronto, a graduate student interested in the auditory mix of European and indigenous 'soundways' in colonial Canada asked whether certain reactions to music are not universal. Doesn't a pounding beat always evoke a physiological response of excitement? Perhaps it usually does, but the degree of excitement will vary from one culture to another and from one period to another according to how accustomed people are to hearing such music and what it signifies for them. For example, in the 1960s the driving beat of Beatles' songs was often experienced as highly disturbing and attributed a vague cultural association with 'savagery'. Today, when early Beatles' songs seem rather charming and innocent to many people, it would even be possible to use one as a lullaby. Our ways of hearing that music have changed.

Particular practices of looking and listening are also shaped by cultural factors. In the modern classroom, the ability to remain still for long periods of time solely looking and listening is a prerequisite for academic success. In cultures in which education is a more active process involving all of the senses and bodily movement, looking and listening would only be one part of the educational process (see Bateson and Mead 1942 on kinaesthetic learning).

In eighteenth-century Paris, going to the opera to listen to the music was thought to be decidedly gauche. 'There is nothing so damnable,' one nobleman declared, 'as listening to a work like a street merchant or some provincial just off the boat' (cited in Johnson 1996: 31). The assumption was that upper-class Parisians were so familiar with musical conventions that they need scarcely attend to performances. What required listening to and watching instead were the conversations that took place and the appearance and movements of the fashionable crowd.

The invention of the telephone, the radio and sound-recording devices enhanced both our power of hearing and the number of things to listen to. Such modern media of communication as film, television and computers bring both sight and sound together to present sensorially-limited but culturally and psychologically powerful representations of the world. Indeed, so accustomed have we become to audiovisual representations that we almost take this pairing of sound and sight as given in nature, rather than by culture and technology. Olfactory-visual or audio-gustatory pairings would hardly seem as convincing.

That sight and hearing, the two most highly valued senses in the West, are mediated by culture may perhaps be readily appreciated. The notion of 'the period eye' and 'the educated listener' are commonplace. To what extent, however, can the senses of touch, taste and smell model and transmit cultural values? This is a subject that has been far less often considered, primarily because cognition is not usually associated with the 'lower' senses in modern culture. Indeed, one clear sign of the cultural importance of sight and hearing in our society is the sheer volume of academic and scientific work dedicated to the exploration of these senses compared to the vastly-reduced interest in the study of the other senses.

To what extent are touch, taste and smell worthy of extended cultural consideration? We know they are of great practical importance and that they afford us sensations of pleasure and pain, but they are typically represented as subjective and private – *chacun à son goût*. Do they have any cognitive value? Can thought be based on tactile sensations, for example? For most of Western history the standard answer would have been no. A person born blind and deaf was generally 'supposed incapable of any understanding, as wanting all those senses which furnish the human mind with ideas' (Rapalje 1887: 3). We now know, however, that this is incorrect. As the deaf-blind Helen Keller famously demonstrated in the early twentieth century, it *is* possible to experience a socially and symbolically-meaningful world through touch, smell and taste alone and to communicate and think using tactile sign language.

There is no reason to think that this ability to transmit and receive ideas through the so-called lower senses is restricted to those who lack the senses of sight and hearing. In fact, it is the contention of this book that ideas are communicated through sensory impressions all the time. There are culturally-modulated ways of touching, tasting and smelling and culturally-meaningful textures, tastes and smells. Within every field of social endeavour, explicit or implicit significance is ascribed to different sensations and sensory practices, whether visual and auditory, or tactile, olfactory and gustatory.

Sense and polysemy

The significance of a sensory act is not necessarily unitary. The way in which a doctor touches a patient during a physical examination, for example, may be taken as primarily a data-gathering process or may have personal meaning for the participants ('This doctor has a caring touch'). However, as we will examine in the chapter on medicine, it also has a particular social history and an important symbolic significance.

Even sensory acts that have recognized social functions have many shades of meaning. A handshake may be variously interpreted as a gesture of friendliness, an attempt to dominate, an act of condescension, an invitation to intimacy, a show of equality, a bridging of differences, the sealing of a contract, or a breach of etiquette. When the Australian Prime Minister Julia Gillard shook hands with Queen Elizabeth II instead of curtsying she was technically committing a breach of etiquette. Within the cultural context of Australia's former status as a British colony, however, what might seem like a simple social gaffe was instead an important symbolic gesture of equality and modernity. When Queen Elizabeth shook hands with a former commander of the Irish Republican Army, the act had very different connotations: it was seen as a dramatic act of reconciliation, 'the ultimate handshake' between persons representing two old enemies.

If the eighteenth-century wit Sydney Smith is a reliable guide, a considerable variety of handshaking styles and significations existed in his day. The 'high official' handshake consisted of 'a rapid short shake, near the chin', in the clerical handshake only one finger was held out, while in the 'rustic handshake', 'your hand is seized in an iron grasp, betokening rude health, warm heart and a distance from the Metropolis; but producing a sense of relief on your part when you find your hand released and your fingers unbroken' (cited in Classen 2005a: 16) The range of connotations that can be communicated by a simple handshake demonstrates that tactile acts are not simply the physical labour that allows us to engage in other socially meaningful acts, such as writing books or creating art, but potentially highly meaningful in themselves (see further Gregory 2011; Smith 2008).

Another reason to attend to the full range of sensory experience and expression is that cultures differ in the emphases they place on different senses and the meanings they give to different sensory acts. This difference can affect peoples' perceptions at a very basic level. In the West, for example, the sun has traditionally been seen above all as a source of light. However, the Tzotzil of Mexico, who emphasize thermal values in their culture, think of the sun pre-eminently as a source of heat, and even call it 'Our Father Heat' (Classen 1993a: 122–26). The Batek Negrito of peninsular Malaysia, who classify virtually everything in their environment by smell, say that the sun has a bad smell, 'like that of raw meat', in contrast to the moon, which has a good smell, 'like that of flowers' (Endacott 1979: 39)

These are particularly striking examples. However, such sensory variation in emphasis and meaning can occur in many subtler ways across cultures, as well. To return to the example of the handshake, in Japan, where non-contact greetings are the rule, the handshake, when performed, is usually done limply. This might well be misinterpreted by a Westerner as signifying weakness, but is in fact a sign of social tact, conveying respect for the other person's bodily boundaries. In countries in which a kiss is a customary social greeting, a mere handshake may seem cold and even offensive. While French President Jacques Chirac bestowed a Gallic kiss on most of the leaders at the Franco-African Summit in 2003, he greeted the Zimbabwean dictator Robert Mugabe with only a lukewarm handshake, signifying France's displeasure with his regime. These kinds of nuances in 'body language' require a full-bodied approach to be properly recognized and interpreted.

So-called lower sensations, in fact, are essential to the investigation of the senses in society. With the exception of the purified audiovisual worlds of modern media, touches and smells and savours are experienced together with sights and sounds. Sensations reinforce each other, play off each other and, at times, contradict each other – as when something that looks heavy feels light or when something that smells delicious turns out to taste disgusting. They are part of an interactive web of experience, rather than each being slotted into a separate sensory box.

The term 'ways of sensing', as used here, underscores the plurality of sensory practices in different cultures and historical periods – way*s* – and the processual nature of perception – sens*ing*. We also intend the term to draw attention to the manifold relations among the different senses, which can be called 'intersensoriality' (see Howes 2005a: 9–10; Smith 2007: 125–28).

This brings us to another key point. Equally significant to the ways in which the senses are practiced are the ways in which a society decides that they should *not* be used: when and what we must *not* see, or touch, or taste. Due to the low status of the 'lower' senses, when such prohibitions concern these senses they often attract little attention in Western society. Does it matter that we can't touch in the museum if we can supposedly learn all that is worth knowing about art through our eyes? Let us begin, however, by at least acknowledging that in certain cases, such as that of the museum, ways of seeing are also ways of not touching. Then let us consider, as we shall in the chapter on art, what such constraints signify, how they arose, what sensory and social formations they favour and what information they withhold.

The politics of the senses

To say that perception is shaped by culture and that society regulates how and what we sense is also to say that there is a politics of the senses. Our ways of sensing affect not only how we experience and engage with our environment, but also how we experience and engage with each other. This is clearly seen when we examine sensory values and practices in relationship to values and practices concerning gender, class and ethnicity, as we shall in Chapter 3. From the dominant male perspective in the West, women have been perceived as desirable to see and touch and hear, but also dangerous. Women were considered morally dangerous because of the temptation to sin they presented, intellectually dangerous because their sensuality threatened masculine rationality, and even physically dangerous, because a woman's seductive touch might sap a man's physical powers. Biblical and mythological accounts expressed and promoted this view: Samson losing his great strength as a result of Delilah's seductions, John the Baptist losing his head as a result of Salome's dance, or Ulysses and his men being turned into animals by the sorceress Circe. Even the pre-eminent exemplar of male rationality, Aristotle, was depicted by legend as losing his rationality when he allowed the beautiful Phyllis to bridle him and ride on his back.

In Western tradition, the sight, sound and touch of men were also understood to be desired by and dangerous for women. However, as men held the dominant position within society, it was the masculine perspective that held sway and was endlessly reproduced in stories and pictures, and supported by religious, legal and social codes. Thus, we find many regulations concerning the containment of women. The closeting of women and their sensoriality was imagined to take care of several problems at once: it removed a dangerous temptation from men's sight and touch, it protected women from masculine desires and from their own sensual passions, and it prevented women from challenging male dominance. One who is not supposed to speak in public or be seen on the street, who is not allowed to hold religious or political office or attend university, will find it difficult to effectively contest her social status.

Women were traditionally adjured to keep their eyes downcast, their hearing guarded, their movements restricted and to generally limit their interaction with the outside world. In a sixteenth-century poem called 'Rule for Women to Brynge Up Their Daughters' the penalties for infringing these restrictions are drastic.

> If they wyll go or gad abrode,
> Their legges let broken bee:
> Put out their eyes if they wyll looke
> Or gase undecentyle.
>
> (cited by Hull 1982: 76)

Cocooned within the home, women were expected to engage in housework associated with the senses of touch, taste and smell while men went out and saw the world.

In the contemporary West it is easy to forget for how long and to what extent women were bundled out of sight and hearing in this way: concealed within the home and metaphorically, when not physically, veiled outside of it. An example of the extent to which women might be hidden away even in the modern West can be found in nineteenth-century Lima (as well as in certain towns of southern Spain), where the traditional wearing of the *saya y manto*, or petticoat and head shawl, left a woman swathed from head to foot with only one eye showing to allow her to find her way around.

The use of sensory symbols to characterize groups perceived as potentially threatening to the social order is widespread. The first part of the process involves rendering a social group 'invisible' by keeping it sequestered, by restricting its opportunities, by limiting its representation and by simply ignoring its presence. The 'absent' group is then represented by simple and potent symbols: the beautiful but corrupt seductress; the coarse, malodorous worker; the greasy, slippery foreigner; and so on.

Social groups can contest their sensory typing and challenge the boundaries of their social containment. This can happen outright, as when a group demands that its voice be heard, or, more subtly, by manipulating symbols and constraints to a group's own advantage. In the sixteenth century, the humanist Lucrezia Marinella took the sensory symbols that were used to characterize women as weak and irrational and gave them new meanings. Women's softness, she said, was not a sign of mental weakness, but rather of their ability to assimilate impressions and information (Classen 2012: 73–74). In nineteenth-century Lima, women used the *saya y manto* to bypass the formalities of an elaborate and constricting toilette and to move and speak freely in public spaces without being recognized: 'She puts on her *saya* without corset ... hides her face with her *manto*, and sets out for wherever she wishes' (Tristan 1993: 31). With the one eye that remained uncovered, such women, it was said, gazed at the men in the streets with 'the impudence of an impenetrable incognito' (Wood 1849: 89).

As some observers noted, this disguise enabled women to arrange assignations almost under the very eyes of their unsuspecting husbands (von Tschudi 1847: 98). Consternation and/or fear of women acting freely without proper male supervision led to edicts being issued against the custom as productive of immorality. However, women in Lima long held onto their *saya y manto* for the liberties it allowed them within a male-dominated society. A practice that was originally intended to guard women's senses and sensuality, therefore, ended up being subverted and deployed for precisely the opposite ends.

Corporeality and culture

Attending to the symbolic power of sensation should not distract us from its corporeality: the warmth of a touch, the pungency of an odour, the brightness of a vision. What makes sensations so forceful is that they are lived experiences, not intellectual abstractions. The Tzotzil *feel* the power of 'Our Father Heat' every morning when the sun rises and warms the cold highlands where they live. A handshake between two former enemies not only symbolizes unity, it is itself a tangible union. Even when sensory references are metaphorical they call up deep physical associations. When the Tzotzil speak of religious rituals as 'hot', they express the perceived power of those rituals through a metaphor that resonates on a basic physical level (Classen 1993a: 124).

Each of the senses has its own particular characteristics. Touch is intimate and reciprocal: when we touch someone, that person feels our touch. Sight, by contrast, operates at a distance and requires no physical interaction. Compared to touch, which *attaches* one body to another, sight is detached. Sound, in turn, is dynamic. We can see things that are completely still, but when we hear something we know that an activity is taking place. There are no still sounds. These different characteristics affect how the senses are used and ascribed meanings in different cultural contexts. In a society that emphasizes detachment and objectivity, sight will likely have a high value and touch may well be viewed with suspicion for its boundary-blurring properties. It would be simplistic to leave it at that, however, for much more is involved in the production of ways of sensing. Cultures elaborate and extend the senses in different directions, as we shall see in the pages that follow. The meaning of the senses is in their use, and usage is everywhere informed by culture. Nevertheless, physical considerations also play a role in how the senses are ranked and understood, and should not be overlooked.

Cultural and personal associations, in turn, affect our physical perceptions. When a metaphorical malodour is associated with a particular social group, people may experience members of that group as actually having a bad smell, even though no distinctive odour is present. Even members of the group being stigmatized may experience themselves as 'bad-smelling' and purchase perfumes to 'upgrade' their sensory and social status (Largey and Watson 2006). Sensory associations can be very persuasive.

We can find this associative process happening on a small scale with many of the minor discriminations we make and preferences we show in daily life. For example, taste tests comparing Coca-Cola to Pepsi have shown that people who express a pronounced preference for one of the two are often unable to distinguish between them when unidentified. Yet, when they know what they are drinking, they affirm that Pepsi (or Coke) tastes better. Clearly, non-gustatory factors are playing a role here. These may include the association of a particular drink with good or bad experiences, the influence of accompanying elements such as packaging design or advertising jingles, and the social values a drink appears to embody. While these factors themselves have no taste, they inflect the experience of taste when brought into play. While the sensuality of perception should not be forgotten in the search for sensory meaning, it is important to keep in mind that the experience of that sensuality is itself shaped by diverse personal and cultural associations.

Phenomenology and psychology of perception

Our own sensory experience provides an essential basis for exploring ways of sensing. However, it is inadequate to rely solely on personal experience for understanding how people everywhere perceive the world. While humans share the same basic sensory capacities, these are developed and understood in different ways. Some of this diversity is based on individual differences, such as the ear training a musician undergoes, but much of it is the consequence of general social conditioning. In the West, as a result of widespread literacy and the importance of visual imagery, we are all given extensive eye-training. Vision is a field of 'productive specialization' (Ong 1991).

In an experiment involving a pair of perceptual tests, Mallory Wober (1991 [1967]) found that Western subjects performed better than African subjects on tests involving visual discrimination but poorer than the African subjects on tests involving proprioceptive discrimination (i.e., knowledge of bodily position). He related the difference in performance to the differential elaboration of the visual and auditory-proprioceptive sensory registers in the two cultures. In Western culture, Wober noted, visual attention has been extensively developed.

> However, Temne and other West African cultures include an elaboration of the proprioceptively and aurally perceived world. Thus, music is an extension of speech, rhythm an extension of movement, beauty a function of grace of movement as much as of configuration of visage, and dance is a regular and favoured form of elaboration of activity, started at an early age.
>
> (Wober 1991 [1967]: 33)

Wober's point concerning how sensory orientations vary across cultures and how contrasting orientations may foster the development of different perceptual skills has been borne out by subsequent research in the field (Chernoff 1981; Geurts 2002; Lamp 2004; Berry et al. 2011: ch. 9).

One particularly influential philosophical approach to the study of the senses is the phenomenology of perception. In this approach the corporeal experience of one particular person – or of one particular person in consultation with like-minded colleagues – is extended to apply to all people everywhere. Such an approach cannot do more than sketch a crude picture of human sensoriality, a picture in which the biases of the phenomenologist will be apparent to anyone coming from a different culture of sensation. In their effort to arrive at a 'prereflective' understanding of our being in the world, phenomenologists leave all the essentialist presuppositions about the 'nature' of the senses that have currency in our culture unquestioned and intact.

There are other critiques one can make of the phenomenology of perception, such as its obliviousness to the politics of perceptual practice, or its preoccupation with language. Michel Serres, author of *Les cinq sens* (1985), had this to say in conversation with Bruno Latour about the fixation on language in the work of Maurice Merleau-Ponty:

> When I was young, I laughed a lot at Merleau-Ponty's *Phenomenology of Perception*. He opens it with these words: 'At the outset of the study of

perception, we find in language the notion of sensation ... ' Isn't this an exemplary introduction? A collection of examples in the same vein, so austere and meagre, inspire the descriptions that follow. From his window the author sees some tree, always in bloom; he huddles over his desk; now and again a red blotch appears – it's a quote. What you can decipher in this book is a nice ethnology of city-dwellers, who are hypertechnicalized, intellectualized, chained in their library chairs, and tragically stripped of any tangible experience. Lots of phenomenology and no sensation – everything via language ... My book *Les cinq sens* cries out at the empire of signs.

(cited in Connor 2005: 318)

True to his word, Serres places corporeal experience itself in the forefront of the phenomenology of perception and, in *The Five Senses* (translated into English in 2008), finds philosophical significance in even so minor an experience as that of cutting his fingernails. He is particularly eloquent when it comes to evoking all the ways he experiences the senses as 'knotted' with each other and mingling with the world. Yet, even this move away from description and towards sensation (physical experience) cannot overcome the limitations of subjective analysis. Indeed, the social is absent from Serres' account. This contrasts with the critical social perspective on embodiment which a number of anthropologists have developed in the course of their fieldwork (i.e. Laderman 1994; Desjarlais 1992, 2003; Stoller 1997; Geurts 2002; Hahn 2007; Romberg 2009)

This is not to say that the phenomenology of perception has no value nor any relevance to anthropology. Phenomenology may be highly informative of a particular approach to the world and it may speak to many people who have had similar experiences. However, it cannot speak for all peoples everywhere.

Traditionally, the study of human perception has been seen as falling within the domain of psychology. (Our earliest books on the senses were classified as psychology even though they had the words 'anthropology' and 'history' in their titles.) Through experimentation, psychologists have explored, among other issues, how the processing of sensory stimuli enables individuals to apprehend and interact with the world. The psychology of perception, however, suffers from the same tendencies to disregard cultural factors and to universalize conclusions as the phenomenology of perception. Like phenomenology, psychological research customarily takes the experiences of urban Westerners as the norm. The authority of psychological research, the appeal of the seemingly clear-cut conclusions it can offer, together with the fact that it is usually addressed to readers who share the same general worldview, means that the sorts of ethnocentric simplifications to which it is prone often go unnoticed and unquestioned.

Pursuing a *cultural* approach to perception requires something more. As Kathryn Geurts states in her book *Culture and the Senses*, it requires

that certain concepts or principles deemed basic by many general psychologists be reexamined for the socially constructed, historically grounded, and culturally variable nature of their makeup. ... These so-called basics include concepts such as 'person' and 'situation' and also principles and processes such as 'representation', 'persuasion', 'knowledge-activation', and 'information-seeking' ... and to this list I would add sensing and perceiving.

(Geurts 2002: 15)

The final chapter of *Ways of Sensing* opens up such a re-examination. It focuses on a topic that is normally only treated within psychology – namely, synaesthesia, or the intermingling of sensations. Standard psychological and neuroscientific accounts of this phenomenon hold it to be a rare neurological condition that causes an affected individual to experience such 'irrational' sensory associations as tastes being linked to sounds or the letters of the alphabet having colours. Our work here reveals that, far from being solely a rare neurological condition, synaesthesia can function as a fundamental vehicle for the production of cultural meaning.

Anthropology and history of the senses

The study of the cultural formation of the senses has been led by anthropology and history. These two disciplines underwent a sensory turn in the last decades of the twentieth century (see, for example, Corbin 1986 [1982], 2005 [1990]; Stoller 1989, 1997; Howes 1991a, 2003: ch. 2; Classen 1993a, 2001). The task of sensory anthropology is to describe and analyse the practices and meanings that are constitutive of the life of the senses in particular societies. It also alerts us to the danger of generalizing across cultures. For example, when scholars such as Marshall McLuhan and Walter Ong began looking at the cultural and cognitive effects of different forms of media (which they defined as 'extensions of the senses') one of the primary distinctions they made was between literate and oral cultures (McLuhan 1962; Ong 1982). Literate cultures were said to be eye-minded, due to writing being a visual media, while oral cultures were said to emphasize the importance of hearing, as a result of the auditory nature of speech. When Western civilization changed from being primarily an oral culture to being a literate culture, it received 'an eye for an ear', as McLuhan famously put it (McLuhan and Fiore 1967: 44).

These observations were useful for breaking the silence surrounding cultural differences in sensory practices, however they were too simplistic. Anthropological research has since shown that just as much sensory variation can occur among oral cultures as between oral and literate cultures (Finnegan 2002; Classen 2005c). One oral society will place great importance on smell (Pandya 1993), another on balance (Geurts 2002). Some will give primacy to the sense of hearing (Feld 1990 [1982]), but there will also be those which place cultural emphasis on the sense of sight. For example, due in part to the religious importance of the visions they experience when taking hallucinogens, the Desana, though a traditional oral society, value sight above all the senses (Classen 1993a: ch. 6). It is precisely this kind of information, brought out by anthropologists and others attuned to sensory difference, that makes it clear that the 'sensory order' of any particular culture must be understood on its own terms (Geurts 2002: 5). Anthropologists must also be attentive to intracultural variation, for there are typically persons or groups who differ on the sensory values embraced by the society at large, and resist, instead of conform to, the prevailing sensory regime.

The history of the senses undertakes a similar examination to that of anthropology, but within the cultures of the past. It offers insights into the sensory worlds of earlier societies and what they meant to the people who inhabited them. It also investigates the factors prompting changes in sensory practices and priorities. This is important for several reasons. Bringing out the sensory dimensions of past cultures makes history more memorable and meaningful (Roeder 1994). It allows us a deeper understanding of how people lived and what motivated their actions (Smith 2007). For instance, to understand the significance of the handshake the rebel leader Wat Tyler gave King Richard II during the fourteenth-century Peasant's Revolt, it is necessary to recognize it as a travesty of the traditional medieval hand clasp, during which a vassal would submissively place his hands *in* the hands of his lord (Classen 2012: 6).

A possible limitation of anthropological studies of the senses is that they may make sensory orders seem static – always informed by the same values and promoting the same practices. The historical study of the senses shows us that sensory orders change over time, at the same time as it reveals the historical underpinnings of contemporary ways of sensing. Furthermore, learning about the sensory differences of the past can help to bridge cross-cultural differences in ways of sensing. When one realizes how important olfactory concepts such as the odour of sanctity and the stench of sin were in premodernity, for example, the attention paid to odour by certain non-Western peoples may no longer seem so unusual and 'exotic'.

Anthropologists have the advantage over historians in that through participant observation they can have first-hand experience of the sensory lives of the peoples they study (Pink 2009). Historians must make do with written accounts, visual images and material artefacts. Those who study more recent periods may also have the benefit of film and sound recordings. While much is inevitably missing from such sources, they can, nonetheless, provide a wealth of information about the sensory worlds of the past.

In this book a joint anthropological-historical methodology is used to explore the life of the senses in society. Rather than take a serial, 'sense-by-sense' approach, as is often done in studies of the senses, *Ways of Sensing* examines how the senses are employed in an array of social domains. These include: art, medicine, politics, law and marketing (or consumer culture). The advantage of this domain-based approach is that it enables us to bring out the dynamic interaction of sensations in a given context and thus contributes to a more holistic understanding of the sensorium.

Both the anthropology of the senses and the history of the senses have sometimes been characterized as subfields of their respective disciplines. It is the intention here to show how they can be relevant to the study of *any and all* cultural fields (see further Herzfeld 2001: 253; Robben and Slukka 2007: 388; Newhauser 2010). The ways in which we engage with art, in which we practice medicine, in which we experience our social roles and systems of justice, in which we manufacture and market products, and in which we make sense of the world, all involve particular ways of sensing.

The sociocultural approach to the study of the sensorium is no longer limited to anthropology and history. It has spread to sociology (e.g., Synnott 1993; Vannini et al 2011), geography (e.g., Pocock 1993; Rodaway 1994; Paterson 2009), urban studies (e.g., Zardini 2005; Degen 2008), archaeology (e.g., Skeates 2010; Day 2013), art history (e.g., Kahn 1999; Di Bello and Koureas 2010; Quiviger 2010), literature (Danius 2002; Hertel 2005; Cohen 2009) and media studies (e.g., L.U. Marks 2000; Finnegan 2002; Bull 2013) – to mention but a few of the disciplines that have converged on the sensorium in recent years. This coalescence has brought the monopoly formerly enjoyed by psychology to an end, and created the conditions for the emergence of a highly productive field called sensory studies (Bull et al. 2006). Sensory studies encompasses visual culture, auditory culture, smell culture, taste culture, the culture of touch and the interrelations among all these different registers, while leaving the door open to the discussion of other faculties (Howes 2009). By taking a cultural approach to the study of the senses and a sensory approach to the study of culture, *Ways of Sensing* aims to increase awareness of this dynamic new field and its interdisciplinary potential. While methodologies and theoretical frameworks may differ among scholars of sensory studies, the growing number of incisive investigations into the social life of the senses has made it clear that sense perception is not simply some pre-cultural, psycho-physical 'information-gathering' process. Our ways of sensing and making sense lie at, and indeed give form and life to, the heart of culture.

Part I
Art and Medicine

1 Mixed messages

Engaging the senses in art

The point that cannot be too strongly emphasized is that ... any information of which the spectator [of art] has need must be information that affects what he sees when he looks at the picture because it is only through what can be seen when the picture is looked at that the picture carries meaning.

Richard Wollheim, 'What the spectator sees',
in *Visual Theory: Painting and Interpretation* (1991)

In the early afternoon the patient is led in by the Chanter and seated in the middle of the painting. As the Chanter sings the prayers and the chorus joins in, he rubs sand from each part of the figures of the gods [in the sand painting] on the corresponding parts of the patient's body.

Margaret Schevill Link, *The Pollen Path: A Collection of Navajo Myths* (1998)

Canny exhibition curators, whose job it is to keep track of the *Zeitgeist* and respond to the popular taste, realized years ago that 'the senses' was a theme that could entice people of all ages and educational levels into the museums.

Robert Jütte, *A History of the Senses: From Antiquity to Cyberspace* (2005)

Viewing art

In the modern world, art is overwhelmingly visual. Whether it is considered an object of beauty, a work of genius, an historical artefact, a creative revelation, a valuable commodity, or a political statement, an artwork is assumed to be directed to the eyes. This is held to be true not only of flat paintings hanging on walls but also of three-dimensional sculptures, and, indeed, of all artefacts considered as aesthetic objects, whether Navajo sand paintings, Japanese tea bowls or Medieval tapestries. As soon as something is classified as art, its non-visual qualities are suppressed, and, as trained spectators, we know that the right thing to do is to stand back and look at it.

This single-sensed understanding of art, although it has deep roots in Western thought, only reached its full fruition in the modern period. Handmade and hands-on culture dominated in the pre-industrial world and art was part of that culture. The artist was a craftsman (or woman) and craftwork was appreciated by how it felt, as well as by how it looked. The intricately carved wood- and stonework of the Middle Ages speaks of this emphasis on tactile values. Paintings, as visually-oriented as they seem to us today, also partook of this hands-on culture. In fact, many paintings decorated objects that were meant to be handled, such as books and chests. The paintings themselves invited inquiring and desiring touches through their illusory representations of three-dimensional reality. Furthermore, in an era in which colours were attributed healing properties and in which brightly-dyed cloths were often expensive and rare, the rich colouring of paintings had a strong tactile appeal. People wanted hands-on contact with luxurious and powerful hues (Classen 2012: ch. 6). Touching religious images – which constituted a large part of premodern art – seemed to provide physical contact with the divine. This was an extension of the practice of touching saintly relics, which was believed to confer both good health and good fortune. The benefits to be gained by simply looking at a statue or a picture of a saint could not compare with the direct transfer of sacrality believed to be effected through a devout touch.

We find evidence of such tactile appreciation of art taking place not only in churches and private collections, but also in the early museums of the seventeenth and eighteenth centuries, such as the Ashmolean in Oxford and the British Museum in London. Some of this hands-on exploration was grounded in contemporary scientific notions of the importance of sensory investigation. According to the seventeenth-century empirical philosopher Robert Hooke, the range of qualities to be examined in an object included:

> Sonorousness or Dulness. Smell or Taste ... Gravity, or Levity. Coarseness, or Fineness. Fastness, or Looseness. Stiffness, or Pliableness. Roughness, or Brittleness. Claminess, or Slipperiness.
>
> (cited in Arnold 2003: 76)

Hooke, indeed, explicitly stated that 'ocular inspection' must be accompanied by the 'manual handling ... of the very things themselves' (cited in Arnold 2003: 76; see also Arnold 2006: 144; Candlin 2010: 67–68).

Empirically minded gallery goers took care to do just that. During his visits to European collections, the English diarist John Evelyn recorded a range of sensory interactions with artefacts. He shook a petrified egg to hear the yolk rattle and a crystal with water inside to see the water move. He lifted an antler to test its weight and he smelled scented wood from the Indies (Evelyn 1955: 471, 516 and *passim*). When applied to an artwork, such sensory investigations provided information not only about surface textures but also about the materials employed. (Investigating a piece of marble, one early curator of the Ashmolean, noted that 'when rub'd or scraped [it] yielded a strong ungrateful smell' [Arnold 2006: 56].) Clearly, just viewing museum objects would have been regarded as an insufficient means of acquiring information.

Some of the handling that took place in museums had aesthetic purposes, particularly in the case of sculpture. The sixteenth-century Florentine historian, Benedetto Varchi, stated that touch alone of the senses could appreciate the artistry of a sculpted work. In the eighteenth century, the German philosopher Johann Gottfried Herder argued that sculpture was the highest form of art precisely because it was perceptible to the sense of touch – a more aesthetic sense than sight, in his view, because of its intimacy and thoroughness (Herder 2002; Norton 1990: ch. 6, see further Nichols 2006; Johnson 2011). From this point of view, manacling the hands of modern museumgoers prevents them from experiencing art at its highest level. For the less sophisticated, a strong inducement to touching statues and paintings would have been their lifelike appearance. This 'reality effect' seemed to enable a museum visitor to pat an emperor, fondle a lion, or touch the sky. In the case of both artworks and artefacts there was also the pleasure of coming into contact with spatially or temporally distant peoples through the objects they had created and used.

It wasn't until the nineteenth century that the museum became the eyes-only space it is known for being today, and even then it required a long process of public education concerning correct museum comportment (Candlin 2010: ch. 3; Leahy 2011; see also Griffiths 2008: 162–72). From a practical perspective, this shift towards pure visuality was necessitated by a need to conserve collections. As museums became more open to the public in the nineteenth century and visitor numbers increased, the risk of damage or theft resulting from handling also increased. However, there were larger cultural forces and trends at work behind this transformation than mere concern for preservation.

Already in the sixteenth century there had been a backlash against touching art when Protestant reformers found kissing and touching religious images to be dangerously akin to idolatry. Such concerns regarding idolatry led to the destruction of thousands of religious images in Protestant Europe (the setting for the formulation of modern theories of art). The Reformation was also critical of sensuality in general, which affected attitudes towards touch as the most apparently sensuous of the senses. While, as we have seen, such attitudes did not prevent hands-on explorations from occurring in the museum, they would nonetheless have led many to feel self-conscious about the ways in which they interacted with art.

It was in the eighteenth century, however, that the privileging of a contemplative sight over an inquiring touch was fully elaborated as a philosophy of aesthetics. The concept of 'aesthetics' was coined by the philosopher Alexander von Baumgarten, who based the word on the Greek term for sense perception. For Baumgarten, aesthetics had to do with the study of the 'plenitude and complexity of sensations', which culminated in the perception of art (Gaiger 2002: 7; Gregor 1983: 364–65). When Immanuel Kant took up the concept, however, he drained it of its sensory plenitude and revised its significance to that of a 'disinterested' contemplation and judgement of beauty. It would be Kant's concept that dominated the development of modern theories of aesthetics (Kant 1911; Howes 2011: 167–69).

Although Kant's philosophy of aesthetics was metaphorically expressed in terms of 'taste', he made it clear that the sense most suited to the disinterested contemplation of art was sight. Both taste and smell were dismissed by Kant as senses that provide only sensations of pleasure or disgust and offer nothing to the contemplative mind. While hearing was praised by Kant for its objectivity, particularly when used to perceive the non-representational sounds of language, it was of little value in the perception of material works of art. Touch, in turn, was always part and parcel of any experience in which it participated and hence could never be disengaged in its perception of objects. The less we are aware of our bodies when we perceive, according to Kant, the freer we are to think and form aesthetic judgements about the thing being perceived. Only sight, the 'noblest' of the senses, seemed to have the detached 'purity' necessary for the task (see Schott 1988: ch. 8; Korsmeyer 2002).

If sight was to be the sensory channel for the proper perception of art, then it followed that art must direct itself to the eyes. One result of this way of thinking was to create a divide between the visual arts and handicrafts. The status of painting was enhanced through its association with the immaterial, 'intellectual' qualities of sight, while that of craftwork, associated with the 'coarse' materiality and functional values of touch, declined (Rée 1999: 353–63).

The Romantic movement of the eighteenth and nineteenth centuries furthered the association of painting with sight by promoting the ideal of the artist as a visionary who gazed down on the world from the solitary heights of genius. The 'down-to-earth' craftsman, by contrast, seemed to require no such visionary genius, but only a skilful touch. Of course, it was understood that painting, like craft, involved manual dexterity, but the emphasis was on a discerning eye. (The twentieth-century art theorist Richard Wollheim would declare: A good artist 'paints with … his eyes' [1991: 101].)

Within the dedicated space of the nineteenth-century museum, the public was confronted with the notion of an art that existed only to be looked at and not touched. Furthermore, the museum made it clear that looking at art was a concentrated act that should not be united to any other activities, such as praying, listening to music, or dining, as would often have occurred when art was situated in churches or homes. This situation could not be made the subject of complaint, however, for it had become an accepted truism that the only meaningful perceptual act that can be undertaken in relation to art is seeing. Rather than wishing to *do* more with art, therefore, all one could wish for was to *see* more. At the same time, the perception of the museum as a 'temple' of art that promoted 'pure' visuality, made it seem the most suitable and highest destination for art. As a result, artists increasingly created works with this end in mind – to be viewed on a gallery wall.

No doubt photography and later film, with their exclusively visual presentations of the world, facilitated the acceptance of this single-sensed view of art. The separation of visual art from other cultural domains that occurred in the gallery was also consistent with a wider fracturing of social and sensory life in modernity, which led to music being listened to in concert halls, meals being consumed in restaurants, and physical activity being undertaken in gymnasiums or playing fields. All aspects of life in the modern world, it seemed, required compartmentalization.

Sensing art across cultures

The culturally-specific nature of the visual exclusivity of Western art becomes apparent when we look at the rich sensuality of many non-Western artefacts and aesthetic forms. (The term 'art' can only be used very broadly outside of the West as many non-Western cultures do not share the Western concept of art.) For the Desana people of the Colombian rainforest, for example, an important element of the aesthetics of basketry consists of the distinctive odours produced by the different vines, reeds, and leaves with which baskets are made.

> Reeds and palm fronds often have a dry, sweetish odor whereas vines can have an acrid pungent smell and a bitter-tasting and irritating sap. Splints, leaves, fibers, and bark have odors that are said to be pleasantly sweet.
>
> (Reichel–Dolmatoff 1985: 24)

Similarly, an important element of the *Tanké Ge* masks produced by the Dan of West Africa is the sound created by the jewellery and other accoutrements attached to the masks (Reed 2004). Japanese tea bowls, in turn, are valued not only for their visual appearance, but also for their rich tactile qualities:

> To hold a tea bowl is to grasp a microcosm of the universe in one's palm. It is to experience through one's fingers the delicacy and soft tactility of its form, the textures of the clay and glaze, its volume and mass, the finish of its foot and the contours of its interior.
>
> (Lewis and Lewis 2009: 191)

These sensory traits are important not simply because they are part of the physical experience of Desana baskets, African masks, or Japanese tea bowls, but because they are a subject of commentary and appreciation by the people who make and use them. And, just as particular designs or images can have religious and cultural associations, so may any other sensory dimension of an artefact. In the case of Desana baskets, 'The odor and shape of a piece of vine link it to the image of a forest woman, a snake, an umbilical cord, or a trance state' (Reichel–Dolmatoff 1985: 43).

The sensory dimensions of such artefacts do not only reside in the objects themselves, but in the ways and contexts in which they are used. Sensory elements are added to Desana baskets when they are used to carry fruit or drain the juice from grated manioc or serve cassava cakes. Tea bowls become fragrant and warm and 'tasty' when they are filled with hot tea. When *Tanké Ge* masks are worn in the performance of a dance they become part of the movement of the dancers and the music of the singers and drummers. The helmet mask made by the Pende people of the Congo is not only worn by dancers but also used as a platter for serving ceremonial meals during rites of initiation.

These are not just incidental background elements, like the colour of a wall on which a painting is hung, but a vital part of the social and aesthetic presence of these artefacts. They situate the artefacts within webs of practice and significance. In the case of the Pende, chiefs are expected to have an acute sense of smell, indicating their powers of discernment, and to exercise control over their speech and appetites. These values are conveyed by the prominent nose and closed mouth on the mask, and internalized by initiates when they ritually eat off the face of the mask (Reed 2004: 98–100; Silverman 2004: 247–48).

With certain artefacts, the process of creation is itself a vital part of their beauty and power. In the West, what happens during the process of creation is deemed to be largely irrelevant to our appreciation of a work of art. It may be interesting to learn that Leonardo kept the sitter for the Mona Lisa in a good humour while she was posing for her portrait by having musicians play for her, but this does not affect the aesthetic and social values attributed to the painting itself. When it comes to art, it is the result – the piece that goes in the gallery, the object that is bought and sold – that matters.

Among the Navajo, by contrast, the songs that are sung during the creation of a sand painting play an essential role in its appreciation as they call on the spirits to occupy their representations in the painting. The entire life of the sand painting, in fact, is one continuous process, epitomized by the shifting nature of the sand from which it is made. Sand paintings are traditionally made to be used in healing rituals. The sand-painter creates the painting by singing and sprinkling different coloured sands and powdered plants on the floor of the Navajo ceremonial house or *hogan*. The design, the specifics of which are up to the individual sand-painter (or in Navajo terminology 'chanter'), consists of stylized images of the Navajo 'holy people' within an appropriate cosmic setting. The patient sits on the sand painting in order to integrate herself with the cosmos represented there and come into direct contact with its vital energy. Sand from the different images is rubbed onto the patient's body so that it may absorb her illness. When the ceremony is over the sand is swept away. Creation, use, and destruction, are all part of a fluid management of cosmic energy. Indeed, the Navajo word for sand painting, *iikaah*, has nothing to do with drawing pictures, but means 'the place where the gods come and go' (Gill 1979; Parezco 1983).

For the Westerner it is frustrating that a beautiful Navajo sand painting will be destroyed the same day it is made. (And certainly no connoisseur of art would ever think of sitting on a great painting!) Such destruction of 'art' runs counter to the Western drive to conserve artworks, both as objects of beauty and as precious cultural and financial assets. The Westerner, therefore, wants to have some way of capturing the sand painting. In order to do so pictures have been drawn of sand paintings and photographs taken of them from the smoke hole at the top of the *hogan* – a position from which the Navajo would never themselves traditionally have looked at a sand painting but which allows the Westerner an all-around view. To satisfy the demand for sand paintings that can play the same role as Western paintings, Navajo artists have created imitation sand paintings, sprinkling sand on boards covered with paste (see Classen and Howes 2006).

For the Navajo, however, the true beauty of the sand painting lies not in the end result but in the act of creation and in the role it plays during the healing ceremony. Once that role is fulfilled the sand painting no longer serves a purpose. In fact, whereas in the West the ideal is to conserve artworks for future viewing, the Navajo believe that sand paintings should not be objects for the eyes. Not only is that not their function, but tradition holds that the images are too powerful to look at for long without danger.

Clearly, other and broader notions of aesthetics inform the creation of non-Western artefacts. The Navajo word for beauty is *hozho*, a term that expresses a dynamic ideal of living in harmony with oneself and the world. *Hozho* is traditionally maintained and experienced through the practice of rituals, such as that of sand painting, or the song ceremonies that form part of the Navajo 'Blessing Way'. The role of ritual artefacts in these contexts is not simply to look beautiful or to feel beautiful, but to help accomplish beautiful transformations within individuals and societies, to integrate and invigorate, to restore balance and order (Witherspoon, 1977; Gill 1979).

The appreciation of Japanese tea bowls, in turn, is informed by the concept of *wabi sabi*, which finds beauty in austerity and mutability, as exemplified by old, weathered objects. The rough texture and uneven form of a tea bowl, along with the changes in colour and texture that have taken place over time and the nicks and scratches it has received (alterations that Western museums strive to prevent and repair in the artefacts in their custody) are considered to contribute to its aesthetic and contemplative value. Like the Navajo concept of *hozho*, *wabi sabi* is an ideal that celebrates sensory and mental engagement with the flow of life. Death and dissolution are essential to this flow, and to the aesthetic experience (see Koren 2008). In the museum neither death nor decay are permitted, a denial of change which creates the illusion of an atemporal world and, incidentally, makes the museum complicit in the Western cult of eternal youth (see Ouzman 2006).

When they are subjected to the static visual regime of an art gallery or ethnographic museum, artefacts can no longer be appreciated through their non-visual qualities (Kirshenblatt-Gimblett 1998: xx). As Daniel Reed writes of one such 'museumified' object: 'The *Tanké Ge* mask that hangs on the wall of the BMA [Baltimore Museum of Art] is just one small (though centrally important) aspect of the visual component of the multimedia manifestation' – music, dance, singing, costume – in which the mask participates among the Dan (Reed 2004: 98).

This emphasis on visual appearance also has the effect of privileging showy artefacts and consigning less eye-catching ones to the museum storeroom. Although they may have rich textures and odours, Desana baskets do not have the 'eye-appeal' of other Native American basketry and thus are less likely to be put on display. According to conventional Western aesthetics, non-visual qualities are precisely what 'drag' a work down by associating it with 'primitive' sensibilities and practical functions. From this perspective, the museum 'ennobles' non-Western art by allowing it to be seen in the same light as 'real' art. An African mask can be regarded as an inspiration for Picasso and not 'just' as a prop for a dance or a tray for a ceremonial meal (Goldwater 1966).

At the same time, however, museums have been conceptualized as 'exposing' the 'true' nature of indigenous artefacts by taking them out of their cultural contexts and placing them in the light – the light of the gallery and, metaphorically, the light of Western rationality. Indigenous peoples were customarily imagined to live in the darkness. This was due both to their presumed immersion in the depths of the forest, and to their supposedly 'unenlightened' modes of life – a darkness that appeared to many to be stamped on their bodies in the colour of their skins. Any emphasis 'savages' placed on tactile, olfactory and gustatory experiences was attributed to their presumed physical and mental darkness (see Brantlinger 1988; Smith 2006). Artefacts taken from such peoples and placed in the museum, hence, were regarded as making a transition from darkness to light, both actually and symbolically. Once in the light they could finally be 'properly' seen for what they supposedly were – pathetic idols, utilitarian craftwork, or primitive art. Even anthropologists trying to situate such artefacts in their original contexts often ended up reinforcing this stereotype. Trying to convey the significance of the large wicker figures created in the Purari Delta of Papua New Guinea, for example, the Australian anthropologist F.E. Williams explained that these 'absurd creations of wickerwork' were actually 'possessed of another meaning in the dimness and obscurity of their own environment' (Williams 1923: 9).

Furthermore, the presence of ethnographic artefacts in Western museums entailed their absence from their cultures of origin, an absence that could have far-reaching effects, particularly in the case of religious artefacts. As F.E. Williams put it with regard to his own region of fieldwork: 'A number of trophies of a certain kind have been won from the Purari Delta by Government or private collectors, the loss of which must have seriously disturbed the religious life of their owners' (Williams 1923: 9). Such 'disturbance of the religious life' of non-Western peoples, of course, was in itself customarily taken to be a strong justification for the appropriation of sacred objects by Westerners. Many an 'idol' surrendered to a nineteenth-century missionary ended up as a museum display.

The use of the term 'trophies' by Williams makes it quite clear that, whether forcibly or otherwise obtained, indigenous artefacts were often regarded as the spoils of conquest. The ethnographic collections of numerous museums, in fact, reflect the colonial reach of the countries in which they are located. By 'capturing' non-Western artefacts and subjecting them to Western aesthetic and classificatory systems, museums asserted their power over them and, by extension, the power of the West over the peoples they represented. Visitors to ethnographic galleries, hence, not only view 'exotic artefacts' or 'primitive works of art' that have been stripped of their original social and sensory values, they also survey captives.

Beyond visual art in the West

While mainstream aesthetics in the nineteenth century emphasized the visual character of art, the counterculture of the day encouraged artists to experiment with sensory multiplicity. In many cases this was accomplished by the relatively simple but still evocative measure of using painting to depict objects or actions suggestive of non-visual sensations.

One influential example of this is Gustave Moreau's *Salome Dancing Before Herod* (1876) which uses the biblical story of Salome's dance to create a lush scene of sensuous, oneiric imagery. Tactile sensations are evoked by Salome's filmy garments and gliding movement, by the contrast between her heavy jewellery and delicate skin, by the sharp edge of the attendant's sword (soon to cut off the head of John the Baptist), and by the ornate architecture. Fragrance is suggested by the lotus carried in Salome's hand, the roses strewn on the floor, the smoke swirling from an incense burner, and by the panther, a traditional symbol of seductive scent, facing Salome on the floor. In the background a lute is played, infusing the scene with imaginary music. The whole of the painting offers a subtle tapestry of contrasting and interwoven colours, washed in glowing highlights and smoky shadows. Salome herself is depicted with her eyes closed, bringing out both the trance-like nature of her dance (she is apparently guided by an 'eye' dangling from a bracelet on her outstretched arm) and the importance of non-visual sensations to mystical transcendence.

In the late nineteenth and early twentieth centuries there was a fashion for depicting scent in art, usually in order to evoke a sense of mystery. Two examples are *Incense* (1898) by Fernand Khnopff, which portrays a shrouded woman holding an incense burner and gazing dreamingly into the distance and *The Soul of the Rose* (1908) by John William Waterhouse, which shows a woman with closed eyes inhaling the scent from a climbing rose. In both cases, and many others, odour appears as a means for bypassing the material, visible world and accessing deeper realities. The habitual use of female subjects in such paintings has much to do with the customary association of women with the senses of smell, touch and taste and with irrationality (Classen 1998: ch. 3).

More adventurous artists of the time attempted to go beyond merely depicting sensory acts or objects to create visual equivalents to odours or sounds. This was expressed most aggressively in the Futurist manifesto of 1913 entitled 'The painting of sounds, noises and smells' (Carrà 1973). In it the young Italian painter Carlos Carrà called for 'rrrrrrreds that shouuuuuut' and 'greeeeeeens that screeeeeeam' and visual renderings of the sounds and odours of such 'unaesthetic' sites as workshops, railway stations and garages.

While the Futurists were novel in wishing to transpose traditionally un-aesthetic sensations onto the canvas, a number of earlier artists had already attempted to make scents and sounds visible in their art. The Dutch-Indonesian artist Jan Toorop, notably, depicted thick strands of sound ringing out from bells and swirls of scent rising from roses in his work *The Three Brides* (1893). More commonly, artists attempted to paint 'musically', through a vibrant use of colour, sweeping strokes and sinuous curves. Eugène Delacroix, whose work was seen by many as 'painted music', was a key figure in this regard. 'Delacroix,' wrote the critic Théophile Silvestre, 'causes red to sound like the clang of war like trumpets, and draws sombre complaints from violets. Thus, in colors, he reinvents the songs of Mozart and Beethoven, and the plaintive melodies of Weber' (cited in Ritter 1879: 33). Another prominent example of this trend was James Whistler, who even gave his paintings musical names, such as *Nocturne in Black and Gold* (*c.* 1874) and *Symphony in White, No. 1* (1862).

Such experiments in transposing non-visual sensations or sensibilities onto a visual plane were inspired in part by the contemporary doctrine of sensory correspondences, which held that sensations belonging to one sensory field had their equivalents in other sensory fields. This was most famously expressed by Charles Baudelaire in his poem 'Correspondences':

> Perfumes, colours and sounds correspond
> There are perfumes fresh as children's skin
> sweet as oboes, green as meadows,
> And others, corrupt, rich and triumphant ...

(Baudelaire 1975: 43)

Non-Western aesthetics also played a role. Western artists revelled in the multisensoriality of exotic lands, whether experienced first-hand or filtered through European accounts, and imagined new ways of evoking sensuality through art. Paul Gauguin wrote of receiving artistic inspiration from the scents and sounds of Tahiti in his journal, which he titled *Noa Noa*, using the Polynesian word for fragrance. It may be that Toorop was influenced in the importance he gave to scent by his childhood in Indonesia, where odours could have considerable cultural significance (see Howes 1988). In keeping with the traditional mind/body dualism of the West, European artists tended to perceive non-Western sensuality in stereotypical terms, as emanating from a non-rational, 'primitive' or 'magical' worldview. In a West that seemed to many to be overly rational, however, this perception had considerable charm.

The synaesthetic notions of sensory correspondence elaborated by Baudelaire and others meant not only that painting could be employed to represent sounds and smells (its ability to evoke textures was well-recognized) but also that other sensory fields could be employed to call up visual sensations. The French composer Claude Debussy argued, indeed, that music was superior to painting in its ability to evoke 'all manner of variations of color and light' (cited in Vallas 1967: 207). Scents were also transformed into music in Debussy's sensory mix, notably in his piano prelude *Sounds and Perfumes Swirl in the Evening Air* inspired by one of Baudelaire's poems. The Russian painter Wassily Kandinsky actively combined colour and music in his 'color-tone dramas', the best-known of which is *The Yellow Sound* (1909), a one-act opera highlighting relationships among sound, colour, and emotion. His country-man, composer Alexander Scriabin, united colours to music in his symphony *Prometheus*, which made use of coloured lighting keyed to musical notes (Miller 2002). Musical scores themselves might be turned into artworks by composers and artists attentive to the visual presentation of music. Along with specifying the tints of paper and ink to be employed in printing his scores, Debussy designed the cover for one of his pieces and asked the Symbolist artist Maurice Denis to illustrate another (Wenk 1976: 3 206). A particularly elab-orate instance of this genre is the *Brahms-Phantasie* (1894), a collection of six of Brahms' scores illustrated with 41 etchings and engravings by Max Klinger.

If there was a correspondence and equivalence among the senses then one radical conclusion was that it should be possible to create forms of art for the nose or the tongue or the fingers, as well as for the eyes and ears. In *Against Nature*, J.K. Huysmans argued that 'it was no more abnormal that an art of selecting aromatic odours should exist, than others which separate out sound waves, or strike the retina of the eye with variously coloured rays of light' (1998: 93). The protagonist of that book, Des Esseintes, does, in fact, create 'perfume concerts' and 'symphonies' of liqueur. An example of an actual attempt at such a performance was the 'melody in odours' entitled *A Trip to Japan in Sixteen Minutes* (performed in 1902), which featured a succession of perfumes (Bradstreet 2010). Japan made a particularly good subject for such an experiment because of its associations with incense and its suggestion of alternative aesthetic possibilities.

In the 1920s, the Futurists investigated the possibility of a purely tactile art form, creating 'tactile tables', multi-textured works that were meant to be felt and not seen. F.T. Marinetti, the founder of the Futurists, made the point that visual artists should not be the ones to develop tactile art, as they were too eye-minded. Later members of the movement would invent a Futurist cuisine that aestheticized the flavours, colours and textures of food (Marinetti 1972, 1989).

Such re-evaluation of the artistic potential of the 'lower' senses, along with the fascination for premodern and Eastern decorative arts, gave a new aesthetic life to craft, exemplified by the Arts and Crafts movement and Art Nouveau. In many cases the work created by members of these move-ments not only united the visual and tactile, the eye and the hand, but also evoked musical and aromatic sensations with arabesques and floral designs. Indeed, the new union of art and craft made it possible to smell (out of) an artwork in the form of a perfume bottle designed by René Lalique or even play an artwork in the form of a piano with curving lines and fretwork bouquets designed by Gustave Serrurier-Bovy. In an exhibition of the new art held in Brussels in 1894, furniture by Serrurier-Bovy, silverware by C.R. Ashbee, and books published by William Morris were exhibited alongside paintings by prominent artists. The opening featured a concert of Debussy's works, in which musical arabesques echoed the visual arabesques of the artworks (Lombardi 2009: 153).

Many artists of the period were inspired by the ideal of the *Gesamtkunstwerk*, or total artwork (Roberts 2011), which advocated engaging multiple senses through a combination of art forms. Cultural prototypes of this were found in ancient Greek drama, in Eastern ritual, and in the synaesthetic rites of the Catholic Church.

There were many forms in which the total artwork might be conceptualized. Richard Wagner saw his own 'music dramas' with their fusion of music, poetry and acting, and allusions to scents and savours, as pointing the way of the future. Debussy, who disliked the 'heavy-handedness' of Wagner's productions, imagined suggestive symphonic poems played in a natural setting where 'the very air, the movement of the leaves, and the perfume of flowers would work together in mysterious union with music which would thus bring all the elements into such natural harmony that it would seem to form a part of each' (cited by Vallas 1967: 11). Alexander Scriabin imagined a monumental symphony to be called *Mysterium*, in which sights and sounds would be supplemented by scents and touches. The performance of this work, never completed due to Scriabin's death, was to take place in India and elevate the audience spiritually, as well as aesthetically. In traditional cultures art was often employed in a context of ritual transformation. For many artists of the late nineteenth and early twentieth centuries, ritual transformation was to occur within the context of art (see Classen 1998: ch. 5)

As the twentieth century progressed, these attempts to combine the senses in art (particularly when they engaged the 'lower' senses) were generally marginalized by mainstream aesthetics. (Their harshest critics, indeed, had found them symptomatic of physical and mental degeneracy, see Nordau 1910 [1895].) Those that *did* become part of the canon were shorn of their unusual sensory dimensions. The tactile tables of the Futurists were transformed into visual icons of modern art. Scriabin's *Prometheus* was performed with no accompanying colours.

The same drive to limit each art form to one sense only also manifested itself in the reception of a number of later works. In the mid-twentieth century, for example, the Abstract Expressionist Jackson Pollock was partially inspired by the dynamics and tactility of Navajo sand painting to develop his revolutionary 'drip paintings'. However, the influential art critic, Clement Greenberg (who argued that the role of the artist is 'to render substance entirely optical'), promoted Pollock's work as an icon of 'pure' visual values (Greenberg 1989: 144; Jones 2005: ch. 5; see further Witherspoon 1977).

A few innovative twentieth-century movements kept the notion of a multisensory aesthetics from dying out completely. One notable example of this was Fluxus, which experimented with engaging the 'lower' senses through artworks and events in the 1960s (Higgins 2002). While they managed to rattle the aesthetic cage, however, these counterculture movements were unable to bring multisensoriality into the mainstream of modern art.

The multimedia museum

What is the state of the senses in the state-of-the-art museum of the twenty-first century? At first glance, not much may seem to have changed – museum exhibits remain predominantly silent, visual spectacles. However, cracks have appeared in this visualist façade, cracks that allow a snatch of music or aroma to seep through, and even a visitor's hand to occasionally insert itself.

To begin with, it should be noted that museums have never been entirely silent and still places, for they are animated by the noise and movement of visitors. These might well be considered unwanted distractions by those seeking to gaze contemplatively at museum pieces, but, like them or not, noise and movement were and are part of a museum visit. The feeling of hustle and bustle in a crowded gallery, the conversations overheard and participated in, even the smell of the galleries, attach themselves to our experience of the visual surfaces on display.

Other sensory dimensions entered modern museums through the introduction of new media technologies, notably films and audio guides. These gave added information about the artefacts being viewed but also, especially in the case of films, encouraged visitors to think of them as having a life outside of the gallery space. Films showed artefacts in non-museum contexts – half-finished in the hands of their creators or employed within cultural settings. Certainly this 'exposure' took something of the 'shine' off museum pieces, for it became more difficult to see them as forever reigning in august and untouchable solitude within the white cube of the gallery. However, as a result, art became a little less of a 'thing' and a little more of a 'process'. When touchscreens were introduced at the end of the twentieth century, visitors were even given something to do with their hands and allowed a slight control over the information purveyed to them.

New kinds of museums also emerged that aimed to engage visitors in sensory experiences, such as participating in an experiment in a science museum or touring a recreation of a nineteenth-century village in an open-air museum. Taking part in historical re-enactments, often of battles, became popular as well (see Hoffer 2005; Smith 2007: 118–23). In this section, however, we will focus on the display of artworks and artefacts in museums.

Perhaps the most obvious case of artefacts being sensorially-impoverished when they become museum pieces occurs with musical instruments. No matter how much an instrument was valued for its *sound* (such as the Stradivarius violin in the Ashmolean Museum), in the museum it becomes a purely visual object. Musical recordings are sometimes employed to help deal with this paradox and give visitors a sense of what selected instruments sound like. These recordings may be experienced by the solitary visitor by putting on headphones or entering a booth, or may be played throughout a gallery to produce a collective experience.

An elaborate example of the latter can be found in the Musée du quai Branly in Paris. This ethnographic museum has an immense collection of musical instruments from around the world housed in a glass tower in the reception hall and displayed in specific galleries. In order to 'give voice' to at least some of the instruments and the musical traditions they represent the museum has invested in two types of media systems. One of these, to quote from the museum's website, offers 'eight multimedia programs … plunging the visitor into the midst of an evening of seduction among the nomadic Peuls of Niger, bathing him in the vocal polyphonies of the Bedzan pygmies of Cameroon, or surrounding him with the processional music of Nepal'. The other, which accompanies the tower of instruments in the reception area, attempts to 'immerse the Glass Tower in a cloud of musical whispers, a perfume of sounds if you like, to bring aural presence to the mystery of the instruments kept there and to remind visitors of the true purpose of the Glass Tower's contents' (Musée du quai Branly 2013). While some visitors might find these 'musical whispers' richly evocative, however, they may also be experienced as alienating, as it is impossible to tell which of the encased instruments in the dimly-lit tower is the one uttering ghostly sounds at any moment.

When Musée du quai Branly talks of enveloping exhibits in a 'perfume of sounds', it is speaking metaphorically. Some museums, however, make use of actual perfumes in exhibitions. Unlike music, odours are usually considered too potentially disruptive, and perhaps even 'contaminating', to enter actual collection rooms. They tend, therefore, to be confined to specially designed 'experience' spaces that contain no actual artefacts. An example of one such exhibit is 'The Trench Experience' at the Imperial War Museum in London in which odours, along with sounds and tableaux of soldiers gave visitors a 'feel' for life in the trenches of World War I. While such 'smell effects' might seem frivolous to some, surveys have shown that they are regarded positively by visitors. The vast majority of respondents to a survey on 'The Trench Experience', for example, felt that smell played a valuable role and had added to their experience and understanding of the exhibit (Crowest 1999).

A more conventional way in which the museum experience has been sensorially enhanced is through hands-on workshops, in which participants are able to handle select artefacts and hear descriptions of their histories and uses. Such hands-on workshops are usually directed at children, with the notion that children are not yet ready to engage in mature visual appreciation and hence require extra sensory stimulation to learn from museum exhibits. Indeed there are numerous children's museums around the world that, elaborating on this principle, replace the static display of art and artefacts with interactive and immersive learning environments. The other main group to whom hands-on workshops or tours have been directed is the visually-impaired, usually as the result of pressure from advocacy groups (Candlin 2010). (A variety of small 'tactile museums' have also been created around the world primarily for the use of the visually-impaired.)

In the cases of children and the visually-impaired, the understanding has traditionally been that, if they were able to see properly, they would not need to handle anything. However, museum curators and scholars are increasingly willing to entertain the notion that 'even' sighted adults may benefit from tactile contact with exhibits. One sign of this is the hands-on tables set up in various galleries of the British Museum that allow visitors to touch a small selection of historical artefacts. It may not seem like much compared to the vast numbers of artefacts that remain hands-off, but it constitutes a break with the notion of sight as the only sense of use in the museum.

It may be that this new consciousness of the value of touch has been stimulated in part by the proliferation of images of museum pieces in our digital age. This, arguably, has decreased the value of the museum piece as a sight and increased its value as a material object. Images of the Venus de Milo may be found anywhere, but only the Louvre possesses the tangible thing. We may not be allowed to touch it, but when we look at it standing in the Louvre we feel its material presence and this draws us to the museum as much as any desire to appreciate its already oft-seen visual beauties. Having a few artefacts on hand that visitors can actually touch increases this sense of the museum as the repository of material authenticity.

Ethnographic museums are often in the forefront of the movement to enrich the sensory life of the museum. An important reason for this is the growing awareness among anthropologists of the loss of cultural and sensory meaning that occurs when ethnographic objects are turned into museum pieces (Classen and Howes 2006; Dudley 2009). One notable example of an attempt to at least figuratively reimmerse ethnographic artefacts in a dynamic environment is the 'Indians of the Rainforest' exhibit created at the Museum of World Culture in Gothenburg in 2005 and then shown at the National Museum in Copenhagen in 2009–10. In this exhibit, artefacts from indigenous peoples living along the Orinoco River in Venezuela were displayed in rooms painted blue or green to evoke the rainforest and featuring blown-up photographs of local landscapes, human faces, and animals, along with videos of daily life in the region. A continuous recording of human voices, bird songs, and other sounds of the rainforest accompanied these images. 'The sensory core of the exhibition is a vast video installation of a waterfall ... which rumbles through the exhibition soundtrack [and] projects ripples of light across the floor' (Wiseman 2010: 252). The evocation of water was intended both to symbolize the immersion to be experienced by the museum visitor and to foreground the importance of water for the peoples of the Orinoco. While not interactive, this kind of multimedia exhibit strives to imaginatively locate isolated artefacts within sensory environments and ways of life.

The 'Mami Wata: Arts for Water Spirits in Africa and Its Diasporas' exhibit recently held at several museums in the United States, offers another example of an attempt to recreate a multisensory environment for the display of ethnographic art. Similarly to the video evocation of water in the 'Indians of the Rainforest', in this exhibit a film of ocean surf with accompanying sound was projected onto a wall. Artworks were further contextualized through videos showing traditional ceremonies involving the water deity Mami Wata and the recreation of one of her altars, with characteristic aromatic flowers (Drewal 2012).

Such immersive exhibits certainly help to engage visitors' interest. One reviewer enthusiastically wrote of the Mami Wata exhibit that it was 'as rousing as a drum roll, as piquant as a samba' (cited by Drewal 2012: 50). The extent to which they convey the particular sensory meanings objects and artworks evoke in their original contexts, however, depends very much on the relevance of the design elements employed and the particular information offered.

Another technique that has occasionally been used by ethnographic museums to bring objects 'to life' is to invite members of indigenous communities to create an artefact within the exhibition space. For a time, at least, (and later on video) museum visitors can observe a Navajo chanter at work on a sand painting or an Inuit carver completing a traditional sculpture. Such displays not only provide information about how particular artefacts are made, they also bring a human touch to museum objects and emphasize the importance of the work of creation, the aesthetic *process*.

The limits of immersion

Significantly, however, such immersive or added experiences are rarely offered by fine arts museums. They are also fairly rare in galleries displaying Western crafts. It is difficult to imagine an exhibition of medieval ceramics employing video installations of rivers to remind visitors of the importance of waterways in European culture, a display of Renaissance silverware with a sonic backdrop of barking dogs and rumbling carriages, or one of Christian icons with a mock altar smelling of incense. It is likewise difficult to imagine an exhibition of eighteenth-century musical instruments accompanied by recorded minuets and giant images from period paintings intended to 'plunge the visitor into the midst of an evening of seduction' among the British aristocracy. It is perhaps even harder to imagine a Western artist being invited to paint a conventional Western scene in a fine arts museum for the benefit of visitors.

Why is this the case? Possibly because of an assumption that visitors to exhibits of Western art and artefacts come equipped with the knowledge needed to place these objects in their settings and so don't require any extra cues. No need to invite an artist to create a painting in a gallery when artists can be seen painting pictures in any Western city.

A more important reason, however, lies in the notion that such experiential additions would distract the visitor from contemplating the aesthetic values of the works themselves and compromise those works' identity as stand-alone objects – 'museum pieces'. In this context, to attempt to blend a prized Western artefact in with the sounds and sights of its place of origin would seem beneath its dignity. It would also challenge the cherished notion of the solitary artist by suggesting a communal basis for the creation of art.

To invite an artist to paint in a museum might similarly seem to displace value from the exhibited works by implying that aesthetic worth should be accorded to the act of artistic creation as well as to the finished product. It would also imply that the painting being made on the spot was the equivalent of the ones hanging on the wall. With ethnographic artefacts it may seem alright to suggest that the work being created by an indigenous specialist is equivalent to the one preserved in a glass case. It definitely would not seem right to suggest that any trained Western artist could create the equivalent of the *Mona Lisa* or any other iconic artwork. Furthermore, just as it is untrue to many non-Western aesthetic traditions to present indigenous artefacts as isolated visual works, it would arguably be untrue to modern Western aesthetics to situate artworks destined for viewing in the gallery within interactive, multimedia contexts. This argument, however, could not be so readily made for Western craftwork, created for use and not just display.

Exceptions, or partial exceptions to this exclusion of the fine arts from interactive or contextual displays *can* be found. A retrospective of an artist's work, for example, might include photographs or film footage of the artist at work. A gallery of contemporary art might invite artists to create works within the gallery space. Occasionally museums are even made out of artists' studios or homes, such as the Musée Rodin and the Musée national Gustave Moreau in Paris. Unlike the customary museum gallery, the home/studio museum allows visitors a sense of the space and place in which an artist worked. Occasionally museums are made out of collectors' homes, such as Sir John Soane's Museum in London or the Isabella Stewart Gardner Museum in Boston, situating works within the context of the collector's life.

One interesting departure from the museological norm of disdaining contextual or interactive exhibits in the display of art dealt with the work of Leonardo da Vinci. The touring exhibition entitled 'Leonardo da Vinci's Workshop' featured large-scale models based on Leonardo's sketches, a range of digitized images of the artist's work – manipulable through touchscreens – a hands-on model of one of his designs, and a video recreation of Leonardo's life providing personal and social context. No original drawings were included in the exhibit, however, and, tellingly, it was shown at science centres – which have a long tradition of interactive displays and are not expected to foreground aesthetic values – rather than art museums.

Although not usually criticized when employed by ethnographic museums (perhaps partly because it can be seen as adding authenticity and partly because of the perception that there is no 'high culture' to safeguard from sensory 'distractions' in such museums), the hands-on, multimedia approach has been censured when used at mainstream museums and historic sites. When the National Trust in Britain announced in 2010 that its new 'Bringing Houses to Life' project would make its historic houses more accessible by taking away 'do not touch' signs, lighting fires in fireplaces, playing music, and providing visitors with period costumes and food, they were accused of 'Disneyfying' these sites to appeal to plebeian tastes. The assumption underlying such criticism was the conventional one that we cannot learn anything of value through the 'lower' senses. The leader of the opposition to the changes, John Goodhall, argued in visualist language that what historic houses should ideally offer is not a taste of, or feel for, but an 'insightful glimpse of' history – which should suffice for 'any discerning, intelligent audience' (Howie and Sawer 2010).

A factor to keep in mind in this discussion is the matter of financing. Museums rely on support from government agencies, corporate sponsors and visitors. The exhibitions they present must appear both worthwhile and engaging in order to attract visitors and funding. The non-visual senses often enter museum settings, therefore, not primarily because of a desire to break with the restrictive aesthetic conventions of the past, but in order to increase a museum's consumer appeal (see Chapter 5 on sensory marketing). Hence, rather than justifying its decision to expand the sensory offerings at its sites as promoting a more dynamic and multisensory model of aesthetic and historical appreciation, all the National Trust could say in its defence was that the changes were necessary to appeal to the younger generation (which presumably manifests an 'infantile' desire to touch), and thus ensure the National Trust's financial survival.

As regards finances, ethnographic museums generally have a harder time finding funding than art museums, for ethnographic objects rarely exercise the lure or carry the cultural weight of Western works of art. Visitor numbers at the Musée du quai Branly – although it is one of the foremost ethnographic museums in the world – cannot compare with those at the Louvre. From this practical perspective, the inclusion of 'crowd-pleasing' videos, music, live performances, and hands-on exhibits may seem more necessary to ethnographic museums than to better-funded art galleries.

Art museums have not completely ignored contemporary multimedia and sensory trends. The only way in which such trends can acceptably enter such museums, however, is in the form of art – not in the form of sensory context for pre-existing artworks. Museums, particularly of modern art, have showcased contemporary works and performances by artists involving an array of odours, flavours, sounds and physical interactions (Jones 2005; Schwartzman 2011). Some such works are intended to place the museum experience itself in a new light. Such artistic interventions range from altering the visibility of collections through coloured lighting or visual obstructions, to reshaping visitors' corporeal experience of the museum by inviting them to run through or lie down in galleries (Candlin 2010; Leahy 2011). In 2006 an unusual kinaesthetic sensation and new visual spectacle were added to the museum experience when artist Carsten Höller installed giant slides in the Tate Modern in London. Such 'sense-bending' works may also, of course, be presented outside of museums. One example is the 'Displace' exhibit created by artist Chris Salter and his team, which sought to stimulate and interrelate all of the senses within a performative environment that was staged in Montreal in 2011 and afterwards in The Hague (Salter 2012; Labruto 2011).

At times, it should be noted, museums have been the sites for uninvited performances. For example, the 'Reclaim Shakespeare Company' protested British Petroleum's sponsorship of a recent Shakespeare exhibit at the British Museum by performing a mock Shakespearean skit in the gallery: 'No more o'this, BP, no more/You mar all with your logo/Here's the smell of oil still/ All these shiny exhibits will not sweeten this soiled hand. Oh, oh, oh!/Out, damned sponsor!' When the performers asked visitors to rip the BP logo from the exhibition programmes, however, they were hustled out of the museum by guards evidently concerned that the mutilation of brochures might lead to the destruction of artefacts (Loeb 2012).

In light of the foregoing discussion, this impromptu performance is notable for a number of reasons. It brought a dynamic corporeal dimension to the usually staid British Museum while giving a contemporary twist to one of the plays highlighted in the exhibit. It suggested a glaring sensory contrast between the 'shiny' and ostensibly pristine exhibit being sponsored by BP and the literal and moral stench of the massive oil spill caused by the explosion of one of BP's drilling rigs in 2010. It brought the usually submerged issue of the role of corporate funding in museums into the spotlight. And it invited the public to respond to the 'ill-sponsored' exhibit by doing more than simply look at it. While an unofficial artistic intervention, the performance by the 'Reclaim Shakespeare Company' creatively challenged many conventional museological assumptions and practices.

Aside from the ways in which conventional museums are confronting and courting change, there are new modes of museological experience being offered by a number of contemporary museums which are as much concerned with facilitating interactions as with displaying objects. One such is the Museo Interactivo de la Música in Málaga. This museum, which encourages visitors to 'please play', provides a range of traditional and electronic opportunities for making and listening to music, including a 'Gallery of Sensations and Experience'. This is a far cry from the music rooms in traditional museums, with their instruments encased in glass. At the nearby Museo Caja Granada Memoria de Andalucía in Granada, visitors can manipulate interactive videos and exhibits dealing with Andalusia's history. The blindingly-white postmodernist architecture itself plays a role, evoking the whitewashed houses and snowy mountain peaks of the region, leading visitors down circular ramps into the depths of 'memory', and dramatically asserting that Andalusia has an imposing future, as well as a storied past. (The advertising campaign for the museum's opening included the slogan 'Welcome Future'.) At the same time, however, a commercial message is being made. The museum is intended to celebrate not only the history of Andalusia, but also the achievements of the Caja Granada bank, which helped finance the museum and whose neighbouring headquarters is constructed in a similar style. The underlying suggestion is that the past and future of the region are in the Company's hands – another kind of manipulation all together (see Campo Baeza 2009).

In conclusion, the senses are indeed infiltrating the museum in many ways and to many ends, both reclaiming lost territory and exploring new domains. As we have seen, it is essential to maintain a critical perspective on this development for the process is hardly unproblematic or bias-free. In fact, the particular biases it brings to light, such as that hands-on exhibits are for children, or that multimedia immersion would be degrading for Western artworks, or that adding a touch of 'sensationalism' is a good marketing ploy, are themselves highly revelatory of the cultural formation of perception.

Bringing new sensory dimensions to museum exhibits needs to be approached mindfully, in terms of what these will communicate and what consequences – a deeper understanding or a broader appeal, attitudes changed or confirmed – might be expected and should be pursued. Before we can do this, however, we need to first recognize that aesthetics is a matter of mixed sensory and social messages, and not simply of unitary visual values. We can then begin to develop truly perceptive ways of presenting and approaching aesthetic and cultural diversity.

2 Sensuous healing

The sensory practice of medicine

Whatever historical evidence were offered to show that a king's touch helps to cure scrofula, readers would tend to be very skeptical, suspecting a hoax or a meaningless coincidence, because they would see no way that such a cure could ever be explained reductively. How could it matter to a mycobacterium whether the person touching its host was properly crowned and anointed ... ?

Steven Weinberg, *Dreams of a Final Theory: The Scientist's Search for the Ultimate Laws of Nature* (1994)

In this scenario Weinberg misplaces the causal action in infectious disease, privileging the mycobacterium as the locus of infection and healing. But the proximate 'cause' of a disease is not simply the virulence of bacteria – it includes the host organism's immune response. ... The King's touch, then, need not act directly on the mycobacterium to have an antibacterial effect, it can act on the thoughts and feelings of the person being touched, mediated by the central nervous system, which in turn modulates the immune system ...

Laurence J. Kirmayer, "Reflections on Embodiment", In *Social and Cultural Lives of Immune Systems* (2003)

One important condition of [Shipibo-Conibo] therapy is the aesthetically pleasing environment into which the shaman and the family place the patient. He is carefully surrounded by an ambience designed to appease both the senses and emotions. Visible and invisible geometric designs, melodious singing, and the fragrance from herbs and tobacco smoke pervade the atmosphere ... This setting induces in the patient the necessary emotional disposition for recovery.

Angelika Gebhart-Sayer "The geometric designs of the Shipibo-Conibo in ritual context", *Journal of Latin American Lore* (1985)

When one thinks of the senses in a medical context, the first topic that comes to mind is that of sensory disorders and how they may be treated. This chapter is not concerned with the senses as 'patients', however, but rather with their role as 'physicians' or avenues for medical knowledge and healing processes. This is an unusual perspective to take in mainstream or biomedicine. In mainstream medicine, technology has to a considerable extent supplanted the role of the doctor's senses in diagnosis, while in treatment the alleviation of pain is often considered the most that should be done for the patient's sensory well-being. And while medicine may be referred to as an 'art', aesthetics is not really considered to play any role in it. In fact, a library or internet search for discussions on the aesthetics of medicine is likely to simply turn up works on cosmetic surgery.

In what follows we will delve into, not the medical history of the senses, but the sensory history of medicine. This chapter traces the ways in which the senses were once engaged by Western medicine and how they became side-lined in modernity. It will also explore the sensory dimensions of an array of non-Western and alternative medical traditions in an attempt to arrive at a social understanding of sensuous healing.

Channelling sensory powers in early medicine

The king's touch: Sufferers of scrofula, their necks painfully swollen, kneel in front of a king to receive a blessed healing touch from his royal hands.

The basilisk's gaze: A monstrous animal, half serpent, half cock, raises his head in anger and looks someone in the eye – a fatal sickness quickly spreads through the victim's body.

These two scenarios illustrate a basic tenet of traditional medicine: that ill-ness could be caused or cured through sensory channels. Belief in the healing touch of a king and the fatal gaze of a basilisk participated in the same model of sensory operations as belief in the cooling virtues of cucumbers or the noxious odour of swamps.

As 'gateways' to the body, the senses seemed eminently suited to receive influences that could either benefit or injure the body. If poisonous foods could be taken in by the mouth, why not 'poisonous' sights by the eye, or 'poisonous' scents by the nose? Sensory qualities were often conceptualized as independent forces that could affect one's well-being. Thus, the author of an early seventeenth century medical treatise asked: 'Does melancholy induce fear and sadness because it is black in colour or because it is cold?' (cited in Thorndike 1934, II: 205).

The assumption was that, not only did illness cause certain sensations, but certain sensations *caused* illness. The opposite of this last notion, as we shall see, was also held to be true: certain sensations could promote health. The attribution of agency to sensory qualities made it important to take such qualities into account when diagnosing and treating disease. A putrid smell emanating from a patient might not simply be a symptom of a particular illness, but a primary cause of the illness (as well as a vehicle of infection). A fragrant scent, in contrast, might prevent and treat disease (Classen et al. 1994: 58–62). To understand the body in health and illness it was essential to approach it through the senses.

The senses in diagnosis

Early Western medicine assigned to each of the traditional five senses a role in diagnosis: The ancient Greek physician Hippocrates held that it was 'the business of the physician to know, in the first place, things ... which are to be presented by the sight, touch, hearing, the nose, and the tongue, and the understanding' (cited by Nicolson 1997: 802). The value of the different senses in diagnosis was similarly emphasized by the second-century Roman physician Galen. The sense of sight was employed to provide information about the appearance of the patient's body and excretions. The scrutiny of urine was especially emphasized and physicians often possessed elaborate uroscopy charts to aid them in their visual assessment. These charts displayed some twenty shades of urinous colour – from clear to yellow, orange, red, brown, and black – which could be matched against the flasks of urine brought to physicians by their patients. The senses of smell and taste might also be used to assess urine samples, along with other body fluids and, in the case of smell alone, the breath. Hearing served to gather useful information by attending to the gurgling and wheezings of the patient's body. Physicians might furthermore check for certain characteristic sounds by thumping on different body parts (Nutton 1993; see further Lindemann 2010: 274).

The physician could also palpate the body to feel for blockages in any of the organs. The sense of touch was most commonly employed, however, to take the patient's temperature and pulse. This last was a complex procedure that took into account strength, hardness, speed, interval, regularity and rhythm. It was recommended that the physician use four fingers to take the pulse because the location of the ailment could be distinguished according to which finger felt the beat most strongly: if the forefinger, then the problem lay in the head; if the middle finger, the stomach was at fault; if the ring finger, the intestines, and if the little finger, the feet. It took elaborate expertise to evaluate a pulse. Galen's facility in this domain was legendary and his treatise on the subject was pored over for centuries by those seeking to emulate him. The profound importance attached to the techniques for taking the pulse and temperature suggest that 'For Galen [and his followers] medicine was above all a tactile science' (Wootton 2006: 63; see also Eleazar 1999; Jenner 2010).

Not all early physicians were as multisensory in their diagnostic practices as Hippocrates and Galen recommended. Certainly pulse reading was considered of great importance, along with the analysis of urine. However, due to a belief in the validity of subjective sensory experience (Wear 2000: 109), many physicians relied primarily on patient accounts of symptoms. These accounts or 'case histories' might then be the subject of consultation with other physicians in order to arrive at a consensus as to the correct diagnosis and treatment. One sixteenth-century print satirizing this custom depicts a group of physicians in earnest consultation with each other but with their backs turned to their suffering patients (Bylebyl 1993: fig. 18).

As literacy became more widespread after the Middle Ages, many people simply sent a written description of their ailment to their physician (see Lindemann 2010: 274–75). When in the sixteenth century Albrecht Dürer wished to be diagnosed by an out-of-town physician, he took the added measure of sending a drawing of his body with an index finger pointing to the painful spot and a sentence stating: 'This is where it hurts' (Schott 2004).

The performance of diagnosis at a distance through a written description, sometimes accompanied by a drawing, became popular during the Renaissance. It had the definite advantage, during a period when society was becoming less communal and tactile, of avoiding physical intimacy between the doctor and patient. Perhaps more importantly, it helped to establish professional medicine as a learned discipline, based on the study of texts, as opposed to the more sense-based folk medicine practised by sometimes illiterate healers. This means of differentiation was crucial because there was often little difference between professional and folk methods of treatment in premodern medicine.

Temperature, flavour and colour

It is, indeed, in the field of treatment that the various senses played their most important medical role.

> [As] the senses provided the most vivid, immediate information about the world, so the linking of the senses to remedies ensured that belief about the particular therapeutic power of a remedy would be stronger because it seemed to be validated by the senses.
>
> (Wear 2000: 89)

Traditional humoral theory, which underlay medical practice, understood the universe to be composed of four primary tactile properties: hot, cold, wet, and dry. These primary qualities were present in the human body through the medium of four basic fluids or humours: blood (hot and wet), choler (hot and dry), black bile (cold and dry) or phlegm (cold and wet). When one of these sensory combinations was overabundant within the body, disease resulted. Many forms of treatment, therefore, aimed to provide a counterbalance. Someone deemed to be suffering from an excess of 'cold' and 'wetness' might be treated with herbal remedies considered to be 'hot' and 'dry'. Bloodletting, purging and cupping were other common means of redressing presumed cases of humoral imbalance. Bathing, exercise and massage, while important in antiquity, were less commonly prescribed in later periods, partly because of their negative associations with sensuality.

Diet was considered to play a central role in maintaining health. The ideal diet was suited to a person's temperament and to the season of the year. Honey, for example, was said to be heating and thus healthful for persons with 'cold, moist' temperaments, and for the general populace in the winter-time. The supposed ill effects of consuming one kind of food might be counteracted through partaking of another with opposite effects. Hence the 'putrefying effect' of eating 'cold, wet' cherries, could be countered with the preservative qualities of a 'good, fragrant wine'.

Sugar, interestingly, was considered to be highly healthful. It was charac-terized as warm and moist and easy to digest, with its beneficial attributes signalled by its pleasurable sweetness. Aristotle himself had stated that 'nothing can nourish the body unless it participates in some sweetness' (Shaw and Welch 2011: 211–12). So beneficial was sugar deemed to be that it played an important role in many medicaments. (Indeed, as it was quite expensive, many people never tasted sugar except in the form of a medicament.) Generally, the flavour of a remedy was taken as a sign of its medicinal properties – a notion that led some physicians to chew their way through gardens, classifying plants by their taste (see Wear 2000: 89; Jenner 2010).

Chromotherapy and healthful music

Turning to the field of sight, visual impressions were thought to leave a mark on the soft interior of the body, particularly on the malleable body of an unborn child. One of the best-known expressions of this belief consisted of attributing a harelip deformity in a baby to the mother having stared at a rabbit while pregnant. What one viewed, therefore, could have definite physical consequences, and this made visual images potentially of relevance in the treatment of illness.

Colours had their own medical significance. In diagnosis, the colour of a patient's complexion might be taken to suggest an overabundance of a particular humour – a red complexion was associated with a surfeit of blood, a yellow one with choler, a dark hue with black bile and pallor with phlegm. In treatment, colours might be employed to heat or cool, stir or soothe. The influential Arab physician Avicenna argued that red moved the blood (which made it inadvisable to look at red objects when having a nosebleed), blue and white had cooling effects and yellow reduced pain and swelling (Graham 1999: 267). Red was generally favoured by physicians and the larger populace as a healthful and protective hue, a view that led to a long-standing predilection for red scarves and underwear (Thorndike 1934: 116).

This kind of chromotherapy played an important role in the therapeutic use of gemstones and metals. Emeralds, for example, were thought to be vitalizing when worn next to the skin or ingested in the form of a powder because of their 'life-giving' greenness. Gold, associated with the powers of the sun, was the most-valued metal and colour. Its highly-positive associations led to gold shavings being added to medicinal preparations of the costlier sort (see Ficino 2006: 113–14). In his *Canterbury Tales* Chaucer jokingly relates of the physician in the party of pilgrims that he loved gold – for its medicinal properties (see Eleazar 1999).

The colour of foods might be taken into account when assessing their effect on the body. Whiteness, associated with purity and delicacy, could be thought to indicate a superior digestibility, as in the case of white bread and white sugar. Red foods, by contrast, were generally considered to be heartening and strengthening. One popular medicament and comfit known as manuschristi offered a synaesthetic blend of healing virtues. Its name – 'hand of Christ' – suggested it would have a healing touch within the body. It was composed of sugar boiled in rose water, combining supposedly healthful flavours with a cordial red tint. In its costlier versions it contained flecks of gold and crushed gemstones, which would have added immensely to its prestige as a sovereign remedy (see Shaw and Welch 2011: ch. 7).

Music also had a role to play in healing, though more of a supportive one. The early medieval encyclopaedist Isidore of Seville held that physicians should be knowledgeable about music because of its healing powers. Different modes of music were classified according to the categories of humoral theory. Calming, 'cool and moist' melodies, for example, might be employed to soothe the passions of an overly hot and dry, choleric individual. The rhythm of the pulse was often linked to ideas of a cosmic harmony based on ancient ideas of the music of the spheres. This notion of the underlying musicality of human beings was brought out by Shakespeare in *Hamlet*:

> My pulse as yours doth temperately keep time
> And makes a healthful music
>
> (3, 4.140–41; see further Hoeniger 1992)

Music was considered particularly useful for mental disorders. This was due both to the belief that its 'airy' nature gave it a particular power over the 'airy' human spirit, and due to its presumed ability to realign the disturbed spirit of the patient with the harmonious music of the spheres (Garber 2008: ch. 4; Thorndike 1934: 261–69).

Odours and aromatics

As regards smell, it's important to note that odours participated in a larger experiential domain which included notions of 'vapours', 'airs' and 'fumes'. Even the sense of sight could be linked with olfactory emissions, for it was thought that the eyes (along with stars) could emit poisonous vapours that would spread disease. This explained the fatal glance of the basilisk and also the dangers of the 'evil eye'. Fragrant scents were believed to ward off the noxious odours of disease. Hence, during times of plague, aromatic nosegays and pomanders were frequently used for protection against pathogenic smells. Even unpleasant odours might be considered protective, if sufficiently pungent. This practice was described in a seventeenth-century poem by John Taylor, which told of one plague-fearing Londoner who

> with a peece of tesseld well tarr'd Rope
> doth with that nose-gaye keepe himselfe in hope.

and another who

> takes off his socks from's sweating feete
> and makes them his perfume along the streete
>
> (see Classen et al. 1994: 58–62)

Although the poem is humorous, it gives a vivid impression both of the anxiety produced by such epidemics and of the power attributed to strong scents.

Numerous aromatics were used in treatment. The scent of the mandrake was said to cure headaches and insomnia. Rose perfume cooled overheated brains, while violet scent reportedly calmed fits. The aroma of eggplants, interestingly, was thought by some to be an aphrodisiac. One medieval manual warned:

> When picking aubergines, married women and virgins should be on their guard against aroused males, for the nature of the fruit is hot and moist and its melancholic odors induce deviations from decent behaviour.
>
> (*Four Seasons* 1984: 36)

For women with problems of infertility, in turn, censing the womb with spices was recommended (see Classen 1998: 69–70).

Aromatics could be utilized in a range of ways: in drinks, as incense, as perfume, as purifying sprays and washes, or strewn on the floor to release their odour when stepped on. The proper administration of aromas was understood to help prevent disease by combatting the invasive odours of illness and by countering conditions that might lead to ill health. Thus in the summer, for example, 'cool' scents, such as that of rose, were advised, while 'hot' scents were recommended for the winter, as laid out in the following (very luxurious) medieval prescription for warming aromas.

> In the rooms strew herbs that suggest hotness, such as mint, pennyroyal, sage, hyssop, bay leaves, rosemary marjoram. Make a decoction of these herbs, adding cloves, cinnamon, and nutmeg, with which to spray one's living quarters. A fire should always be lit with fragrant wood like laurel, rosemary, cypress, juniper. Burn incense over hot coals: cinnamon, laudanum, nutmeg, citron rind, myrrh.
>
> (*Four Seasons* 1984: 91)

Despite such extensive use of aromatics, not everyone felt that they were adequately employed by physicians of the day. The essayist Michel de Montaigne wrote in the sixteenth century that: 'The doctors might, I believe, derive more use from odours than they do, for I have often noticed that they make a change in me and work upon my spirits according to their properties' (cited in Classen 1993a: 21).

Odour and/or flavour played an especially important role in the alchemical philosophies of the Renaissance. Humoral theory customarily considered odour and flavour to be secondary properties, arising from combinations of the fundamental qualities of hot, cold, wet and dry. As regards their presence within the body, each of the four humours was deemed to have a particular savour: blood was sweet, choler was bitter, black bile sour, and phlegm salty or insipid. The alchemists, however preferred to emphasize flavour over thermal properties, taking as their authority Hippocrates, who declared that:

'There is in man salt and bitter, sweet and acid, astringent and insipid, possessing powers of all sorts' (Coulter 1975: 414; Pagel 1984: 23). The Renaissance physician Paracelsus associated flavours with different kinds of pain:

> Sour and bitter make two kinds of pain, biting and sharp also two kinds, and none of these is identical with the other. For in the same way as a flavor is obnoxious to the tongue, so also is it in open lesions obnoxious to the flesh. For, though there is no sense of taste in these places, they still feel the pains.
> (cited in Coulter 1975: 415)

The alchemical philosopher and physician Van Helmont, however, held that odours constituted the active principle in health and illness, attributing to them a 'universal creative and generative role' (Pagel 1982: 74). According to this viewpoint, simply inhaling a remedy might prove sufficient, since the essence of a medicament was held to reside in its smell (Coulter 1975: 414–27).

Cosmotherapies

Whether based on humoral theory, alchemy, or ancient notions of the harmony of the spheres, sensory healing was often integrated into a model of the cosmos. In fact, the form and functions of the human body were understood to be related to and affected by the form and functions of the cosmos. In the popular image of the 'Zodiac Man' all the different parts and organs of the body were shown to be under the influence of a particular astrological sign or planet. The senses were divided up among the planets as well, although, since there were more planets than senses, this required a certain 'sensory multiplication'. In the arrangement suggested by Ptolemy in the second century, Saturn was deemed to govern the right ear and Mars the left, Jupiter reigned over touch, the Sun ruled sight, the Moon taste, Venus smell, and Mercury speech (which was sometimes included among the senses) (Tester 1987: 23, 61–62, 67).

Different sensory properties – colours, flavours, perfumes, musical notes, and so on – were likewise linked in chains of sympathy with particular planets. There was some disagreement about which property went with which planet. In the sixteenth century, Gerolamo Cardano classified Mars with blueness and saltiness, Venus with whiteness and sweetness, and Saturn with blackness and bitterness. In the more conventional arrangement of Geronimo Cortes, on the other hand, Mars was red and spicy, Venus was blue and musky, and Saturn was black and acid (Schrader 1975: 325–27). According to this system, each planet regulated the operation of its corresponding sensory properties on earth. The list of things associated with the Sun by the philosopher Marsilio Ficino in the fifteenth century included gold colours, myrrh, amber, balsam, honey, saffron, cinnamon, cocks, swans, lions and 'people who are blond, curly-haired, prone to baldness and magnanimous' (Ficino 2006: 115).

This link between sensory properties and cosmological structure, emphasized in the Hermetic philosophies of the Renaissance, might be taken into account when diagnosing and treating patients and often determined which sensory qualities would be selected to treat an illness. For instance, if a disease was classified as Saturnine in nature – characterized by chills, greyish skin colour, and mental depression – the physician might well decide to combat it with odours associated with the hot, bright Sun, such as myrrh and cinnamon. This infusion of solar scents would help to instil in the patient a properly balanced cosmological and sensory order. From this perspective, the stars might well need to be consulted before the nature of an ailment or its proper treatment could be determined. An interesting example of such 'cosmo-therapy' practised preventively can be found in the case of Pope Urban VIII. When in 1628 an imminent eclipse was taken to predict the pope's death, the Hermetic philosopher Tommaso Campanella tried to counter the malevolent astrological influences by surrounding the pope with jewels, perfumes, colours and music corresponding to the supposedly benevolent planets Jupiter and Venus. As the pope survived the eclipse, the ritual could not be deemed unsuccessful (Burke 1974: 105).

The most sought-after form of sensory healing in premodernity, however, did not come from the domains of medicine or philosophy, but from that of religion. In the Middle Ages (and long afterwards in many countries) pilgrims streamed to shrines with the hope of being healed by coming into contact with saintly relics. It was believed that any ailment, no matter how dire, might be cured by a simple tactile transmission of grace. Different saints and shrines were recommended for the cure of different diseases. Saint Apollonia was appealed to for toothache, Saint Lucy for eye ailments and Saint Sebastian for the plague. As described at the start of this chapter, monarchs (who, although not saintly, ruled by divine right) were believed to cure scrofula with a touch in England and France. A special rite was established for this purpose, which attracted large numbers of hopeful sufferers (Thomas 2005; Classen 2012: 50–51, 158–59).

Nor was touch the only possible medium for divine healing. Stories told of people cured by an odour of sanctity, by a holy voice or by a saintly vision. As physicians generally shared the religious sensibilities of their patients, however, these sacred techniques of healing were not seen as challenging secular medical practices. They rather pointed to God as the ultimate source of health and wholeness and thus the supreme physician.

Directing and displacing the senses in modern medicine

A certain distrust of the medicinal value of sensory qualities arose in the six-teenth and seventeenth centuries. Traditionally it had been assumed that what looked good, smelled good, tasted good or sounded good was likely good for one's health. While there was always the danger of excess, the body gave warning of having had too much of a good thing by experiencing sensations of surfeit or disgust.

Influenced by the Protestant emphasis on asceticism and by new develop-ments in medicine, however, pleasurable sensations were increasingly

suspected of being misleading, either affording no benefits or actually en-
gendering harm. Just as it was becoming more affordable, sugar, for example,
began to lose its reputation as a sovereign remedy and acquire its modern one
of unwholesomeness. Sweets henceforth would become a guilty pleasure
(Shaw and Welch 2011, see generally Mintz 1986). Bright colours, rich
perfumes and melodious tunes became similarly suspect – if they were
conducive to moral corruption, as the stricter Protestants claimed, could they
really be good for one's health? Should not medicine, like life itself according
to more sober thinkers, be painful to be beneficial? 'The physic [medicine]
must make us sick that doth us any good', commented one seventeenth-
century Puritan with sad resignation (Wear 2003: 74). This perception of
medicine as a 'bitter pill' effectively dismissed the notion of there being an
important aesthetic dimension to medical treatment.

Reformers also denounced as superstitious such religious practices and phenomena as touching relics and the odour of sanctity, thereby greatly reducing
the role of sacred acts and objects in healing. This opened the door to considering a range of related medical practices, such as the king's touch, as similarly
based on superstition (although natural explanations for seemingly supernatural
healing abilities were also sought for a time [see Classen 2012: 159]).

The clinical senses

With the rise of empirical philosophy in the seventeenth and eighteenth centuries, the focus of medicine changed from the human being as a microcosm
of the universe, to the human being as an organic 'machine'. To learn why a
machine is not working properly one does not consult the stars nor rely on
ancient authorities, one examines its insides (see Wear 2000: 447). In medical
terms this led to a growing emphasis on the study of anatomy and the practice
of surgery. In sensory terms it would eventually lead to a decline in the significance attached to the subjective sensations reported by patients and a sharp
increase in the importance of direct observation by the physician. It was by
opening up the body to the medical gaze that its murky inner secrets were
exposed and the old order of medical 'superstition', with its elaborate sense-
based theories and practices, demolished.

The settings for the performance of this new clinical model of medicine
were the clinic, with patients lined up in beds for easy observation, and
the medical theatre. This latter was the site where lectures were made visible
through the dissection of cadavers on the demonstration table.

> To teach sound knowledge ... the instructor [had to link] correct terms
> with what the pupil *saw*. The other senses, such as touch in anatomy or
> smell in materia medica, certainly provided data supporting the impres-
> sions given by sight, but these secondary sensations were rarely discussed
> or described explicitly during the lectures.
>
> (Lawrence 1993: 170)

In response to the demand for visual access to the inner body, advances in anatomical illustration were made by William Cheselden, William Hunter and other eighteenth-century anatomists, who built on the work of previous illustrators. Striving for representational accuracy, these illustrators sought to develop artistic styles so transparent that their depictions were taken as literal visual truth. Thus, William Hunter confidently stated that: 'Representation in the imitative Arts is a Substitute for reality.' This premise enabled him to claim that a well-drawn picture could give 'an immediate comprehension of what it represents' (cited in Kemp 1993: 85, 118). The fact that odours and tactile sensations came to be viewed as 'secondary sensations', is not surprising, given this reduction of 'reality' to that which meets the eye. (In fact, 'clean' and 'clear cut' anatomical illustrations helped purify anatomy of its 'messy' tactile and olfactory associations.) These new ways of understanding the body were hotly contested by many physicians who preferred older or other models, but over time they came to dominate medical thinking.

At the turn of the nineteenth century the 'anatomico-clinical method' advocated by Xavier Bichat of the Paris Clinical School further emphasized the importance of extending the power of sight to the interior of the body. 'Open up a few corpses,' wrote Bichat, 'you will immediately dissipate the darkness which observation alone could not dissipate' (cited in Foucault 1973: 146). Through correlating the lesions revealed by post-mortem examination with the symptoms manifested by the patient during illness Bichat and his contemporaries were able to cast the underlying conditions of disease – and also life – in a whole new light (Barnes forthcoming). Henceforth, what clinically-trained physicians would see when examining a living patient was a corpse, due to their perception of the living body being mediated by the image of the dissected body. And, as a mere 'corpse', the patient would have little active role to play in the healing process.

The new technology

Another major development in modern medicine concerned the adoption of new technologies for diagnosis: 'machines' for investigating the organic 'machine' of the body. These initially met with some resistance, partly due to doubts concerning their accuracy, but also on the grounds that they distorted or devalued the 'God-given' sensory abilities of humans. The microscope, invented in the seventeenth century, was considered by some to distort the view of the world which God has deemed most suitable for human eyes (see Knellwolf King 2008: 113). Not until the nineteenth century did it become an important tool for diagnosis. When it did, however, it enabled the medical gaze to penetrate even more deeply into the body, to the level of the cell, which became the new site for pathology (Barnes forthcoming).

Similarly, the thermometer ('fever-stick'), while likewise invented in the seventeenth century, only became a standard medical tool in the mid-nineteenth. Resistance to its adoption was based not only on its originally clumsy design, but on its usurpation of the diagnostic role of the hand. Long-celebrated as a masterpiece of divine design (O'Rourke Boyle 1998), the hand was deemed to be the 'perfect instrument' with which to gauge hot and cold, wet and dry. No human invention, it was thought, could compete with the hand's subtle tactile perceptions (Wootton 2006: 54).

The stethoscope, invented in the nineteenth century, was more readily adopted. A key reason for its acceptance by the medical profession, however, would seem to have been that it provided a more discrete alternative to laying an ear directly on a patient's chest. Much discussed was the fact that, thanks to the new device, doctors need not have their sensibilities offended in the course of examining malodorous patients, and female patients need not be distressed by an infringement of their bodily privacy (Nicolson 1993; Porter 1993). It was this capacity for appeasing sensibilities and neutralizing a morally ambiguous situation by maintaining distance, rather than any new information it made available, that most commended the stethoscope for adoption.

These examples indicate that developments in the practice of medicine are not solely due to advances in knowledge or technology. Rather, the so-called scientific reasons for the adoption of a given discovery sometimes complement and sometimes compete with other considerations – moral, aesthetic, epistemic – and it is the totality of considerations that determines acceptance.

Along with these new technological aids to diagnosis, the late nineteenth-century physician had a new human instrument to depend on – the nurse. The nurse, in a way, became the doctor's senses externalized in a female body (an eminently suitable form according to gender ideologies that associated women with sensuality). With her trained senses, the nurse was expected to record relevant sensations and communicate them effectively to the attending physician. Never, however, was she to 'cross the line between nursing observation and medical diagnosis' (Sandelowski 2000: 87; Meade 1936). The nurse's senses were supposed to feed into the physician's mind, not into her own.

The one precision instrument that fell within the domain of the nurse and became closely associated with her was the relatively straightforward thermometer. Any attempts to provide nurses with training in more complex technologies of analysis were met with suspicion by physicians. One declared that:

> What patients required was not a nurse who could write a thesis about urinalysis or how to test for hydrochloric acid in stomach contents but, rather, one who could fluff their pillows, feed them, and report on their condition to the doctor.
>
> (cited by Sandelowski 2000: 87)

Many of the new tools for observation and diagnosis expanded the role of sight and downplayed or obviated the use of the other senses. This was in keeping with the new importance given to sight in clinical practice and in modern science and philosophy generally. Instead of being ascertained through touch, body temperature could be read from a thermometer. The

composition of body fluids was no longer judged by smell or taste, but ana-
lysed under a microscope. Visual readings of the pulse were produced by the
sphygmograph, and of the heartbeat by the electrocardiograph. The stethoscope was unusual in its continued reliance on a non-visual sense. However,
even the stethoscope might be perceived as metaphorically extending the
physician's gaze. In the words of one commentator, it placed 'a window in the
breast through which we can see the precise state of things within' (Barnes
forthcoming; see also Lachmund 1999: 433–34). A range of new medical
technologies from the X-ray to all the recent forms of imaging technology
(such as CT and PET scans and Magnetic Resonance Imaging or MRI) continued the trend of channelling information about the condition of a patient
through the medium of sight alone.

The nurse, herself, although expected to register multiple sensory impressions and regarded as the 'hands-on' counterpart to the 'overseeing' physician
came to be conceptualized as an instrument of vision. 'The trained nurse was
to be all-seeing: to take all the "visual opportunities" available to her and to
maintain "visual control" of her patients' (Sandelowski 2000: 72). Nurses were
also in charge of ensuring that the patients under their care did not offend
visitors and, in particular, physicians, with any unpleasant body odours. (An
early antiperspirant marketed to nurses, among others, for this purpose was
called Mum, suggesting both the feminine, motherly nature of odour management and the importance of 'silencing' odours – 'Mum's the word' was
one of the product's slogans.) This practice helped delete odour from the
sensory signs to be taken into account in medical diagnosis.

As regards the underlying causes of illness, these lost their sensory attributes
in the nineteenth century and became a matter of the actions of microbes,
genes and cells in the twentieth. This transition was in keeping with a general
move away from sense-based theories and methods in the sciences (L. Roberts
2005). The older thermal, olfactory or flavourful accounts were not entirely
without modern counterparts. Temperature still had a fundamental role to
play in biology, physics and chemistry. Van Helmont's olfactory model of the
cosmos provided a basis for modern theories of gases. Sugars and acids would
be deemed the building blocks of DNA. However, in modern science sensuous qualities were no longer accorded any objective reality (Classen 1998:
109). As regards representation, visual images and diagrams would come to
serve as the predominant way of relating to the workings of the world
through our senses.

The decline of sensory healing

The treatment of ailments in modernity focused on isolating and treating the
diseased organ or tissue, either through surgery or, increasingly, following
the rise of laboratory methods, through pharmaceuticals. In this transition, the
senses withdrew from the medical scene as media of well-being. One by one
the traditional sensory remedies were deemed unfounded by the medical

academy: hot and dry remedies were of no use against diseases that had been determined to not really be cold and wet in nature: flavours played no role in the efficacy of medicines; music was not a useful treatment for insanity; odours neither caused nor cured disease; and, the touch of kings or saints had no healing powers.

Sensory forms of healing were not discarded all at once or altogether. 'Aromatic elixirs' were widely sold for medicinal purposes in the eighteenth and nineteenth centuries, and though they may not have explicitly been deemed to heal through their scent or savour, they still carried more than a whiff of the old way of thinking about them. Inspired by the importance of friction in ancient medicine, 'flesh brushes' for stimulating the skin and blood became a common item of toiletry. Thermal baths were popular both for their medicinal value and for their sociality. Electrical charges experienced a vogue as a supposed means of restoring vitality. Within the domain of folk healing many of the old sensory remedies survived or were reinvented as alternative therapies. One of the most elaborate of the modern attempts to harness sensory powers for therapeutic purposes was undertaken by James Graham in the late eighteenth century. Graham created a 'Celestial Bed' that combined music, colours, odours, clockwork images, mirrors and magnetism in order to help couples conceive (Williams 1975: 188). Although Graham might have been out of tune with contemporary medical theories, he certainly understood the popular appeal of a rich and evocative sensuality.

On the whole, however, such sensuous treatments were left behind, if not denounced outright as quackery, as medicine progressed. The chemical and surgical remedies offered by modern medicine aimed to alleviate or cure the patient with as little affront to his or her sensibilities as possible. Pills were swallowed without being tasted. Painkilling drugs deadened the sensations of illness, injury and surgery. In a medical model where the body is an organic machine, there is little point in trying to engage patients through their senses. In much of modern medical treatment, therefore, *anaesthetics* became more important than aesthetics.

Sensuous healing in Tibet, the Andes and the Amazonian rainforest

While Western medicine has moved away from sensory theories and therapies, these still play a fundamental role in many non-Western medical systems. Acupuncture, qijong and ayurvedic medicine are among the many practices that have become known in the West as ways of promoting physical and mental well-being through corporeal techniques. Many other medical systems, practised in both large- and small-scale societies, also have rich traditions of involving the senses and the body in the promotion of health and healing (see, for example, Roseman 1991; Laderman and Roseman 1996; Hinton et al. 2008; Romberg 2009), although much more work needs to be done in this area to bring out just how. In this section we look at three of those traditions – one from Tibet, one from the Andean region (which we ourselves have investigated) and one practised by the Shipibo-Conibo people of the Amazonian rainforest.

Many medical systems consist of a blend of local and introduced beliefs and practices. Ancient Greek medicine (and hence premodern Western medicine) was heavily influenced by medical theories coming from the East – which helps explain the many similarities between traditional Asian medicine and early Western medicine (see Kuriyama 2002). The indigenous medical traditions of the Andes merged with the medical system introduced by the Spanish during the colonial period. Tibetan medical knowledge is based on Indian Ayurvedic medicine, with influences from China and indigenous practices. In such cases it can be very difficult to separate out the different strands. For example, are the categories of hot and cold that are so important in Andean medicine indigenous, or were they adopted through the influence of Western humoral medicine? In any case, the inhabitants of a region will take their medical system as a whole, without worrying about what parts come from where.

Tibet: the Tree of Health and Illness

The discussion of Tibetan medicine presented here is largely taken from Terry Clifford's seminal work, *Tibetan Buddhist Medicine and Psychiatry* (1984; see also Lauf 1977; Govinda 1983). Tradition states that the Buddha took on the form of the Medical Buddha Vaidurya and gave the medical teaching known as *The Four Treatises*. These form the basis of Tibetan medicine. The Medical Buddha is depicted as residing in a crystal palace in the middle of a healing paradise. In each of the four directions there rises up a medicinal mountain. To the north, for example, rises 'Snowy Mountain', on which grow white sandal-wood, camphor, aloes, and other medicines that combat hot diseases. It is said that the perfume of these plants can help to lower the temperature of fevers. In the south lies the 'Thunderbolt Mountain', where hot medicinal plants that combat cold diseases flourish. These include red sandalwood, pomegranate and black pepper. Their perfumes are considered to raise the temperature of the body. The image of the four mountains provides a richly-evocative means of presenting and situating the wide range of medicaments employed in Tibetan medicine.

Another image used in the teaching of medicine in Tibet is that of the Tree of Health and Illness, which offers an organic model for learning and ordering the major elements of the medical system. This tree is said to have three roots. The first root or division, deals with physiology and pathology, the second root with diagnosis, and the third root with therapy.

As in the West, medical training in Tibet relies heavily on the study of medical texts, of which there are many volumes (most as yet untranslated into Western languages). However, textual study is supplemented by hands-on training with patients and by the study of medicinal herbs and the preparation of medicines. One prominent Tibetan physician recounted that an important test in his final year of study consisted in identifying different herbs by taste and smell alone – a field in which Western medical students are not expected to possess any competence (Donden 2000: 10; see also Good 1994: 74).

Tibetan medicine distinguishes three basic types of vital energies or humours that influence conditions of health and illness. These are loosely translated as wind, phlegm, and bile. The physical constitution of individuals are thought to be dominated by one of the three. The different parts of the body are also associated with one or another of the three humours in Tibetan medicine. In terms of the senses, hearing and touch are linked with wind, sight with bile, and smell and taste with phlegm. Disorders are characterized by an excess of wind, phlegm or bile. Wind disorders produce aches in joints, irritation and insomnia; bile disorders cause headaches, fever and backache; phlegm disorders bring on vomiting, heaviness and coldness.

The three trunks that grow from the diagnostic root in the Tree of Health and Illness deal with Visual Observation, Tactile Observation, and Questioning or Oral Communication. Central to the first two forms of observation are urine analysis and pulse-reading. Urine is examined in terms of its colour, clarity, density, temperature and odour. Normal urine, for example, is said to be 'white with a yellowish tinge like the colour of freshly-melted butter; it is light, with a bad odour; the steam is normal ... after the odour has disappeared, the sediment is blue with a yellowish tinge' (Clifford 1984: 105). Pulse-reading distinguishes many different kinds of pulses that correspond to particular medical conditions.

When approached by a patient, the Tibetan physician tries to establish whether a disease is caused by wind, bile, or phlegm. In order to do this, visual and tactile observations are supplemented by information provided by the patient. This last area is outlined in the Questioning Trunk of the Tree of Health and Illness. The Wind Branch of the Questioning Trunk prompts physicians to inquire concerning such 'windy' symptoms as yawning and shivering, sighing and stretching, cold chills and aches, and dulled sensory perceptions. The other branches suggest other bodily conditions to be discussed.

The particular constitution of a person is carefully considered by Tibetan physicians when prescribing medicaments. The three elements of wind, phlegm, and bile must be kept in balance within the body, according to the patient's personal constitution. The person with a wind constitution tends to be small, lively, sensitive to cold, and a light sleeper. The bile-type is medium-sized, proud, and impatient. The phlegm-type is tall and heavier, has greater powers of endurance, and tends to sleep deeply.

Tibetan treatment involves diet, behaviour and medicaments taken internally or applied externally. A large part of treatment regimens concerns the gustatory and tactual (or physical) powers of foods and medicaments. There are six tastes – sweet, sour, salty, bitter, pungent and astringent – and eight tactile qualities – heavy, oily, cool, bland, light, rough, hot and sharp. The first are thought of as the taste of a medicament, indicating its active principle, the second as the effect it will have on the stomach.

As a treatment for wind diseases, for example, the patient is advised to take medicines and foods that are sweet, sour and salty in taste, and sticky, heavy and soft in texture. For wind, it is furthermore recommended that one should be massaged with oils and relax in a dark, warm place with a friend who tells 'sweet' stories. Sensually appropriate treatments are similarly prescribed for the other two categories of illnesses and types of constitution.

Tibetan healing is effected by reintroducing equilibrium into the body, rather than by treating any particular organ or symptom. Pharmacology is very important in this process, while surgery plays a comparatively minor role.

The most popular ways of administering treatment are the so-called gentle methods. These include inhaling incense, taking herbal baths, drinking teas, and being massaged with aromatic butters. Incense is thought to be particularly important for psychiatric ailments caused by wind. One all-purpose psychiatric incense contains aloeswood, frankincense, nutmeg, cubeb, juniper and myrobalan.

In certain cases a physician may determine that a disease is the result, at least in part, of an ill deed committed by the patient in this or a previous life. In such a case treatment must be supplemented by repentance and virtuous action by the patient (Donden 2000: 17).

The Andes: the cosmic body

In contrast with Tibet, the Andean region of South America does not have a tradition of literacy. The medicine of the region, therefore, is not learned through texts, but through apprenticeship to established healers, through personal experience, and through revelation, as in the form of dreams and visions. A lack of standardizing texts and medical academies means that Andean healing techniques, although sharing common principles, vary in their specifics from one locality to another.

The model of the body underlying Andean medicine highlights the importance of the movement of fluids and airs within the body and between the body and the environment. This corresponds to larger models that present both society and the land as bodies that require the circulation of goods, energies and fluids to be dynamic and productive. On the largest scale, the entire cosmos is conceptualized as a body with structures and processes similar in principle to those of the individual body, and similarly requiring a balanced exchange of fluids and forces to be integrated and animated. An illness afflicting a particular person, hence, is often considered in terms of how it may be affected by disruptions within these larger bodies. The ultimate goal of Andean medicine is not simply to ensure a corporeal equilibrium, but rather to bring about a balanced and productive interchange of fluids and forces (Bastien 1985; Classen 1993b).

The Andean general practitioner (for there are also specialists) determines the nature of an ailment through observing and consulting with the patient. Divinatory aids to diagnosis, such as reading coca leaves, are also frequently used. These are intended to help the healer and patient know not only where the problem lies within the patient's body, but also how it originated.

This knowledge is essential for, if a treatment is to be effective, it must be directed at the ultimate cause of the illness, as well as to its physical symptoms.

In a complex case, therefore, treatment will have two dimensions: one will address the presumed underlying cause, which may be sorcery or an offended ancestor or deity, and the other will aim to cure the ailments of the patient. In both cases, sensory elements are employed, for these are regarded as powerful avenues of communication and agents of transformation. For example, a ritual of atonement for an offense committed against the ancestral spirits will involve prayers, chanting, ritual movement, incense, and offerings. Treatment directed at the patient may similarly involve a range of sensory stimuli.

Andean healers have traditionally had access to a wide variety of plants for their cures. This is due to the nature of the Andean environment, which supports very different plant life at different altitudes and locations. Medicinal herbs are generally classified as either 'hot' or 'cold' according to the effect they are presumed to have on the body. They are administered to patients by healers in a variety of ways, the most common method being in the form of a tea. Such teas are believed to work upon the patient both through being swallowed and through their aromatic vapours. Aromatic plants may also be burnt to produce an incense, or employed in fragrant baths or in massage ointments. As in Tibet, Andean healers must be able to identify herbs by taste and smell alone, not least because, when dry and crushed, they often look very similar (see further Classen and Howes 1998).

In the case of a serious illness, an attempt will often be made to treat the patient through all of her or his senses. This is the case with 'susto' – fright sickness – a common ailment in the region, as in other parts of Latin America. Susto is said to occur when a person, and particularly a child, suffers a strong fright, which has the effect of separating the soul from the body.

Susto produces sensations of weakness and nervousness and may lead to crying and vomiting. The healer usually visits the place where the fright occurred, if this is nearby, and attempts to lure the soul back to its body by calling out the name of the patient. The healer will also drag a piece of the patient's clothing on the ground to leave a trail for the soul to follow home. During this ceremony it is important that there be complete silence, for even the bark of a dog is said to be enough to scare the already frightened soul away again.

In the meantime, the patient will have been treated with a range of therapies. The sufferer from susto is kept warm in bed and given aromatic herbal tea to drink. Incense composed of a variety of substances, such as rosemary, rue, and sugar, is burnt in order to soothe the patient, attract the wandering soul, and keep away evil spirits. The patient may also be massaged in order to alleviate the physical disturbance resulting from susto. Prayers to Pachamama (Mother Earth) and to Christian saints will invoke supernatural aid on behalf of the patient. Finally, a bright red charm, often in the form of a bracelet, may be used to strengthen the patient's resistance to evil forces. This multisensory therapy creates a pleasant aesthetic environment in order to encourage healing in the patient. At the same time, it integrates the patient into the healing process through all of her or his senses.

The Amazonian rainforest: the mingling of sensations

In the Amazonian rainforest the mingling of sensations is essential to many healing traditions. This emphasis on synaesthesia is undoubtedly influenced by the widespread use of the hallucinogenic ayahuasca brew, which produces experiences of sensory interconnections. The ayahuasca-imbibing Desana of Colombia, for example, hold that colour forces animate the world. These colour forces are believed to combine with temperature to produce odour, which then gives rise to flavour. Disease is thought to 'muddy' the chromatic energies within the body. The Desana healer therefore concentrates on restoring a healthy spectrum by invoking and employing a range of hues and related sensory stimuli (Classen 1993a: 131–34).

The mingling of sensations is also central to the medical traditions of the Shipibo-Conibo (an amalgamation of two neighbouring ethnic groups), who live in the Amazonian region of Peru (Gebhart-Sayer 1985). At the start of a healing session the healer, under the influence of ayahuasca, sees the inner body 'pattern' of the patient. A sick person's body pattern appears 'like a very messy design' or mixed-up pile of garbage, and its pathological aura is said to have a vile stench, which is the mark of the attacking spirits (*nihue*) causing the illness. The healing ritual involves both the restoration of a healthy body pattern and the neutralization of the pathogenic aura through life-enhancing fragrance.

The shaman begins by brushing away the 'mess' on the patient's body with a decorated garment and fanning away the miasma of the attacking spirits with his fragrant herbal bundle, all the while blowing tobacco smoke. He then takes up his rattle and shakes a rhythm. Following this, he perceives whole 'sheets' of luminescent geometric designs, in the form of delicate arabesques, drawn by the hummingbird spirit, hovering in the air, which gradually descend to his lips. On reaching his lips the shaman sings the designs into songs. At the moment of coming into contact with the patient, the songs once again turn into designs that penetrate the patient's body and, ideally, settle down permanently. However, the whole time the healing design is being sung onto the body of the patient, evil spirits will 'try to ruin the pattern by singing evil-smelling anti-songs dealing with the odor of gasoline, fish poison, dogs, certain products of the cosmetic industry, menstrual blood, unclean people, and so on', and thereby smudge or contaminate it (Gebhart-Sayer 1985: 171). It may take up to five sessions for the design to come out 'clear, neat, and complete' and the cure to be finished. (If the design does not settle down permanently, the patient is said to be unlikely to recover.)

Such medicinal songs are accompanied by herbal treatments for, as in the Andes and Tibet, plants are central to the healing practices of the Shipibo-Conibo. In fact, Shipibo-Conibo healers claim to acquire much of their knowledge directly from plants. During the period of training, an apprentice healer will drink an infusion of a particular plant before going to sleep. The spirit of the plant is then said to take the trainee on a voyage of discovery during his or her dreams. The next day, the student consumes more of the plant and then has a session with a medical master, who helps interpret what has been communicated during the night and conveys information about the practical application of the plant. In this fashion, initiates in medicine are thought to acquire – and embody – a complete knowledge of herbal powers. Each plant is said to have both beneficial and harmful uses. The student who focuses on the latter, it is believed, will go on to become a sorcerer rather than a healer. The spirits of the plants themselves are said to decide when a course of study is complete through a visionary communication (Caruso 2005).

Aspiring healers will also spend much time training their voices in order to acquire the melodious tones which will most effectively penetrate and reorder the patient's body in a song session (Caruso 2005: 248). A healer's songs are held to be stored in his medicine vessel. It is important for this vessel to be carefully guarded from evil spirits, for they will try to pry open the lid and allow the 'therapeutic power' of the songs to escape. 'This power is imagined as the fragrance of the design songs or the aromatic gas fizzing from fermenting yucca beer' (Gebhart-Sayer 1985: 172).

The visual designs into which the songs transform are said to originate in the colourful markings on the skin of the cosmic anaconda Ronin. These geometric designs are deemed to have both beautiful and protective properties, and, along with being evoked in the healing songs, are woven into textiles, drawn on pots and house posts, and painted on faces. The Shipibo-Conibo term *quiquin*, which means aesthetic and appropriate, is used to refer to pleasant auditory, olfactory and visual sensations. The shaman operates by 'synaesthetically' combining *quiquin* 'to form a therapy of beauty, cultural relevance, and sophistication' (Gebhart-Sayer 1985: 162).

As in the case of the Navajo and their sand paintings (discussed in the previous chapter), the Shipibo-Conibo incorporate a rich multisensory aesthetics into the practice of healing. The synaesthetic interrelationship of the designs, songs, and fragrances used in the healing rituals is well illustrated by the following lines from a shaman's healing song:

> The (harmful) spirit ...
> swirling in your body's ultimate point.
> I shall tackle it right now
> with my fragrant chanting.
> ...
> I see brilliant bands of designs,
> curved and fragrant ...
>
> (Gebhart-Sayer 1985: 172)

In the healing rituals of the Shipibo-Conibo, therefore, we encounter an orchestrated sequence of sensory transformations – a visual motif turns into a musical pattern, which can in turn be perceived as a perfume – which has as its ultimate purpose the transformation of disease into well-being.

Cosmic and sensory integration

The ways of healing found in these three non-Western medical traditions share certain characteristics. One of these is cosmic integration: all three are grounded in a belief system that encompasses the natural, human, and sacred realms. This grounding imbues the experience of disease and that of healing with meaning. The cures work in part by resituating the patient within a meaningful and orderly cosmos (see Lévi-Strauss 1963; Laderman and Roseman 1996; Hinton et al. 2008). This holistic approach to healing means emotional and even social disorders, along with physical disorders, can be addressed by medical specialists.

If the disease itself cannot be cured, therefore, at least the patient and family members are able to make sense of and deal with it within a comprehensive *cosmic model*. Patients belonging to the same culture as the healer share the same underlying concepts of health and illness, have knowledge of many of the plants and other medicaments employed in treatment, and feel comfortable within the familiar sites used for healing. Entering a healing situation, therefore, does not mean entering an alien sensory and conceptual world, as it does for many patients who are treated by Western medicine.

A second common theme is that of *sensory integration*. Sensory integration refers to the ways in which different senses are stimulated and interrelated in healing. In the non-Western traditions we have explored, we find that careful attention is paid to the aesthetic dimensions of the cure and there is a concerted attempt to deliver complementary treatments and messages through a variety of sensory channels. It is usually considered important for a patient to be attentive to these sensory dimensions so as to actively participate in the process of healing. In the words of a healer from the Himalayas: 'If the patient is asleep, she won't get better' (Desjarlais 1992: 197).

It would be overly idealistic to see indigenous medical systems solely as ways of promoting physical and social well-being. Such systems may also cause physical harm, may uphold social inequalities, may employ fraudulent healers, may promote the collection of endangered plants and animals, and so on. They are not, by virtue of being indigenous, problem-free. They do, however, testify to the remarkable variety and complexity of the sensory worlds of medicine and the ways in which these integrate people with their social and physical environments.

Postmodern medicine and the senses

Hospital aesthetics and patient–physician interactions

Unlike the historical and cross-cultural traditions discussed above, contemporary Western medicine, or biomedicine, makes little attempt to be aesthetically pleasing or to engage patients through their senses. One key indication of this can be found in the pre-eminent site for the practice of healing in modernity – the hospital.

The hospital is a decidedly unaesthetic place. Indeed, for many confined in its grim interior, the hospital must seem more a 'house of correction' for deviant bodies than a house of healing. Hospital rooms are drab and uniform. Gleaming and threatening instruments for administering to or prying into ailing bodies abound. Indeed, the hospital may seem more designed to accommodate medical technologies than to cater to human sensibilities. Hospital food is notoriously unsavoury. Odours are musty or antiseptic. The acoustic world of the hospital is populated by the chatter of staff, the bustling of trolleys, the white noise of the ventilation system, and an assortment of electronic sounds given off by diverse monitors. Tactile contact is often perfunctory, outside of the context of physical therapy. Hospital clothing is neutral-coloured and shapeless – signalling the loss of identity individuals must undergo within the institution – a loss of identity further fostered by the sense of the hospital as a place of social exclusion rather than a central social institution. Outdoors, pleasant environments are lacking as vehicular access and parking take priority over green spaces.

In this setting, the bouquet of flowers brought by a well-meaning visitor often constitutes the solitary attempt to enliven the sick room with a breath of colour and fragrance. However, for many hospital patients the one bright spot, the one homey element, and the one avenue of escape from their over-whelmingly disengaging environment, is the television set on the wall of their room – a sensory technology to compensate for the abject lack of sensory and mental stimulation (see Fuqua 2012).

This lack of attention to hospital aesthetics may be attributed to practical considerations, such as the maintenance of cleanliness or budget constraints. However, it clearly indicates that the sensory and aesthetic experiences of patients are not held to be crucial to their treatment for or recovery from illness. If nothing else, this creates an alienating divide between bodily well-being and sensory well-being. The place where you go to get well is the place that (aesthetically if not actually) sickens you.

It is not only the drab and alienating nature of the hospital environment that leaves patients feeling disengaged, however, but also their interactions with physicians. Patients often feel dehumanized by the gaze of the doctor, who seems to see them more as a body (a corpse) or a body part (the liver in room 202) than a person. Even more troubling may be the fact that physicians spend more time looking at the results of diagnostic tests than interacting with the patients themselves, giving the impression that those patients have been transformed into series of tell-tale numbers or X-ray images. This tendency is a consequence of the rise of laboratory medicine, which meant that physicians, confident in the accuracy of laboratory tests, no longer had to spend lengthy periods of time questioning patients or conducting physical examinations:

> No more would it be necessary to spend time at the bedside meticulously percussing the chest to outline the heart, or moving the stethoscope

slowly from place to place over the chest listening for sounds that would indicate a lesion. Instead, a swiftly written order to the X-ray department would produce the evidence needed.

(Reiser 1993: 268, see also Borell 1993: 259)

As a result of this technologization of medical perception and diagnosis, patients may well feel that the brief time they spend in visual, auditory, and tactile contact with a physician is insufficient. While this impression might not be true in terms of what is needed to make an accurate diagnosis, it is true as regards the creation of a satisfactory patient–doctor relationship and the performance of socially and emotionally important 'ritual' aspects of the physician–patient encounter (see Porter 1993; Reiser 1993).

Moreover, the aura of certainty and objectivity that surround new medical technologies, from the X-ray to the MRI scan, make the images they produce seem like the final word on the patient's condition. Little room is left for discussion when faced with the apparent 'photographic' proof of a condition produced by these visualizing technologies (see Joyce 2008: 153). Significantly, in recent decades, even the task of interpreting such data has been technologized to a degree through the development of computer programmes capable of diagnosing certain diseases.

During the little time that they do spend with physicians, patients often feel that they are not being heard and that, in turn, they are not being fully informed about their conditions in language they can understand. This situation, eloquently described by Jay Katz (1984) in *The Silent World of Doctor and Patient*, is responsible for another of the common sensory and social malfunctions of contemporary medicine – that of miscommunication.

Bringing the senses back into medicine

Contemporary medical treatment, as discussed above, is primarily chemical and surgical. While it aims to enable patients to return to the physical and social activities important to them, it does not itself usually offer meaningful or sensorially-stimulating experiences leading to recovery. Time spent in treatment is 'empty time' and therefore best passed as quickly as possible. Compare taking prescription drugs for arthritis with a treatment that might be recommended by a Tibetan healer: herbal tea, massage, and 'relaxing in a dark, warm place with a friend who tells stories'. While not all ethnomedical treatments are pleasant or painless, this contrast highlights a potential difference between non-sensuous and sensuous treatment regimes.

But what of the matter of efficacy? Is not contemporary biomedicine, with all its shortcomings, immeasurably more efficacious than traditional medicines? This is a complex issue. In terms of treating specific physical ailments, modern Western medicine has definite advantages. However, there are still occasions when it seems to be trumped by indigenous medical traditions (apart from the fact that a number of the drugs used in modern medicine were first found within such traditions). To return to the example of arthritis, one interesting study compared the perceived efficacy of a Western treatment for the disorder with a Tibetan treatment among patients in a Tibetan community. The former treated the patients with Western medications while the latter regimen focused on behaviour, herbal remedies and diet. The study found that a majority of patients considered the Tibetan treatment to have been more successful at restoring mobility, although the Western treatment was said to be good for dulling pain (Ryan 1997). It would be interesting to see if Western patients would come to the same conclusion or if cultural preferences are playing a role in the experience.

In any event, the issue of efficacy is not straightforward. In biomedicine it usually concerns how successfully a particular physical ailment is cured or particular physical symptoms alleviated. In many traditional medical systems, other goals are often sought as well, such as the social and spiritual integration of the patient and the upholding and transmission of cultural values.

To elaborate on this last point, if an Andean patient visits a clinic and is prescribed a course of drugs for a particular disorder, this may be more effective at curing the disorder than traditional Andean methods employing herbal teas, censing, ritual acts and prayer. However, it will be a complete failure at engaging the patient in a meaningful and stimulating sensory and spiritual enactment of bodily and cosmic wholeness. It will also create a rupture in an age-old tradition of ethnopharmacology and treatment. Who in the community knows what is in the pills being taken or how it works to heal the body? By contrast, indigenous treatments, while perhaps less effective at curing the specific ailment, will foster broader and more culturally-relevant notions of well-being and will contribute to the development of local medical traditions making use of local resources. The benefit of a medical treatment, therefore, may depend on much more than its ability to cure a specific physical ailment in a particular individual.

The Western medical academy is not entirely oblivious to the concerns that have been raised here. For example, there is considerable discussion of how to improve the quality of the verbal communication between doctor and patient. (One motivating factor behind such discussion is the threat of lawsuits by patients holding they were inadequately informed by their doctors of the potential risks of a given treatment [Berg et al. 2001].) There is also an incipient interest in refreshing medical perception by bringing a visual arts sensibility into clinical reasoning. A programme along these lines at Cornell University used painted portraits to help medical students improve their visual discernment and recognize emotional and character traits in their patients (Bleakley et al. 2003).

This aesthetic approach also enters into treatment on the margins of medicine, through visualization techniques and creative arts therapies. There is even innovative research being carried out in what could be called 'museum therapy', which explores the benefits that handling museum artefacts might have for patients (Chatterjee 2008: Part IV). Such art-based therapies usually locate

the source of the benefits to the patient in the effects of psychological suggestion or creative expression, rather than, as in many indigenous therapies, in
potent forces within the visual images, music, or objects themselves.

Aside from arts-based therapies, certain forms of sensory therapy, such as
therapeutic touch, have also occasionally passed through the hospital doors
(Pratt and Mason 1981; Krieger 1979). This usually occurs through the
medium of nurses, the traditional hands-on caregivers. Sensory integration
therapies, in turn, are increasingly recommended for the treatment of 'sensory
disorders' associated with autism and related conditions (Bogdashina 2003).

For the most part, however, the public demand for sensorially- and emo-
tionally-engaging medical regimes, for practitioners and practices that work with
the body and not simply on it, is ignored by mainstream medicine. To meet this
demand a variety of alternative and complementary treatments have proliferated
in the West. Some of these, such as acupuncture, come from non-Western
systems. Others, such as aromatherapy and spa treatments, were developed in
the West. In the latter case elements from non-Western traditions may be
incorporated and perhaps given a quite different significance and use. For
example, the Las Ventanas al Paraiso Spa in Mexico offers such healing treatments, supposedly based on 'ancient indigenous Mexican cures', as 'the Nopal
Anti-Cellulite and Detox Wrap', and a 'Nopal Pineapple Smoothie' for internal
cleansing (Henry and Taylor 2005: 231). (Elements of Western medicine may
similarly be given a new meaning within non-Western contexts – as, for
example, when Tibetan nomads understood a physician's stethoscope to be a
healing instrument that could cure through touch [Schrempf 2007: 105 n28].)

Complementary and alternative therapies encompass a wide range of sensory practices. Sound therapy can involve drumming, chanting, playing or
listening to music, or even the use of sonic vibrations that can scarcely be
heard, as in crystal therapy. Tactile therapies include anointing and laying on
of hands within religious contexts, massages of different sorts, dance and
movement therapies, saunas and thermal baths, and therapeutic touch, which
involves manipulating the patient's 'energy field' rather than directly touching
the body (see Barcan 2011). Aside from their sensory and aesthetic attractions,
such therapies appeal through their holistic dimensions, and, in certain cases,
by allowing the patient to take an active role in the healing process. The
medical pluralism of contemporary society that makes this wide range of
therapies available, however, also leads to treatments being taken piecemeal,
thereby reducing their holistic value.

Whatever the benefits of any of these therapies, there is evidently a deep
desire for sensorially-engaging medical practices and environments. The historical and cross-cultural evidence, as well as the popularity of contemporary
sensory therapies, signals the central role of the senses in the experience of
well-being and healing. It is insufficient simply to label such therapies as
'misguided' or 'unscientific' in comparison with the practices of biomedicine.
Even in the world of drugs, surgical procedures and hospital wards, the senses
continue to matter. Many patients make judgements about their medications

(which in turn affect how regularly these are taken) based on the simple colour of the pills – red is good for the heart, pink is sweet, and so on (More and Srivastava 2010). Other studies have found that listening to music after surgery reduces sensations of pain and that having a hospital room with a view of nature can speed recovery (Sternberg 2009). Humans are sensuous beings who respond emotionally and physically to the world of sensations and their associated meanings in whichever period or culture they live. The question is whether the medical academy can find a way to engage our senses productively in the process of healing and remedy its sensory and aesthetic malaise, or whether the field of sensuous healing will continue to be the exclusive domain of alternative and ethnomedical therapies.

Part II
Politics and Law

3 The politics of perception

Sensory and social ordering

Here you come to the real secret of class distinctions in the West ... It is summed up in four frightful words which people nowadays are chary of uttering, but which were bandied about quite freely in my childhood. The words were: *The lower classes smell.*

George Orwell, *The Road to Wigan Pier* 1958 [1937])

It's certain that having Spaniards, Poles and Portuguese work among us causes less problems than having Muslims or Blacks ... Imagine a French worker ... living next to a piled-up family with one father, three of four wives, and some twenty kids, bringing in 50,000 francs from welfare payments, without working of course. If you add to that the noise and the smell, well!, it drives the French worker mad.

Jacques Chirac, Mayor of Paris (1991)

Tens of thousands of people in [Singapore] said they would cook or eat curry on Sunday in a protest highlighting growing anger over increased immigration. The campaign began after an immigrant family from China complained about the smell of curry from a Singaporean neighbor's home and local officials brought about a compromise.

Harry Suhartono, 'Singaporeans' culinary anti-immigration protest: curry' (2011)

How are the senses used to order society? While the role of the senses in other social fields, such as art or medicine, may seem fairly obvious, the domain of politics can appear too bound to ideas and institutions to have much to do with sensory perception (see Panagia 2009). Yet, as the quotes above indicate, and the discussion below will show, the senses do come into the matter, and in very important ways.

The phenomenon of nationalism, for example, can never be adequately comprehended simply as an adherence to certain political ideals or social communities. It is always at the same time an attachment to particular tastes, smells, sounds and sights, which themselves carry cultural values and personal memories. However, while a few authors are attending to the subject (i.e., Edensor 2002, Trnka et al. 2013), the conceptual cupboard of many works on nationalism is entirely bare when it comes to sensuous considerations.

The social control of perceptibility – who is seen, who is heard, whose pain is recognized – plays an essential role in establishing positions of power within society. Such control is exercised both officially and unofficially, and determines not only *who* is perceived, but also *how* they are perceived. Renaissance sumptuary law, for example, dictated what colours, fabrics and styles of clothing were reserved for the elite. Even when apparel is not legally regulated, differences in clothing may serve as customary ways of marking group distinctions such as gender, class, ethnicity, and occupation. Such systems of sensory classification are fundamental to upholding social divisions and hierarchies, as well as to constructing ethnic identity.

Although the importance of sensory markers and practices in systems of social categorization is less recognized today, they have not lost their relevance. Indeed, many ongoing struggles for social reform have prominent sensory dimensions. These include the fight for women's voices to be heard in politics, the battle to end social discrimination based on skin colour, the quest for greater access for persons with disabilities, the endeavours to have alternative sexual orientations recognized, and the struggle for greater legal and cultural weight to be given to animal sentience.

While at first glance social and political issues might seem to have little to do with the life of the senses, a second look reveals how deeply they are intertwined. Sensory ways, models and metaphors inform our notions of social integration, hierarchy and identity. The senses are directly put to political ends through acts of marking, excluding, punishing or exalting particular individuals and groups. The following pages discuss a range of historical, cross-cultural and contemporary concepts and practices concerning the role of the senses in social ordering to reveal the insights offered by a sensory approach to political culture.

A history of the senses in society

Tactile rites and sensory symbols

Sensory markers and practices have a long history of being used to order and integrate society. In the Middle Ages, when communal life was valued over private life, a range of sensory practices – or 'ways of sensing' – worked to incorporate individuals into the group. Circle and line dances, with the participants holding hands, were a popular form of entertainment. At meals people sat pressed together on benches and ate out of shared bowls. Bathing was similarly often a communal affair, with neighbours joining for a soak in the bath house. The all-important hearth provided those who gathered around it a tangible sense of the inclusive warmth of fellowship. Even at night, individuals were seldom on their own as separate bedrooms were rare and beds (and body warmth) were usually shared. To be expelled from the group into the cold and dangers of the outside world was one of the worst punishments that could be imposed on a member of a community (Classen 2012: ch. 1).

Religion was likewise a collective affair, with Church rituals providing key occasions for promoting social solidarity. During the celebration of Mass, participants exchanged a kiss of peace as a mark of fraternity. Confession, in turn, was usually a communal rite, and penance was often communal as well. In fact, conversion to Christianity was often itself a matter of joint action, since whole populations converted along with their rulers or at the behest of their conquerors, in a number of cases.

While an emphasis on communal integration may go together with an egalitarian approach to society, it does not preclude the establishment of social hierarchies. Medieval lords might eat with their men and sleep together with their servants, yet there were numerous signs pointing to their superior status. Luxurious clothing of velvet and silk, in contrast to the rough wool that chafed the skins of the poor, was one. A rich aroma of perfume provided another distinguishing mark. In Cervantes' classic, a half-clothed madman in the woods is identified at once by Don Quixote as a person of quality from the perfume emanating from his torn doublet (I: 9). Tones of voice and niceties of speech could identify members of the upper classes without any external signs being necessary. An elevated bodily position was a further sign of an elevated social status. Riding on horseback put one above the walking peasants. Sitting at a raised table set one above the mass of diners below. Being bowed or kneeled to similarly emphasized one's higher status. These were seen and felt signifiers that made the social order readily and physically apparent to all.

During the premodern period, handclasps and kisses were both common social greetings and important ritual signs. Exchanging a 'holy kiss' during Mass signalled the brotherhood of all Christians. Ritually placing one's hands in the hands of a superior was a key act of vassalage. Joining hands in marriage signified the physical and social bonding of the bride and groom – and also, according to ancient tradition, that the bride was being *handed over* to the groom. A handclasp or a kiss was a fundamental way of sealing a contract between two parties, signifying their concrete commitment to the terms of the bargain. When a touch of a hand or a kiss came from a holy person or a monarch (the 'royal touch'), it might be attributed healing properties, as personal touch was envisaged as transferring spiritual force from one body to another.

Along with such corporeal practices, however, groups within society could be distinguished by sensory associations. Traditionally in the West the upper classes were associated with the 'higher' senses of sight and hearing. They were the rulers or overseers, they made themselves heard in political affairs, they were educated and literate. The lower classes, by contrast, were linked to touch, taste and smell, which were deemed 'lower' senses – dedicated to manual labour and the basic feeding and care of the body. Workers, in fact, were often referred to simply as 'hands', a term that reduced their social being to a single sense. Centuries later Dickens would say of workers that they were 'a race who would have found more favour with some people, if Providence had seen fit to make them only hands' (Dickens 1854: 75).

Women, as discussed in the Introduction, also tended to be allied with the 'lower' senses of smell, taste and touch. This was in keeping with the customary association of women with bodily concerns. Men – and the senses of sight and hearing – were, by contrast, associated with the faculty of reason and the mind. Just as the association of the 'lower' classes with the 'lower' senses was taken to signify that the former were destined to work with their bodies, rather than their minds, so were women expected to eschew mental labour for 'body work'. This meant, basically, taking care of their families and homes, cooking, cleaning, sewing, nursing and nurturing. Thus, one seventeenth-century housekeeping manual listed the skills which a 'complete' woman ought to possess as 'skill in physic [healing], cookery, banqueting-stuff, distillation, perfumes, wool, hemp, flax, dairies, brewing, baking, and all other things belonging to a household' (Markham 1986: 8). Upper-class women might engage in a refined version of such 'women's work', embroidering, arranging flowers and 'tastefully' adorning themselves and their homes. However, their realm was still imagined to be that of the 'proximity' senses and the home (Classen 2012: ch. 4).

The biopolitics of the senses

The sensory typing of social groups was not thought simply to be a matter of associations and markers (so that, with the right clothes and perfume, a peasant might be transformed into a knight). People were believed to be *made* for their social roles. Hence, peasants were imagined to have coarse skins to signal – and enable them to endure – the coarse physical labour and hard living conditions for which they were suited. The weak eyes and soft bodies attributed to women were deemed to indicate that they needed to be guided by men and to stay within the protective shells of their homes (Classen 1998: 71–75). This biopolitics of the senses – conferring social values on sensory (or pseudo-sensory) traits for political ends – emphasized the futility of rebelling against one's lot in life. A coarse peasant could no more transform himself into a fine nobleman than a human could learn to fly.

The pseudo-biological sensory markers of social status included speech, which was often deemed to manifest innate characteristics. As speech was taken to be *the* sign of rationality in Western culture, its mode of use was taken as revelatory of the speaker's mental capacities. Women were represented as possessing an overabundance of speech, a virtual flood of words, which testified to their chaotic passions and readily disordered minds. Peasants and workers used coarse, vulgar language or else few words at all, indicating a weak intellect. Any speechless beings, from animals to infants to deaf-mutes, were traditionally considered to be lacking in all but the most basic mental capacities. As regards the deaf, those who were mute from birth were thought incompetent to handle their affairs and consigned to a 'perpetual legal infancy' (Peet 1857: 7; Rée 1999: 94–95). Their ability to speak meant that the blind did not suffer the same social and legal penalties as the deaf. They were, however, stigmatized as unintelligent and sensual due to their lack of vision and reliance on touch (Weygand 2009).

Another sensory field in which a blurring of real or supposed physiological traits with social features often occurred was that of smell. Odour associations have played an important role in differentiating and ranking social groups. George Orwell, as noted in the quotation at the head of this chapter, went so far as to declare that 'the real secret of class distinctions in the West' was that '*The lower classes smell*' (Orwell 1958 [1937]: 127). The sanitary reformers of the nineteenth century wrote about the stench and filth of the masses in excruciating detail, but even the most explicit language was inadequate to convey its intensity: 'No pen or paint-brush could describe the thing as it is. One whiff of Cowyard, Blue-Anchor or Baker's Court [London slums] out-weighs ten pages of letter press' (Lord Ashley cited in Mighall 1999: 68). As in the cases described above, this supposed malodour was not thought of simply as the result of external conditions, such as filthy living conditions, but as an intrinsic characteristic. Orwell wrote that even "lower-class' people whom you knew to be quite clean – servants, for instance, were faintly unappetizing. The smell of their sweat, the very texture of their skins, were mysteriously different from yours' (Orwell 1958 [1937]: 128). This perception of the intrinsically repulsive nature of the 'lower orders' played a powerful role in convincing the 'higher orders' to keep their distance (see Corbin 1986).

Malodour was likewise an assigned trait of other marginalized (and therefore potentially 'corrupting') groups within society. Traditional medical theories as well as popular belief attributed a malodour to women (Classen 1998: 85). Jews were likewise said to emit an offensive odour, a *foetor Judaicus* – the only cure for which was baptismal chrism or, more dramatically, drinking the blood of a Christian (Marcus 1972: 166). One study of 'caste' in the Southern United States in the 1930s found that:

> Among beliefs which profess to show that Negro and white people cannot intimately participate in the same civilization is the perennial one that Negroes have a smell extremely disagreeable to white people ... White people generally regard this argument as a crushing final proof of the impossibility of close association between the races.
>
> (Dollard 1937: 378)

'Race-hatred, religious hatred, differences of education, of temperament, even differences of moral code, can be got over,' observed Orwell, 'but physical repulsion cannot' (1958 [1937]: 128).

Stigmatizing people with repulsive associations effectively made them social outcasts. At the same time, the bad smell associated with a social group signalled its potential, in spite of all safeguards, to disrupt society.

The senses modernized and nationalized

Coordinated bodies

In the modern West the old tactile modes of social bonding no longer worked. For one thing, individualism made people less willing to enter into physical contact with their neighbours. Individuals, or at least members of the middle and upper classes, were now more reluctant to have their corporeal boundaries infringed: they sat on separate chairs, slept in separate beds, and bathed separately. This emphasis on individualism extended to mental states, with personal piety, for example, gaining importance over communal worship (Lebrun 1989: 75–86).

Furthermore, in modern Europe the right to rule was no longer deemed to be vested in the body of any one individual. It was rather an impersonal public office. The role of a personal touch in governance was hence diminished. This was not an easy transition. In fact, in a number of countries, most notably France, it required directly destroying the body of the monarch (Connerton 1989: 7–9). It also required a certain retraining of sensibilities. When complaints were made in seventeenth-century England concerning the loss of the 'royal touch' after Charles I was deposed by the Parliamentarians, a Republican humorously suggested that the Great Seal of Parliament might be touched instead. The intent was evidently to throw the practice into ridicule (Thomas 2005: 357).

The older emphasis on social solidarity through tactile bonds was replaced by a new stress on social uniformity through corporeal discipline. One no longer had to kiss or eat or play with one's neighbours, but rather to act in unison with them: to get up at the same time, go to work or school at the same time, sit or stand there for long hours engaging in repetitive labour, and return home at the same time to undertake similar, if often solitary, tasks and recreations. The particular functions of different workers might well differ, much more so, indeed, in the highly-specialized society of modernity than previously. However, the ideal was that they would intersect with each other in the coordinated fashion of the factory production system to create efficient social and material wholes. The reward for such concerted labour came in the form of social respectability and, more tangibly, the wondrous consumer goods produced by the industrial system.

The influence of the printing press and the printed word on this social and sensory shift was suggested by Marshall McLuhan (1994 [1964]: ch. 18; see also the qualified version of this thesis in Anderson 1991). McLuhan noted that print recreated speech as sequences of detached but homogenous units: typed letters. Due to the centrality of language in shaping self and society, he argued that this widely disseminated new form of communication helped to create a modern individualistic but uniform social order (as well as fostering an increased visual orientation). How influential the spread of print culture was in promoting this new social order is a matter of debate. However, it is likely that the lengthy and arduous process of learning to read – to transform the fluidity of speech into series of discrete visual symbols – did support new ways of envisaging the world, especially when undergone at a young age by schoolchildren.

While the printed text provided a model for thinking about society as an orderly agglomeration of individuals, the military drill offered a training method for the creation of disciplined and coordinated bodies. Developed in the late 1500s, military drill became widespread in subsequent centuries. Young men, often possessing a range of idiosyncratic behaviours when they entered the army, were rigorously trained to carry out basic manoeuvres in unison until they could perform the motions like clockwork. The clockwork analogy is an important one, for not only were drilled battalions acting with synchronized precision seen to be more effective than individual warriors (however strong and skilful) acting with spontaneity, they were also seen to be more effective workers in the new factories, which likewise demanded an untiring, synchronized mechanical precision (Classen 2012: 167–73).

As large standing armies had become the norm among European states, this mechanized 'reconstruction' of the body became a common experience for young men. The army, however, was not the only place in which to experience the drill in modernity. Prisons also employed drills of various sorts to exercise and discipline the bodies of inmates. Perhaps most importantly, schools, which had become major state institutions with the introduction of compulsory education in the nineteenth century, also made use of drills and drill-like routines. In schools, pupils were trained at an early age to behave in a synchronized, orderly fashion on command. Even reading and writing could be regarded as a form of 'eye-drill' and 'hand-drill'. As occurred in the army and the prison, any deviations from the prescribed routine were harshly punished. However, at least in theory, within the mechanically-minded society of modernity such deviations were not to be regarded as 'evils' that required condemnation and extirpation, but rather, as 'malfunctions' that required correction.

Ensuring the performance of the correct corporeal techniques necessitated pervasive surveillance, a sensory and social characteristic of contemporary society (Foucault 1995). The eventual goal was the development of an internalized self-discipline, which would keep workers at their tasks day after day, instead of, as was a problem in the early decades of the factory system, only when they felt the economic necessity. 'This penchant for idleness,' observed one industrialist, 'is certainly a cause for the failure of many manufacturing establishments' (cited in Classen 2012: 171).

Creating the sights, sounds and savours of home

Not only need citizens be hard and steady workers in the modern state they must also be nationalistic – ready to serve the state because of their attachment to a national identity. The growing sense of bodily boundaries in modernity coincided with a growing attention to national boundaries. In both cases a new emphasis on visual representation had a role to play. On the one hand, the increased prevalence of portraits and mirrors made people more aware of themselves as discrete, visually-bounded entities. On the other, the production and mass dissemination of national maps presented the state as a similarly bounded and integrated whole.

With the rise of the nation-state the forging of unifying national identities became imperative to overcome regional differences, transcend feudal allegiances and bind citizens to new notions of collectivity and homeland. The promotion of national languages, through state schools and through mass media, was essential in this regard, as was the construction of nationwide networks of transportation (see Robbins 2008: 113–21; Weber 1976). Sensory rituals and symbols were also well-suited for this purpose. They had the dual advantage of countering the disembodied impersonality of the state and of impressing the values of nationalism directly on the individual sensorium. In a political variation of Ignatius of Loyola's popular 'Spiritual Exercises', which asked devotees to meditate on the life of Jesus through all of their senses, citizens were asked to conceptualize the life of the state through a full range of sensory symbols.

In a number of countries, broadly-shared sensory symbols already existed that could serve the purpose of nationalism. This was the case, for example, where there was a state religion, such as that of the Church of England, with distinctive aesthetic traits and corporeal practices. Where practices with the potential for widespread appeal – musical forms, dances, cuisines – were centred in a particular region, these might be more broadly disseminated and given a new nationalistic significance. Hence the hopak dance of the Cossacks became the national dance of the Ukraine, the tango of Buenos Aires the national music and dance of Argentina, Devonshire cream tea became a British culinary institution, and so on. The underlying notion, which formed a key element of Romantic nationalism, was that such patterned sensations made visible, audible, tangible or gustable, the national 'soul' or ethos. As regards music, for example, we find this conveyed by Herder's notion of the *Volksgeist* – the spirit of a people which expresses itself on a sonic plane as a representative musical form (Curtis 2008: 28).

Aside from making use of pre-existing sensory cultures, however, nation builders also worked to create and institutionalize evocative new sensory symbols that could serve to represent the state and rally its citizens. As noted above, the map of the state, along with being a practical scale model of a nation's geography, provided a potent symbol of territorial integrity, sovereign power, and enclosing boundaries. As an iconic model, the national map made the extent and integrity of the state not just a matter of hearsay to people who knew little of the distant places and peoples it encompassed, but of seeming visual evidence.

The key non-functional sensory symbols of statehood were national flags, anthems and colours (which were often, but not always, derived from flags). In addition to these, flowers, trees and animals sometimes served as official or unofficial national symbols. These, although customarily employed in the form of visual symbols, might also have auditory, olfactory or gustatory dimensions. In the case of England, for example, a lion's roar might evoke the lion as the national animal, while rose perfume could suggest the traditional Tudor rose emblem. In the case of Canada, the sugar maple as a national emblem resonates on a number of sensory registers. The red colour of its leaves in autumn echoes one of Canada's national colours, the leaf appears on the national flag, and the tree's sap provides the characteristically Canadian savour and scent of maple syrup.

Whether they have been officially adopted by the state or acquired national significance through a more informal process, politically-encoded and widely-shared sensory symbols – sung anthems, waving flags, echoing church bells, traditional savours, verdant landscapes – can be as effective at inducing citizens to adhere to a national ideal, and even risk their lives in its defense, as any amount of 'rational' discourse. 'The portrayals of the nation that stirred people into action were oral, audial and visual ... a matter of symbols, songs, images, reports and rituals' (Smith 1998:139).

The popular British song of World War II, 'There'll Always Be An England', for example, associated England with 'a cottage small/beside a field of grain' and challenged the listener to come up with similar scenes worth fighting for that might be evoked by the colours of the British flag: 'Red, white and blue; what does it mean to you?' Even commercial products could serve as sensory icons of nationalism. During the Second World War, soldiers from the United States declared that they were fighting 'as much to help keep the custom of drinking Cokes as [they were] to preserve the millions of other benefits our country blesses its citizens with' (cited in Mintz 1996: 28).

However, for such sensory symbols to achieve cultural potency they had to be associated with nation-building events, achievements, and stories: battle triumphs, sports victories, cultural institutions, national mythologies. Mass media – novels, newspapers, radio, film, television – played a vital role both in promulgating the sensory icons of nationalism and in associating them with inspiring triumphs and homey values. National festivities, in turn, brought patriotic symbols into the homes and bodies of citizens – potentially making every inhabitant a flag waver, an anthem singer, and a consumer of cake iced in the national colours. The pleasure, wonder and gratitude experienced on such celebratory occasions could be at least partially transferred onto ideals of citizenship.

State institutions, notably schools, which bring all of the nation's children into their rooms, served as regular providers of sensory symbols of nationhood; the flag flying outside the building or standing in a corner of a room, the national anthem sung each morning in the classroom. Schoolchildren may be encouraged to draw explicit connections between their sensory experiences and their national identity. One current primary-school book promoting patriotism in the United States prompts teachers to ask: 'What does America smell like, taste like, look like? What does it feel like? What does it sound like?' (Hart 2002: 19). Natural symbols, such as trees and flowers, in turn, have the potential to elicit patriotic sentiments outside of public institutions and nation-affirming events. In the case of such symbols any garden or any forest, if it contains the plant in question, may evoke a sense of patriotism.

Another important way in which national and cultural identities have been incorporated by individuals is through everyday ways of sensing and acting: techniques of walking, eating, greeting, talking, gesturing, looking, touching, and so on (see Fox and Miller-Idriss 2008). As discussed previously, social institutions such as schools, armies and workplaces, along with mass media, help to ensure a general uniformity of such practices across a nation. This ideally makes it possible for citizens to feel physically at home anywhere in the state (at least among members of their own class).

As a result it is not only this flag, this music, this emblem, or even this landscape, this language, this meal, which signifies the homeland, but also this way of greeting a friend, this way of sitting down to dinner, this way of gesturing. Visiting another country where customs are different – people kiss or bow instead of shaking hands, look down instead of looking one in the eye, sit on cushions instead of chairs – induces a sense of physical unease and alienation. This makes one's own country the place where one 'fits in', not just socially, but on a very intimate, physical level and, by extension, it makes it the place where things are done 'right'.

The politics of perception in modernity

Constructing and deconstructing sensory typologies

Aside from being employed to create modern sensibilities and national identities, the senses have been put to a broad range of social uses in modernity. A biopolitics of the senses was employed in the United States to help justify the enslavement of Africans. The dark hue of African skin was said to indicate a benighted mind and its supposed toughness was deemed to make Africans 'wholly suited to the demands of outdoor manual labor' (Smith 2006: 15; see also Dias 2010).

A similar form of biopolitics was used in England to justify the hard lot of the working classes. Workers were likened to beasts, they were the 'swinish multitude' in Burke's infamous and decontextualized term, and could therefore be presumed to be as insensitive to suffering as animals were conveniently taken to be. 'Brutes, and brutish men, are commonly more able to bear pain than others', noted the natural philosopher Nehemiah Grew complacently in 1701 (cited in Day 1884: 82). A nineteenth-century writer made the link between low social status and sensuous 'brutishness' clear: 'The lower we descend in the social scale ... the nearer we approach to the brute, devoid of any thought beyond sensual necessities and gratifications, destruction, and reproduction' (Ford 1839: 48). In other words, the lower classes were characterized by a supposed irrationality that manifested itself in 'base' gustatory and tactile appetites.

Members of such low-status groups were customarily denied any individuality. Just as animals were often presumed to lack individual characteristics and exist only as exemplars of a type, so were Africans, workers or, for that matter, women. 'The worker' was interchangeable with any other worker, 'the negro' with any other negro and 'woman' with any woman. This view made it unnecessary to take the particular sensibilities or abilities of any one member of the class into account and also perpetuated a notion of these groups as amorphous masses, always threatening to 'swarm over' society.

The perceived lack of individuality within low-status groups became an especially important issue in modernity for, as the upper classes strove for greater individuation and privacy, the working classes often retained and reworked older ways of life that emphasized social solidarity. These ranged from sharing benches, while the middle and upper classes had moved on to the use of individual chairs, to engaging in communal storytelling rather than reading in private, and to a 'dangerous' insistence on organizing themselves into trade unions. This emphasis on group cohesion could be taken as further evidence of the 'lower orders' corporate tactile propensities.

The force of sensory categorizations was such that even those reformers who attempted to challenge the 'sensotyping' of marginalized social groups often found it hard to completely escape the typologies. At the start of *Oliver Twist*, for example, Charles Dickens took pains to point out the superficial and circumstantial nature of the signs which marked a person's station in life.

> What an excellent example of the power of dress young Oliver Twist was! Wrapped in the blanket which had hitherto formed his only covering, he might have been the child of a nobleman or a beggar; it would have been hard for the haughtiest stranger to have assigned him his proper station in society. But now that he was enveloped in the old calico robes ... he was badged and ticketed, and fell into his place at once – a parish child – the orphan of a workhouse – the humble, half-starved drudge – to be cuffed and buffeted through the world – despised by all, and pitied by none.
>
> (Dickens 1850: 14)

However, the reader soon learns that rough clothes and harsh treatment cannot affect Oliver's refined sensibilities, delicate appearance and upper-class speech, which are the intrinsic signs of the orphan boy's gentle blood. (In this context one can appreciate the radical implications of Shaw's suggestion in *Pygmalion* – better known to many as *My Fair Lady* – that a working-class woman's speech and manners can become ladylike through training.)

In his classic account of the life of factory workers in nineteenth-century England, Friedrich Engels depicted the 'Saxon' English working classes as degraded by external factors, but the 'Celtic' Irish as inherently base. Their 'savage' nature, according to Engels, kept the Irish mired in a life of crude tactilities. They were on 'too low a plane' to attempt any work above manual labour. They were content to sleep on rags amid refuse. In their desire for crude comforts they cast even the doorposts and flooring of their huts into the fire. Worst of all, seemingly, was the Irishman's intimacy with the pig: 'He eats and sleeps with it, his children play with it, ride upon it, roll in the dirt with it ... ' (Engels 1971: 106). This fellowship with 'livestock' placed the Irish firmly within Burke's 'swinish multitudes' in Engels' mind.

Despite their blind spots, Dickens, Engels, and other social reformers attempted to make the plight of the working classes visible and audible to those who had little knowledge of their living conditions or who had learned not to regard them. A reviewer of *Oliver Twist* (who would have preferred not to have such 'offensive' scenes and language thrust onto his consciousness), acknowledged that Dickens 'opens up a new world' of poverty to his well-off readers (Ford 1839: 48).

Speaking for oneself

The working people, for their part, made themselves very visible and audible – and at times tangible – during the nineteenth century through demonstrations and riots. The essayist Charles Lamb commented after one outbreak of working-class discontent: 'It was never good times in England since the poor began to speculate on their condition. Formerly they jogged on with as little reflection as horses. The whistling ploughman went cheek by jowl with his brother that neighed' (Lamb 1886: 44). Unlike Engels, who was revolted by how the Irish and their pigs apparently formed a seamless whole, Lamb was evidently nostalgic for an idealized past in which the peasantry shared the speechless, tactile world of farm animals.

Women constituted another social group that increasingly made itself heard, seen, and felt in the nineteenth and early twentieth centuries. Women demanding the right to vote marched in the streets, carried banners and beat drums. They chained themselves to the railings of government buildings, were carried off to prison, went on hunger strikes and were, in response, force-fed.

The two main arguments against suffrage for women were that women belonged at home and that they lacked the physical force necessary to defend their country's laws and borders. Both of these arguments had strong sensory dimensions. The first reinforced women's association with the intimate 'lower senses' and the second relied on the customary trope of women as soft and delicate. The conception of Parliament itself as a pseudo-battlefield supported the notion of politics being men's work. In the eighteenth and early nineteenth centuries this conception was corporealized in the fencing stance taken by speakers in the House of Commons.

One pro-women's suffrage cartoon caricaturized the notion of women belonging at home, with its concomitant denial of visual power to women, by having a 'primeval woman' asking 'Why can't I go out and see the world?' and a 'primeval man' answering 'Because you can't. Woman's proper sphere is the cave.' The suffragist Laura McLaren adeptly alluded to women's traditional domestic labours to counter an MP's use of the insufficient-force argument:

> And yet this Member had that morning ordered a number of women in his household to get out of bed while he was comfortably sleeping. He was then roused from his slumbers by the knock of a woman; he donned a shirt that a woman had made and that a woman had newly washed ...

he went down to eat the breakfast which a woman had prepared, and walked out to go to the House of Commons over steps which a woman had knelt to scrub ... And yet he was not aware that the greater part of the dirty, disagreeable, monotonous and ill-paid work of the whole of this country is performed by women, and proclaimed to an applauding House that woman have no physical force at all!

(cited in Tickner 1988: 180)

This passage is striking for the way it brings women's work into visibility and uses it as proof of women's physical eligibility for the (by comparison) rather light duties of Members of Parliament.

Colour played a particularly important role in the suffragists' battle for public visibility. The most prominent organization promoting suffrage in England, the Women's Social and Political Union, used purple, white and green, which were said to stand for dignity, purity and hope. 'The usefulness of "colours" lay in their universal application. Anything in any combination of purple, white and green could become a symbol and reminder of the cause: a button, a pamphlet, a dress, a procession, a decorated hall' (Tickner 1988: 93). Without having to say a word, therefore, a woman wearing a dress or scarf in the movement's colours proclaimed the cause in 'a new language' that could be understood 'by the most uninstructed and most idle of passers-by in the street' (Tickner 1988: 93).

Along with the women's movement, a number of later twentieth-century social movements, including the civil rights movement, indigenous rights movements, and disability rights movements, each made the point that different bodies and different ways of life should not be penalized through social and legal discrimination. As with the women's movement, an important first step for such groups was to increase their public visibility. For people with physical disabilities this meant, in part, demanding that material barriers to their access to public spaces be removed. In other cases it entailed participating in public protests and parades and occupying off-limits zones, such as 'whites-only' restaurants.

One technique frequently used to upset sensory and social hierarchies in modernity was that of assigning positive values to traits which have been viewed negatively. We can see this in the 'Black is beautiful' movement that countered stereotypes of African bodies as unattractive, or in the positive characterization of the working classes as being 'down-to-earth' – honest and practical – rather than lowly and dirty. Such reversals of the values attached to sensory markers worked as much to boost the self-image of the marginalized group itself as they did to improve its public image.

Controlling sensory difference

As in the case of the women's movement, these attempts by marginalized groups to fashion new roles and images for themselves have often resulted in a social backlash. Societies have customarily made use of three basic methods for dealing with threatening differences (whether deemed to be physical, ideological or cultural in nature): containment, elimination, and assimilation. The first method aims to place a threatening group within a contained space; for example, women within the home and ethnic groups within ghettos. The sensory and social differences attributed to these groups are tolerated, at times even celebrated (i.e., the warm, nurturing domesticity of women), so long as they remain contained. When the group appears to be transgressing its space, when it is seen and heard and felt and smelled in the wider society (or when it provides a convenient scapegoat for social ills) efforts are usually made to put it back in its 'place', where its visibility and audibility are concealed by social, and sometimes physical, walls.

When a group is considered so disturbing that it is not deemed to have any place within society, attempts may be made to eliminate it entirely through exile or annihilation. The latter may be physical (i.e., sterilization or genocide) or social (i.e., prohibiting the practice of a religion, removing children from parents). The harshness of this method means that it requires a strong moral justification, namely that the religious, social or even biological survival of society depends on it. In actual fact, however, more practical motives, such as wishing to appropriate the property of the stigmatized group, may also be involved.

The third method for dealing with potentially destabilizing groups is through social and/or physical assimilation (e.g., intermarriage). Assimilation works to 'safeguard' society by making marginalized social groups stakeholders in the system and by minimizing their perceived difference. The entry of marginalized groups into previously off-limits domains is contingent on their conforming to the dominant models of behaviour. For example, women are 'allowed' into previously masculine fields so long as they behave like men, and non-Western ethnic groups are 'allowed' to hold political office in Western countries so long as they act like 'whites'. Where differences cannot be entirely overcome the idea is that they will at least be suppressed, with each member of a marginalized group becoming, as it were, a ghetto of one, hiding her or his own distinctiveness.

Social assimilation may be forced on a group, whether or not it wishes to participate in the dominant culture. This was the common fate of many indigenous peoples in the Americas. An example of this can be found in the work of Richard Henry Pratt, an ardent nineteenth-century campaigner for the assimilation of Native Americans in the United States. Dedicated to transforming the 'Indian' 'in all ways but color into a white man', Pratt supported the forcible suppression of Indian identity. 'Kill the Indian and save the man', he infamously declared. Such 'killing' involved stripping Native Americans of their clothing, language, and traditional lifestyles and ensuring, to the extent possible, that they looked and sounded, felt and thought like Anglo-Americans (Churchill 2005).

Assimilation is often a measure of last resort for societies under pressure from disenfranchised groups and their supporters. This is due to the concerns that it will result in the overthrow of the social order, or at least 'contaminate' society with alien bodies and values. For example, during the debates over women's suffrage the concern was often raised by those opposed that allowing women to vote would make society more effeminate – 'softer' and 'weaker' in sensory terms – and even invite foreign invasion (Tickner 1988: 155). Assimilation may also occur, however, because the differences that initially kept a group marginalized no longer seem that important in contemporary society, or because perceptions of that group and its symbolic attributes have changed – i.e., women no longer seem so 'soft', or 'softness' now appears to be a positive quality.

Sensory metaphors have played an important role in conceptualizing and justifying these different responses to social difference. A powerful sensory image that responds to prevalent concerns will go far in promoting particular social policies and practices. One common metaphor presents society as a body. This is a highly useful image for suggesting organic unity, inter-dependence and hierarchy. It also offers the compelling feature of being an image with which everyone is intimately familiar: it is not, therefore, just something to think about, but something to *feel through*. In the social-class version of this model, the head represents the ruling class and the feet or, as we saw above, the hands, represent the workers. In the gendered version, the head traditionally represents men, and the body women. All of the parts are necessary to the whole and so long as each plays its 'proper' role all is said to be well. However, when one part attempts to usurp the place of another a monstrous aberration is said to result (see, for example, Knox 1572).

Groups that are not deemed to have a functional role within society by the dominant ideology are often conceptualized as an abscess in the social body. So long as the group/abscess is regarded as relatively sealed off from the rest of the social body it may be tolerated, although it will likely be stigmatized as morally and physically repulsive. When, for whatever reason, it is seen as spreading into the whole of society, 'poisoning' or 'infecting' it, however, an attempt will be made to suppress it. This is usually considered by the dominant group to have a purifying and healing function, removing a source of 'corruption' from society, and eliminating an 'eyesore', an 'earsore' or a 'thorn in one's side'.

The stigmatization and treatment of Jews in Western history, culminating in the Holocaust, offers perhaps the most notorious example of this approach. Anti-Judaism in Nazi Germany was the result of historical prejudice, rising ethnic nationalism that demonized so-called inferior peoples, and anxieties concerning the social prominence of Jews following their enfranchisement and assimilation into mainstream society in the nineteenth century.

Making use of long-standing stereotypes, the Nazis insistently portrayed Jews as sensorially and morally repulsive. The following lines from Hitler's *Mein Kampf* are a typical example:

> The cleanliness of [Jews], moral and otherwise, I must say, is a point in itself. By their very exterior you could tell that these were no lovers of

water, and, to your distress, you often knew it with your eyes closed. Later
I often grew sick to my stomach from the smell of these caftan-wearers ...
All this could scarcely be called very attractive; but it became positively
repulsive when, in addition to their physical uncleanliness, you discovered
the moral stains on this 'chosen people'.

(cited in Classen et al. 1994: 173)

Once the threat posed by 'unhygienic' Jews to the health of the social body
was established by such spurious means, their eradication became a 'hygienic'
necessity. 'National Socialism is nothing but applied biology,' proclaimed
Deputy Leader Rudolf Hess (cited in Classen et al. 1994: 173; see further
Smith 2012).

A melting pot or a salad bowl?

Metaphors promoting social integration must offer sensory imagery sufficiently
potent to counter negative typologies of social difference. One such metaphor
is that of the 'melting pot'. This thermal metaphor was popularized at the turn
of the twentieth century as a way of describing the molding of immigrants
into 'Americans' in the United States:

> America is God's Crucible, the great Melting-Pot where all the races of
> Europe are melting and reforming! ... Germans and Frenchmen, Irishmen
> and Englishmen, Jews and Russians – into the Crucible with you all! God
> is making the American.
>
> (Zangwill cited by Gerstle 2001: 51)

The immigrant experience, according to this model, was, willy-nilly, one of
extreme 'heat' dissolving differences (with a suggestion also of removing
impurities). The depiction of God as the Great Smelter of new citizens added
a touch of the sacred to the process, in keeping with visionary ideals of the
United States as a 'promised land' (see further Chidester 2005).

The melting pot, while referring to the process of melting down metal in
order to forge it anew, has often been taken to signify a cooking process, a
kind of boiling and blending of everyone into one soup. The antithesis to this
model of social integration is the recent 'salad bowl' model. Whereas the
'melting pot' metaphor conveys the notion of heat fusing difference into
unity, the salad bowl model presents a cold integration of ingredients that
retain their separate identities:

> An alternative model of a multiethnic and multicultural society is that of a
> salad bowl ... wherein each ingredient in the tossed salad retains its own
> color, texture, taste, and identity ... Salad dressing of oil and vinegar
> would induce a smooth and tasty blending and unity of the salad.
>
> (Kim and Kim 1998: 115)

In the salad bowl metaphor, the nature and acceptability of the 'dressing' is itself a matter of concern: 'Can ideals of justice and tolerance, even love and peace, become a universally accepted "house" salad dressing?' (Wilson 1993: 10).

This model works well to counter negative images of 'others' as ugly, disgusting, putrid, and sickening by presenting them as visually attractive, tasty, fresh, and good for us. It also conveys the notion of a culturally-diverse society as something that must be 'eaten' and therefore internalized. However, as a 'cold' dish it offers little in the way of emotional appeal (and certainly no hint of God as the Great Salad-Maker). Consequently, it would probably do nothing to convince those who feel that society is being fractured by sectarianism or that cultural diversity is being 'shoved down our throats' of the value of a broad social mix. The notion of shared social values as mere 'salad dressing' to help the mix go down, in turn, offers a weak metaphor of social cohesion. It also raises the question of which group will provide the 'smoothing' and unifying dressing.

Various other dishes have been proposed in place of salad as a metaphor of social integration, such as the following suggestion for a 'stir-fry' social model.

> Appropriately enough, this dish is a foreign import to US shores, a seasoned mix of vegetables and meat or seafood typically stirred together in a wok over an open flame. The image better reflects the heat generated in the process of immigration and mutual adaptation. But more important is what happens to the ingredients. They do not lose their distinctiveness; this is no melting pot. You can always tell the broccoli from the chicken, and even from the green peppers or the cauliflower. But the ingredients cannot remain wholly unchanged either. A well-cooked stir-fry subtly changes the constituent parts and makes them part of a unified single dish.
> (Martin 2000: 30)

This proposal makes a painstaking attempt to find the right recipe to cook up – but not blend – the multicultural society. It points, however, to the limits of such models in a culturally diverse society, for the image of a stir-fry has little hope of appealing to everyone's tastes (and, indeed, with its inclusion of animal flesh, might appear exploitative in its very basis to members of vegetarian cultures).

A lack of general appeal is also a drawback with the salad bowl metaphor. For example, one study of food habits among Asian-Americans recorded an informant saying: 'Who eats a salad while eating soup and noodles? Oh yes, the Americans. Those white folks. Oh well, maybe this is something we might have to learn if we live here until we are old.' Another responded: 'Oh no, they can force me [to] speak English, but they cannot make my tongue like the taste of salad dressing' (Manalansan 2007: 188). Sensory metaphors of society must feel right to the people intended to employ them, as well as sound right to politicians and academics, to achieve cultural salience at a popular level.

Sensory and social orders across cultures

Easter kisses and cultural mosaics

There is considerable variety in the sensory practices and symbols employed to represent and to order society across cultures. On a broad scale, however, they may all be thought of as variations on a theme: that of making social cohesion and hierarchization a matter of corporeal perception and action.

Even in the West we can find important differences among countries. For example, the sensory and social shifts that occurred in Northern Europe in modernity did not happen in precisely the same way or time in the rest of Europe. Many nineteenth-century travellers to Russia were astonished at the amount of social touching and kissing that still went on in that country. This social tactility was intensified during Easter, when all family members, friends and acquaintances were expected to greet each other with a kiss. The practice occurred not only within social circles but also on an institutional level:

> In the army, every general of a corps (of 60,000 men) must kiss all its officers, and in a like manner every commander of a regiment all the officers of that regiment and a select number of privates to boot. The captain kisses individually all the soldiers of his company, who mustered for this special purpose. The same system prevails in the civil department: the head must kiss all his underlings, who hasten to visit him on Easter Sunday morning.
>
> (Kohl 1843: 163)

Far from being superficial air kisses, these were 'downright hearty smacks'. High rank was no excuse for avoiding one's tactile obligations, for even the tsar was expected to kiss 'the meanest sentry in his palace' (Kohl 1843: 164). Along with its religious associations, such a practice pointed to the continuing importance of tactile rituals and bonds in a society that maintained strong feudal structures.

Differences likewise existed among Western countries as to the metaphors and models for social integration that were employed. For example, whereas the dominant model in the United States has been that of the 'melting pot', in Canada that of the 'cultural mosaic' has had more prominence and acceptance. In his book of 1938, *Canadian Mosaic: The Making of a Northern Nation,* John Murray Gibbon depicted culturally-diverse Canadians as colourful mosaic pieces that fit together while remaining distinct:

> The Canadian people today presents itself as a decorated surface, bright with inlays of separate coloured pieces, not painted in colours blended with brush on palette. The original background in which the inlays are set is still visible, but these inlays cover more space than that background, and so the ensemble may truly be called a mosaic.
>
> (Gibbon 1938: viii; see further Porter 1965)

This mosaic imagery was influential in the implementation of various policies promoting multiculturalism during the twentieth century. It conveys neither the revolutionary fervour of 'the melting pot' nor the healthy and contemporary social diet of the 'salad bowl', but it does offer a sense of solidity and order with a colourful variety of cultural distinctions.

Even if some Canadians might have desired more of a fused identity than the 'mosaic' allowed, this was never entirely possible due to the existence of 'two founding nations' in Canada, the French and the English. Arguably, this divided identity is not only framed in the Canadian constitution but has also become part of popular culture, as evidenced in iconic Canadian works of music, art, and literature (see Howes 1990, 1991b). The mosaic model, then, can be seen as a multiplication of this primordial social dualism, which never quite allows Canadians to think in the unifying tactile terms of the United States, as expressed in its unofficial motto *e pluribus unum* – from the many, one.

The mystique of blood in Japan

A similar range of similarities and differences in the ways the senses are put to social ends exists in non-Western societies. One interesting case is offered by Japan. In the late nineteenth century, the concept of 'blood' gained importance in Japan for promoting notions of social cohesion and order. Significantly, this was the period when Japan was recreating itself as a modern state and required unifying metaphors. An early twentieth-century Japanese eugenicist promoting ethnic 'purity' declared: 'There is nothing that talks more substantively than blood. There is nothing that binds together human beings more intrinsically than blood' (Robertson 2002, 2012: 101).

The notion of all Japanese being of one blood, 'protected' from racial intermixture by their island geography, supported the idea of Japan as an ethnically – and therefore culturally – unified state. In order to preserve this social ideal, citizenship was based on the principle of *jus sanguinis*, right of blood, or ethnic descent, rather than on the basis of having been born in Japan. The strong emphasis on ties of blood in Japan has been called 'hemato-nationalism' (Robertson 2012).

This ethnic nationalism is otherwise expressed through the metaphor of the extended family. The state is conceptualized as a 'family-state' (*kokka*), which includes all Japanese citizens, symbolically united by blood. The emperor serves as the 'father' of the 'family-state' and is a key symbol of social unity. In Japan, where the word 'self' means 'one's part of the whole', considerable value is given to the sublimation of one's personal wishes and identity to that of the group, whether this is the family, the 'family-state' or the 'corporate family' for which one likely works in modern Japan.

One of the ways in which blood is thought to 'talk' in Japan is through 'family likeness'. This notion assumes that all Japanese, being 'related by blood' will have a similar physical appearance (Weiner 1997). Conversely, even if a person is legally a Japanese citizen, if he or she does not look ethnically

Japanese an assumption will be made of 'foreignness' (Arudou 2012). Uni-formity in dress plays a further role in emphasizing the importance of 'family likeness', with uniforms being popular in schools and in many companies.

A range of tactile and kinaesthetic practices help to enforce the sense of familial solidarity. As in the feudal culture of the premodern West, we find communal practices emphasized in Japan. Bowls of food are often shared during meals, leading to the expression 'we eat from the same bowl' to convey a sense of interdependence. Communal bathing, in turn, is a tradi-tional part of Japanese culture, helping to cement social bonds among family members and friends. Co-sleeping among family members is also common, facilitated by the close arrangement of bed mats in the family room (which, in the typically small Japanese living quarters, serves as a living room by day and a bedroom by night). In a transformation of the English term 'kinship', this social bonding through physical intimacy – although not necessarily involving direct touching – has been called 'skinship' by the Japanese (Odin 1996: 289; Donahue 1998: 150; Daniels 2010).

Such forms of immersive social intimacy contrast with the otherwise low-contact nature of Japanese culture. Individuals, for example, do not touch – shake hands or kiss – when meeting, but rather greet each other with a bow. One nineteenth-century European resident of Japan noted the lack of social touching, even between parents and children, with surprise:

> After babyhood there is no more hugging or kissing. Such actions, except in the case of infants, are held to be highly immodest. Never do girls kiss one another; never do parents kiss or embrace their children who have become able to walk. And this rule holds good of all classes of society, from the highest nobility to the humblest peasantry ... [And] hand-clasping is an action as totally foreign to Japanese impulse as kissing.
>
> (Hearn 2006: 90)

However, collective corporeal uniformity is pursued through the widespread implementation of calisthenic routines. These popular exercise drills, with accompanying songs, have been used both to promote patriotism and create a sense of social solidarity. During the militarization of the country prior to and during World War II, Japanese ideologues went so far as to invest each move-ment in calisthenic routines with nationalist significance (Igarashi 2000: 49).

Popular radio broadcasts of exercise routines in present-day Japan ensure that large numbers of people are doing the same movements at the same time across the country, and thus in kinaesthetic harmony with each other. When practiced in schools and companies, calisthenics aim to promote group loyalty and syn-chrony, as well as improve health. Blood in this case can be said to talk by moving multiple bodies in the same way at the same time. This is an example of com-munity being sensed, not simply imagined (as in Anderson's [1991] usage).

The Japanese flag, depicting a red sun on a white background, resonates with the symbol of blood through the colour red – considered very auspicious in Japan – and through the emperor's legendary descent from the Sun goddess. The Japanese can thus see themselves as having a family relationship with the Sun through the emperor's blood line. This symbolism is often rendered edible on ritual occasions. A red plum on a bed of white rice, for example, is a common ceremonial dish that conveys the appearance of the flag and at the same time makes use of two foods very closely identified with Japan – rice and plums. To eat this dish is to literally consume the Japanese identity.

The cherry blossom, commonly regarded as Japan's national flower, is another key symbol of Japanese identity with ties to the rhetoric of blood. The cherry blossom can be seen as having a tinge of blood due to its light pink colour: 'it is this very warmth of life which has made the cherry blossom the symbol of the Yamato [Japanese] spirit' (Kiernan 2007: 482). The cherry blossom also has the characteristic of being particularly beautiful when massed, rather than on its own, hence serving in floral form to represent the value of the social collective.

During the Second World War, cherry blossoms came to be identified with warriors who spilt their blood in defence of their country, falling in their prime like the ephemeral flowers. A popular wartime song declared that 'In flowers it's the cherry, in people it's the warrior'. Squadrons were named after different types of cherry blossoms, cherry blossoms were painted on military planes, and kamikaze pilots carried cherry blossom with them to their deaths (Ohnuki-Tierney 2002: 163–66). The symbolic qualities of cherry blossoms extended to their fragrance. It was said that, just as the fragrance of the blossom lives on after it falls, so the warrior's repute will live on after death (Orbaugh 2007: 227).

Japan and the odour of the other

In Japan, foreigners were often conceptualized, at least by traditionalists, as polluting: bringing 'bad' smells, looks, touches, tastes and sounds into the country and potentially disrupting its mythologized social, biological and sensory unity. Among the negative sensory signs of foreignness, particular prominence was given to bad smells. In 1853 when Japan was forcibly opened to foreigners by the United States, one nationalist poet declared that:

> Only the cherry blossoms take not on the rank barbarian stench
> But breathe to the morning sun the fragrance of a nation's soul
> (cited by Samuels 1999: 77)

While many Japanese adopted Western fashions due to their association with 'progress' (one song lyric humorously proclaimed: 'If you strike a head with Western-style hair ... you hear the sound of civilization'), foreign ethnicity remained suspect (Ohnuki-Tierney 2002: 63).

In contemporary Japan, non-Japanese often face difficulties finding housing due to concerns that they will 'contaminate' apartments with malodour. Any Japanese who is perceived as associating too much with foreigners is liable to be labelled *gaijin kusai* – 'smelling like a foreigner' (Stronach 1995: 55).

The Japanese emphasis on ethnic homogeneity does not, however, preclude the existence of internal divisions and their associated sensory markers. The *burakumin* were historically the lowest class in Japanese society, working in 'defiling' trades, such as butchery, which were associated with bloodshed and death. Sumptuary laws dictated what colours of clothing these social outcasts could wear and assigned them leather badges as signs of their defiled status. Attempts were also made to contain the *burakumin* within separate ghettos or villages outside cities.

With the creation of the modern state of Japan in the late nineteenth century, such segregating practices were outlawed. However, the social stigmatization of *burakumin* has not entirely disappeared. A bad smell and polluting qualities remain associated with members of this class, due not only to their traditionally bloody occupations but also to their own supposed 'bad blood' – which is also said to result in their children having deformities or birthmarks (Orbaugh 2007: 190; McCormack 2012: 118). Such prejudices have resulted in a reluctance to employ or marry persons considered to belong to this class (an identification usually made on residence within a traditional *buraku* neighbourhood).

A more recent mode of distinguishing groups in Japanese society is by blood type. Popular psychology in twentieth-century Japan associated different blood types with different personality traits. This practice has now become widespread, leading to a variety of products (soft drinks, bath salts, chewing gum) being marketed expressly for different blood types, and even different educational approaches and jobs being specified as appropriate for particular blood types. Indeed, it has become common for blood type to be requested on employment applications in Japan. Within the political realm, a politician's blood type can be used to indicate his or her suitability or unsuitability. The result is frequent stereotyping of people by blood type, with people of less well-regarded types sometimes suffering discrimination.

Type A blood is particularly associated with Japanese ethnicity and national character. It is prominent among the Japanese population and is said to produce a group-oriented person. Type B blood, by contrast, is less common in Japan and is often linked to non-Japanese Asians. It is said to produce an individualistic person. When the Japanese Minister for Reconstruction, Ryu Matsumoto, was forced to resign recently due to certain 'socially-insensitive' remarks he had made, he blamed his abrasive B-type blood for his failings. Even the idealized homogeneity of the Japanese people through shared blood, hence, has its internal divisions and hierarchies (McNeil 2011).

The global sensorium

Cultural curries

In the nineteenth and twentieth centuries the sensory, social and technological complexes of modernity and nationalism – industrialization, national armies, state schools, modern media of communication, literacy, transportation networks, national languages, currencies, maps and emblems – were promoted around the globe by modernizing elites. Although these institutions, practices and symbols were reshaped to some extent by local influences, they none-theless had a homogenizing effect on ways of sensing. A citizen (particularly a male citizen) could work at a factory in France or in Australia, speed along railways in Spain or in Canada, practice military drills in Argentina or in Japan, read a newspaper in Egypt or in India. Ironically, therefore, the precise insti-tutions that were employed to create distinct nations, also laid the basis for a transnational uniformity.

Along with the core perceptual experiences of modernism, a range of European corporal techniques were exported abroad during this period. In nineteenth-century India, British educators attempted to promote 'manly' virtues and overcome the tactile barriers separating castes by encouraging boys to participate in contact sports (Sen 2005). In the twentieth-century, Western marketers hoped that exposure to practices of physical intimacy in Hollywood films would lead to greater sales of personal hygiene and beauty products in India: 'When you want to be physically closer to people a lot, then you tend to want to look better, smell better. So the market [in India] will grow for cosmetics, perfumes, after-shaves, mouthwashes, and so on' (cited in Classen and Howes 1996: 180). In twentieth-century Japan the occupying US forces promoted the practice of social kissing with the notion that it would make for a more open and democratic society (Buruma 2004: 135–36).

Through processes of colonization, commerce, immigration, and other forms of cross-cultural contact, sensations and sensory practices have spread across the globe. While this flow of sensation has often originated in the West, however, it is by no means one way. Western countries have also been exposed to a wide variety of non–Western sensory influences, from Asian food and medical practices to African art and music. Similarly, sensory and social influences have long circulated among non–Western societies themselves, as they have among Western countries.

Whatever direction they travel in, however, the sights and sounds and tastes of elsewhere are often divested of the particular associations they had in their cultures of origin and imbued with new values in their cultures of reception. A good example of this is provided by the global trajectories and cultural transformations of curry. In its country of origin, India, curry has no general-ized significance for it is a Westernized catch-all term for a range of distinct dishes that are associated with different regions, social classes, medicinal values, and often religious practices (see, for example, McGilvray 1998: 27). In Britain the taste of curry, first introduced by colonial administrators home from India, came to represent exoticism, ethnicity, a savour of imperial power, a test of virility when the curry was highly spiced, a threat to Britain's sensory and cultural integrity, and, recently, even Britain's new, multicultural national dish (i.e. Panayi 2008; Highmore 2010).

In Japan the taste of curry, through its association with the British who brought their version of it into the country, originally had elitist connotations of Western progressiveness, power and sophistication. It also provided a disguise for the beef being fed to (previously largely vegetarian) Japanese soldiers in the hope that it would endow them with Western-style military might (Ohnuki-Tierney 2002: 64–67). Eventually it would become a comfort food, simple to make (according to Japanese methods), hot and filling, and requiring none of the aesthetic refinement or attention to ceremony of Japanese dishes (Collingham 2006: 253). A general uniformity of sensations across cultures, consequently, does not necessarily signify an equal uniformity of values.

Neither does the greater sensory integration of cultures prevent foreign sensations from continuing to be viewed with suspicion. When they are linked to immigrants, in fact, they often arouse anxieties concerning an invasion of alien physicalities and lifestyles. Such threatening sensations may belong to any perceptual field, however smells often carry particular social weight due to the transgressive qualities of odour and its associations with ethnic identity and physical hygiene. Occasionally these olfactory markers of foreign origin are primarily symbolic, as when black South Africans characterize immigrants from other African countries as bad-smelling, due to their perceived inferiority, or when descendants of Koreans living in Japan are said to be malodorous because of their foreign ethnic origin (Mwakikagile 2008: 67).

At times, however, olfactory markers of foreignness are based on actual odours associated with the group, particularly those of ethnic foods. Returning to the example of curry, the spicy scents of the dishes cooked by immigrants from the Indian subcontinent, while highly appreciated in many countries, have also sometimes been the focus of anti-immigrant sentiment. In England, the view that 'Asians' smell of curry has contributed to discrimination and ghettoization. 'One woman accounted for her desire to leave the Birmingham street where she had lived for more than thirty years by saying, "I want to get away from the Asians … It's not the colour I'm against, far from it … [But] all the houses reek of cooking curry"' (Buettner 2012: 152). While it is simple to characterize such attitudes as 'racist', the issues are more complex. They relate not only to negative ethnic stereotypes but also to antipathies to olfactory difference (or to any strong odours entering public spaces in 'deodorized' societies), and to fears of sensory and cultural colonization and of losing the 'sensescape' of home.

The situation may also be reversed, with immigrants criticizing the 'unpalatable' sensory characteristics of their new countries. Using the example of curry again, this occurred recently in Singapore. As described in the news account given at the head of this chapter, complaints by Chinese immigrants concerning the scent of curry wafting from their Singaporean neighbours touched a local nerve. Curry is a traditional dish in Singapore, thanks to influences from India and from British colonizers. In view of this, these complaints raised a public outcry against 'cultural suppression' by Chinese immigrants. A 'Cook a Pot of Curry' day was organized with the intention of filling the country's air with the 'nationalist' scent, defying the sensibilities of 'outsiders'.

Such examples indicate that, while there are many instances of sensory fusions across cultures, these fusions still have particular political histories and local cultural meanings. They also indicate that, despite the growing globalization of sensation in contemporary culture, sensory differences remain a source of social tension and social tensions continue to be expressed in terms of sensory difference.

Indeed, the more sensations and values are fused and homogenized across cultures, the more likely it is that 'recalcitrant' sensory and social difference will stand out as a deviant anomaly. In this sense early nineteenth-century Europe, where one could find, and must necessarily tolerate, such sensory and social difference not only in every country, but almost in every county and city, was far more conscious of cultural diversity than contemporary global society – in which one expects to access the same food, the same modes of transportation, the same commercial networks, the same notions of individual rights, the same media of communication and the same news wherever one goes.

Tribalism, individualism and the senses in the electronic age

In the mid-twentieth century Marshall McLuhan predicted that the instantaneous communication enabled by new media would result in print-based nationalisms being replaced by a new global 'tribalism'. This new tribalism, while dependent on modern technology, would partake of the synthesizing, interactive and communal nature of traditional tribal societies. As regards the senses, the new modes of communication would favour the interpersonal senses of hearing and touch over the detached sense of sight due to their immediacy of expression and impact and to their integrating properties. 'We are moving out of the age of the visual into the age of the aural and tactile,' McLuhan declared (1994 [1964]: x). The sociologist Michel Maffesoli would later agree, emphasizing in *The Time of the Tribes* (1996) that a synthesizing tactility had replaced visual detachment as the dominant sensory model of contemporary social ordering.

The development of the personal computer and the internet, and the immense popularity of social networking sites such as Facebook, can be seen as bringing this new 'tribal' sensory and social order about in some respects. While internet users may divide up into many 'tribes' based on their particular interests, rather than merge into one global community, they do nonetheless all participate in the immediacy of electronic information-sharing. Online communities, in turn, have something of the sociality of a village get-together. Internet theorists following a McLuhanesque line of thought hence argue that 'the acoustic all-at-once-ness that marked face-to-face communication has been retrieved' and that 'electronic mediation does not support self-standing individuality because it is primarily a tactile form of engagement with the world' (van Loon 2008: 112–13).

There are several difficulties with this paradigm, although it is not entirely invalid. One is the assumption that tribal societies all experience the world through the same sensory mix, so that all, being non-literate, give the same priority and value to the auditory and tactile. As discussed in the Introduction to this book, tribal cultures, in fact, make use of a range of different sensory models and techniques to order society (see further Classen 1993a; Finnegan 2002; Geurts 2002), many more, indeed, than the limited sensory repertoire of electronic media permit.

Along the same lines, this paradigm assumes that people everywhere use electronic media in the same way with the same consequences. Studies indicate, however, that there are cultural differences in such use and in its perceived effects. While the internet and electronic media are often associated with collectivism in the West, for example, in Japan they have been seen as promoting personal distinctions and 'electronic individualism' (see Hjorth 2011: 115–16).

In traditional societies, internet experiences similarly may well not match the popular Western and academic notions of a new, collective, electronic orality. One study of e-mail use by members of a traditional Mohawk community in New York State found that it brought disturbing dimensions into their interchanges with family and friends. E-mail users in this community described how seeing their words written on the computer screen gave rise to a process of reflection and revision, which was antithetical to oral dialogue and even carried a taint of 'scheming'. They also manifested an awkward consciousness that, when they communicated through e-mail, they were first of all interacting with a machine, whose requirements – inputting the correct commands, responding to prompts – needed to be 'satisfied'. People felt they had to 'maintain pace with the machine', which introduced a mechanical dimension to interactions (MacDougall 2012: ch. 3).

Referring to electronic communication as a form of tribal tactility, furthermore, seems rather feeble when compared to the physical impact of actual tactile contact. Mensa Otabil, a Ghanaian pastor and educator combatting the divisiveness and violence he associates with tribalism in his country, makes the contrast in forceful terms: 'You have been told your ancestors were proud warriors. Yes, they were killing people and killing elephants. Well, my friend, we don't kill people now. We are now on email, we are now on the internet' (cited in Gifford 2004: 126).

Here the internet is evidently seen as a distancing – and civilizing – medium compared with the potentially violent immediacy of tribal life in Ghana. Although this is a negative characterization of tribal immediacy, one can see how traditional forms of corporeal bonding would also be obviated by internet use. Electronic modes of communication, in fact, could only seem tactile to a society long accustomed to eking out as full an imitation of multisensory life as possible from audiovisual media.

This is not to say that the internet, while not itself a tactile form of interaction, cannot promote the performance of tactile acts in the material world. However, by its emphasis on visuality, it also fosters the transformation of actual tactile acts into electronic imagery. Indeed, for many in the electronic age, an act does not attain its full realization until it is posted as a visual image on the World Wide Web. This can apply to everything from tourism to social gatherings, and from sexual acts to acts of violence. An example of the last is the recent phenomenon of 'happy-slapping' in which an assault is initiated and filmed by camera phone in order to be circulated as a video. It is this visual publicizing, and not the actual tactile experience or its consequences, that gives significance to actions and social importance to actors in the minds of the participants.

The problem with the comparison of online interaction with face-to-face interaction is that, while it may have some of the same immediacy, it lacks any physical encounter. In traditional societies spoken exchanges are not only multisensory, involving sight, and often smell and touch, as well as hearing, they also always occur in the physical presence of the speaker. Furthermore, unless one blocks one's ears, what is spoken can only with difficulty be ignored. Sound penetrates. This is what gives speech its particular psychic and corporeal impact and makes it such a strong medium of social integration. Electronic communications, on the other hand, are for the most part disembodied visual fragments, which do not carry the impact of the physical presence of their senders and can be left unseen and unattended.

Furthermore, unlike in a tribal society, one can generally select and deselect one's cyberspace community. This does not mean that people do not become emotionally involved or even obsessed with their online groups, but rather that there is far less compulsion to interact with any specific group, to obey any group's norms, or commit oneself to its defence. While a cyberspace community can provide important social support, one does not usually depend on it for one's material survival, the way one does with a traditional community. These characteristics of electronic media may well yet change. Participation in particular online groups may become compulsory, as well as necessary for both our social and physical survival. The internet may acquire a tactile, and even olfactory, presence as digital technologies broaden their sensory scope. Such developments would give online communities more of the feel of real-life societies.

All of these developments, however, would not necessarily transform online communities into tribal collectives, for they in fact promote a variation of the coordinated individualism characteristic of Western modernity. People do similar things at the same time – both in their physical use of electronic devices and in their online activities – and rely on a network of co-users, but they nonetheless manifest a strong sense of individual identity and importance. The photographs on Facebook visually shout 'Look at me!'

Furthermore, although internet users may appear to function like 'tribes' (or like 'herds' – stampeding towards the latest viral video), there is no possibility of participants simply fusing with the group. In an extension of the surveillance politics of modernity, internet users are singled out as individuals with particular consumer preferences or social profiles by marketers and government watchdogs alike.

The omnipresence of surveillance means that there is also less possibility of losing oneself in a crowd in the physical world. The rioters in England in 2011 were captured on video by surveillance cameras and camera phones, enabling individuals to be identified and arrested. Such identification involved, in part, using 'face-recognition' technology to match photos of rioters with pictures they had posted of themselves on Facebook or similar sites. Even when faces were obscured, visual identification was still possible in certain cases. 'We can identify people based on how they walk, their height, their clothes, shoes, all manner of things,' said the chairman of a surveillance camera association in London (Potter 2011). Bodies can press together and voices can blend together, but sight picks individuals out from the crowd. Whatever new sensory and social orders are fostered by electronic media, therefore, visual demarcation and individualism are unlikely to lose their social and political significance.

Electronic media and technologies have dramatically changed and continue to change the life of the senses. Word of mouth has become word of eye as news and commentary flicker on screens around the globe. Crowds can be convened and social protests arranged with an astonishing alacrity. Physical bodies can be put to one side and complex new identities adopted, at the same time as the crudest physical stereotypes are massively promoted in online texts and images. Harassment and bullying can occur without one physical touch, as can intimacy. Whatever forms of actual and virtual tactility are fostered by new media, however, the regulated individualism normalized in the nineteenth century is unlikely to lose its social and political significance in the electronic age.

4 The feel of justice

Law and the regulation of sensation

And by smelling in awe of the Lord.
and not what his eyes see will [the Messiah] judge.
and not by what his ears hear will he decide.

Isaiah 11:3

Pende chiefs ... are expected to have an extremely refined sense of smell, by which they can distinguish the odors of ritual and civil violations and the perpetrators.

Raymond A. Silverman, 'The olfactory', in *See the Music, Hear the Dance* (2004)

Most plain view cases involve the sense of sight and, more, recently, the sense of touch ... Plain odour, however, has not been clearly established thus far as a legal doctrine by Court decisions.

Rolando V. Del Carmen, *Criminal Procedure: Law and Practice* (2010)

Law, through its conventional association with reason, has been seen as opposed to, or at least situated outside, the realm of the senses – although very much involved in its regulation. This duality has been particularly noted as regards the fields of law and aesthetics: 'Art is assigned to imagination, creativity, and playfulness, law to control, discipline, and sobriety' (Douzinas and Nead 1999: 3; see also Manderson 2000).

This opposition of law and aesthetics has been challenged in recent years by a number of works exploring how the two fields interact: 'the ways in which political and legal systems have shaped, used, and regulated images and art, and ... the representation of law, justice, and other legal themes in art' (Douzinas and Nead 1999: 11). This chapter takes a broader approach, looking not just at the aesthetic, but at the sensory dimensions of law and how these relate to ways of sensing and making sense within culture.

As the quotations at the head of the chapter demonstrate, there can be wide divergence, as well as similarities, in how different cultures view the role of the senses in law. The following are among the questions to be addressed here: How are notions of justice informed by sensory models? What values do the aesthetics of the courtroom uphold? What kinds of sensory experiences can be taken into account as evidence? When do sounds or smells constitute public nuisances? Can there be property in sensations such as colours or textures? How do indigenous cultural traditions challenge and suggest alternatives to the sensory assumptions of the Western legal system?

Perceptions of justice

The senses of sight and hearing dominate Western perceptions of justice. Legal systems are customarily transmitted through visual texts or oral traditions. Visual and auditory evidence generally takes precedence over evidence based on other sensory experiences. Legal proclamations are diffused through printed notices or, in older times, by public criers calling out 'oyez' or 'hear ye'. The performance of justice itself is often conceptualized as dependent on 'seeing clearly' and 'hearing both sides'. The public acknowledgment of justice having been performed, in turn, is agreed to necessitate its audibility and visibility. 'Not only must Justice be done, it must also be seen to be done,' exclaims the modern aphorism.

There, are, however, exceptions to this audiovisual rule that are by no means trivial. The traditional image of the blindfolded figure of Justice holding scales in one hand suggests a very tactile notion of justice. The image indicates that sight would introduce a bias into the practice of justice by taking into account social status based on visual markers, whereas touch will ignore such markers and reach an impartial decision on the weight of the evidence alone. The other hand of Justice is often depicted holding another very tactile instrument, a sword. This indicates that Justice not only judges impartially, but also punishes impartially (and severely, as a sword is no mere disciplinary rod). This icon with its representation of justice as tactile would come to be exported around the world with the spread of Western legal traditions.

Lady Justice is usually shown standing erect and still, to emphasize the righteousness (with its connotations of straight and upright) and immutability of the law. A different perception of the figure is presented in Franz Kafka's novel *The Trial*, however. In the novel the protagonist K sees a painter working on an image of Justice and asks: 'But aren't there wings on the figure's heels, and isn't it flying?' The painter explains that he has been asked to combine the blindfolded figure of Justice holding scales with the image of the winged goddess of Victory (although winged feet would actually suggest the messenger god Mercury). K responds that it's not a good combination: 'Justice must stand quite still, or else the scales will waver and a just verdict will become impossible' (Kafka 1977: 177). However, the reader soon learns that in Kafka's surrealist world justice does 'move about', always eluding the grasp of those who seek it. Indeed K finds that, as the painting progresses, the image comes to look like the goddess of the hunt, conveying an image of Justice stalking, capturing and killing her 'prey'.

Kafka was certainly not the only writer to manipulate the traditional image of Justice to convey certain notions about the practice of law. It has, in fact, been a highly popular icon both for portraying justice and, with certain alterations, for portraying the miscarriage of justice. The latter is often done through shifting the sensory values presented: showing the scales to be unbalanced, for example, or depicting Justice to be blinkered rather than blindfolded (Resnik and Curtis 2011: ch. 1)

Significantly, the original model of 'Lady Justice', the Roman goddess 'Justitia', was not depicted blindfolded. The notion of a deity of justice who cannot 'see' what she is doing would have been unappealing to the Romans. It is also the case that taking visual markers of social status into account was important in Roman justice as one's status determined one's legal standing. For example, only male citizens were legally permitted to wear togas. Wearing a toga in court, therefore, indicated that one was a Roman citizen with all the associated rights. One first-century case reveals the importance of such visual markers. Faced with the situation of a Greek man claiming to be a Roman citizen, the Emperor Claudius allowed the man to wear a toga when pleading his case, but obliged him to don Greek apparel when contrary evidence was being presented (Boatwright 2012: 68).

In the Middle Ages, when blindness signified lack of judgement and even sinfulness, Lady Justice likewise had no blindfold. It was in the Renaissance that her sight was first veiled. This coincided with the figure becoming a representation of human, rather than divine, justice, for the latter would presumably require no blindfold to be fair (Resnik and Curtis 2011: 70; see also Jay 2003: ch. 9).

One Renaissance emblem offering a different sensory representation of justice depicted a sightless king surrounded by counsellors or judges without hands. The interpretation here is that the monarch, like Lady Justice, is not influenced by visual worldly considerations. In the explanatory text, he is said to judge 'according to what is said in his ear' emphasizing the aural dimension of justice. The judges are depicted without hands to show that they do not receive bribes and that no favours, in turn, can be received from their hands. This representation brings out a more negative image of touch as self-interested and prone to favouritism. However, the judges are still said to have a good sense of balance, indicating that 'balance', at least, retains its importance as a metaphor for fair dealing (Resnik and Curtis 2011: 41–45).

The ostrich provided a popular zoological emblem of justice (although, unlike Lady Justice, not one to be seen outside the world's courthouses today). An ostrich feather was a traditional symbol of justice and impartiality among the ancient Egyptians because, unusually among birds, the barbs of the feathers on one side of a shaft are the same length as those on the other. More dramatically, the ostrich was believed able to digest even the hardest of materials. This transformed the ostrich into a symbol of the ability of justice to deal with even the most difficult cases (Raffield 2004: 16–17).

This further example of the perceived 'relationship between corporeal sensations and decision making' (Resnik and Curtis 2011: 79) brings perceptions of eating and digesting into the sensorial imagery of justice. Such a gustatory/visceral association with justice was also central to biblically based notions of justice and righteousness. 'Blessed are they that hunger and thirst after righteousness, for they shall be filled,' declares Jesus in the Gospels (Matthew 5:6).

According to Christian doctrine, the first unlawful act was the eating of the forbidden fruit by Adam and Eve, which alienated humans from God. The ritual consumption of bread and wine, the body and blood of Christ, in the Eucharist, by contrast, effected a reconciliation of humans with God. The Church Father Augustine explained that, as Jesus himself embodies divine justice, through eating and sharing his body, our hunger for justice is satisfied. The Eucharist also provided a powerful model of a just society: in the Lord's Supper all share the 'food' equally. Thus a meal could serve as a model for the restoration of wholeness to a community fractured by iniquities and inequities (as will be discussed in an Amerindian context below).

The sense of taste was by no means neglected in theological considerations of the consumption of justice. Partially basing himself on Psalm 33:9 – 'Taste and see that the Lord is sweet' – Augustine came up with the notion of a 'palate of the heart' capable of tasting spiritual sweetness. This, he said, allows us to savour the 'sweetness' of divine justice, and therefore find delight as well as satisfaction in its consumption. The concept of an interior sense of taste which delights in spiritual sweetness was taken up enthusiastically by subsequent medieval theologians (Posset 2004). During centuries when many people were hungry much of the time, the notion of divine justice (and more generally God) being 'delicious food' had a powerful resonance.

The sense that may seem the least amenable to informing perceptions of justice is smell. This is because in the modern West we tend to associate smell with intuition, ephemerality and idiosyncratic personal memories. In pre-modernity, however, this sense was often conceptualized as able to perceive essential truths. Thus, when it came to judging, smell could cut through appearances and reports (this fruit looks good and is said to be good) and ascertain the true state of affairs (it is, in fact, rotten).

This notion of smell informs the quotation from Isaiah given at the head of this chapter. In a statement that is hard on modern audiovisual sensibilities, it is suggested that the Messiah will judge people by his sense of smell, rather than by sight or hearing. The next verse, continuing in an olfactory vein, proclaims that, 'with the breath of his lips he shall slay the wicked' (Isa 11:4). This might seem to be just a rather unusual metaphorical device, except for the fact that we find similar ideas expressed in historical accounts and practices. One intriguing historical reference occurs in the Babylonian Talmud. This reference concerns Bar Koziba, leader of a Jewish revolt against the Romans in the second century, and said by some Jews to be the messiah.

> Bar Koziba ruled for two and one-half years and said to the rabbis, 'I am the messiah.' They said to him, 'Of the messiah it is written that he smells and judges. Let us see if he can do so.' When they saw that he was unable to judge by scent, they killed him.
>
> (Green 2011: 246 n106)

This account indicates that allusions to messianic powers of smell could be taken literally.

In Western history certain saints were reputed to have a supernatural acuity of smell. Both the fourth-century Saint Hilarion and the sixteenth-century Saint Philip Neri, for example, could supposedly smell and identify human sins. The eighteenth-century Mary Margaret of the Angels similarly was said to be as good at 'scenting out and discerning hidden sins as a hunting dog scents out game' (Classen 1998: 48). This belief in the efficacy of the sense of smell in discovering hidden sinfulness was rooted in the popular notion of moral corruption producing an actual malodour, just as holiness reputedly produced a perceptible odour of sanctity.

In the nineteenth century, Friedrich Nietzsche claimed to have a similar ability to sniff out 'corrupt' souls, although he expressed it in a more modern language of 'physiology' and 'psychology'.

> My instinct for cleanliness is characterized by a perfectly uncanny sensitivity so that ... the inmost parts of every soul are physiologically perceived by me – *smelled*.
>
> This sensitivity furnishes me with psychological antennae by which I feel and get a hold of every secret: the abundant *hidden* dirt at the bottom of many a character.
>
> (Nietzsche 1989: 233)

Nietzsche's usage offers a strong suggestion of how a reputed ability to smell 'hidden' moral corruption could be used for political ends to single out and exclude (or 'purify') individuals and groups. As we saw in the previous chapter, this did indeed happen in numerous cases, notably in the Nazi stigmatization of Jews as malodorous.

The use of sensory metaphors and models for notions of justice and judging can be found in cultures around the world. Corporeal metaphors of straightness, uprightness, balance and evenhandedness are commonplace. Among the Igbo of Nigeria, for example, the expression 'to keep the hand straight' means to speak the truth and act fairly (Ndukaihe 2006: 268). Even taste and smell play a role in shaping perceptions of justice across cultures. Whereas justice, or at least the justice of God, was said to be sweet in the West, in China it was associated with a bitter taste. In traditional Chinese medicine, in fact, governmental functions are assigned to different organs. In this scheme the 'minister of justice' is the gallbladder: 'a righteous, unbiased and selfless official' said to be endowed with great courage. The consumption of bitter bile (sometimes from the gallbladders of executed criminals) was traditionally considered a useful way to increase one's personal courage and decision-making capacities ('Medical Anthropophy in China' 1830; Yu 2009: 118). As regards olfactory notions of justice, a prominent non-Western example is the long-standing custom in a number of African societies of smelling out witches.

Such sensory metaphors and models play an important role both in the conceptualization and practice of justice. They may also, as noted above, contribute to injustices. The ongoing custom of 'witch-smelling' in parts of Africa, for example, has led to many people (often women) being assaulted and even killed for supposedly practicing witchcraft. Due to this, as well as to negative Western attitudes towards 'primitive' beliefs, the custom of smelling out and disciplining witches is illegal in a number of African countries. Local peoples adhering to traditional beliefs, however, have stated that they would be better served if the courts would punish the witches, whom they hold responsible for misfortunes, rather than their assailants (Niehaus 2001).

In the contemporary West the use of allegorical images to represent justice greatly declined. A potent symbol of this decline is presented in Dickens' *Bleak House* in which the old-fashioned lawyer, Mr Tulkinghorn, has on the ceiling of his out-of-date office an allegorical image 'in Roman helmet and celestial linen' whose only purpose seems to be to 'make the head ache' (see Ribner 1999).

However, the ongoing life of sensory metaphors and models for justice can still be seen in fields ranging from the civil rights movement to global justice movements. The image of the fairly divided meal – sometimes expressed as 'equal slices of the pie' – remains highly popular. Over the past 50 years this ideal of tangible, edible justice has been extended to ever more groups within society and even to some outside human society, as in the ecological justice movement.

The notion of justice being blindfolded has likewise retained its social importance as more groups are included among those to whom justice should be impartial. (Indeed, this image has become such a cultural icon that a blindfold is sometimes mistakenly assumed to adorn even those statues of Justice that have none, i.e., Gibson 2009: 32.) One influential contemporary variation on this model is the 'veil of ignorance' concept, which advocates 'blinding' oneself to oneself, or putting aside personal considerations when determining principles of justice (Rawls 1999).

Ironically, for those who are actually blind, the image of a sightless justice may be thought to wield a double-edged sword. On one side, the image seems to present a rare positive view of blindness. Furthermore, the disabled are now often included among those groups theoretically protected from discrimination by Justice's blindfold. However, the fact that Justice is not portrayed as actually blind – 'presumably when Justice is off duty she can see' (Kleege 1999: 26) – may seem to leave the blind still outside the pale of even metaphorical social utility. And in fact, as one social historian of blindness notes and as we shall discuss further below, the blind are often excluded from jury duty: 'though Justice is blind, the jury should be sighted' (Kleege 1999: 26).

The senses in the courtroom

Another important way in which perceptions of justice are shaped is through our experience of judicial settings. In a materialization of the aphorism that 'not only must justice be done, it must also be seen to be done', a recent English guide for court design states that 'court buildings need to be seen to be there and seen to be public' (Mulcahy 2012: 170). In other words, court buildings must be visually prominent and appear accessible (see Resnik and Curtis 2011: 168).

Other sensory qualities, however, are also required of the traditional courthouse. It needs to convey a sense of solemnity and authority to inculcate feelings of respect in the people who view and enter it. In order to impress on society that the justice system is not something to be taken lightly, court buildings are usually designed to look massive and heavy. Employing stone as a building material conveys notions of the social weight of the edifice and the enduring nature of the principles upheld within. Tall pillars suggest both moral rectitude and the awe-inspiring forms of ancient temples. Ascending stairs imply the need for elevating one's thoughts to a higher plane and submitting one's will to a higher authority. All of these values are conveyed both visually and through the tactile/kinaesthetic experience of approaching and entering the building.

The conventional courtroom similarly shapes the experience of those who see and enter it. The abundance of wood suggests dignity and tradition. The benches and boxes convey a sense of order and separation of roles. Courtroom design further functions to control sight, sound, touch and movement.

Security screening, the use of bulletproof materials, and, in some courtrooms, the bolting of furniture to the floor, are aimed to reduce the dangers of physical assault. A railing customarily prevents spectators from interacting with the actors in courtroom proceedings. In fact, in order to avoid what has been called the 'nightmare' of the public mingling with judges and defendants, different routes of passage are now carefully designated within courthouses for the visual, auditory and tactile separation of the different kinds of participants in the proceedings (Resnik and Curtis 2011: 173). If worse comes to worse, 'panic buttons' can be pressed to call for help and even, in some cases, activate closed-circuit television monitors, which will convey and record the nature of the problem.

Clear views are ideally maintained within the courtroom so that justice may 'be seen to be done'. However, no one should be able to see in from outside for reasons of confidentiality and security. Similarly, speech must be readily heard by all within the courtroom but not by persons outside it. The formal clothing worn by judges and lawyers, from full legal dress with wigs and robes to business suits, offers a visual cue to the seriousness with which the proceedings are to be regarded (see further Brigham 2009; Mulcahy 2012).

The senses are engaged not only by the material characteristics of the courtroom, but also by the acts performed within it. The kinds of acts and movement allowed within the courtroom, however, vary according to judicial traditions.

> Americans often feel that the English courtroom, with its wigs and gowns and its scarlet and ermine, looks like purest theater ... But think about it for a moment and you'll realize that the English court is almost entirely *static*. The barristers are anchored to one spot. They either stand up or sit

down. ... An American courtroom, by contrast, is a positive kaleidoscope of movement.

(Evans 2010: 44)

The suggestion here is that in the United States the desired 'theatrical' effect of the traditional visual symbols of the courtroom is achieved instead through the drama of movement.

Speech, of course, is at the centre of all this drama. The legal principle of oral immediacy mandates that:

> Even in instances where written material is produced in court ... the actual hearing of the proceedings in court is conducted orally: there is the oral reading of the relevant written material, the oral arguments, the oral exchanges between the court and the lawyers, ... the oral evidence at the trial, the oral judgment of the court.
>
> (Jacob 1987: 19–20)

As regards the non-linguistic sounds of the courtroom, one traditional auditory, tactile and visual act involves the rapping of the judge's gavel. This 'hammers home' the authority of the court and signals the opening and closing of a court session (the last use giving rise to the expression 'to beat the rap', meaning to avoid sentencing).

One rarely discussed but often memorable element of the sensory atmosphere of the courtroom, is its odour. Historically, the courtroom was often permeated with the odours of unwashed prisoners, which doubtless contributed to a perception of criminality being ill-smelling and the administration of justice a nasty business (see Corbin 1986: 276 n30). Mark Twain noted in 1865 that the police court of San Francisco was 'the infernalest smelling den on earth' (2003: 172). Charles Dickens described a typical nineteenth-century courtroom as smelling 'close and unwholesome' (1850: 173). The presence of bewigged barristers and judges would not have helped the situation, for their awe-inspiring wigs were notoriously foul-smelling.

Given that malodours were associated with disease and that in the eighteenth century an outbreak of 'gaol fever' had resulted in several deaths in the Old Bailey courthouse in London, the practice arose in London of adorning the courtroom with sprigs of rue – the strong scent of which was held to ward off the invasive odours of disease. Along with fragrancing the courtroom, these sprigs provided defendants in the dock with something to handle. In 1840, a 17-year-old accused of trying to assassinate Queen Victoria spent his hours in the dock 'picking, rubbing and smelling' the rue (Murphy 2012: ch. 6). In 1849 a woman being tried for murder angrily picked up some of the rue in the dock 'and threw them vehemently over the wigged heads of the "learned" gentlemen' (Thornbury 1881: 468).

One twentieth-century literary example of courtroom odour comes from Egypt, where it had an impact on the rise of nationalism. It appears in a fictionalized account by Mahmud Tahir Haqqui of an incident in which Egyptian villagers were put on trial for attacking British officers. In a heavily symbolic moment the Anglicized Egyptian prosecutor asks to have the 'malodorous' peasants sprayed with English cologne to render them less 'obnoxious'. This rescenting of the villagers is only a temporary expedient, however, for the prosecutor's ultimate demand is for 'the execution of all the foul-smelling accused' (Selim 2004: 98).

Contemporary courtrooms may not be as malodorous as those of the nineteenth century, but odour in the court can still be an issue. When one Kansas judge complained recently about the malodour in her cramped courtroom, the commissioner overseeing courthouse facilities responded bluntly that it wasn't coming from the room: 'It's the clientele' (Work 2011).

If odours still inhabit modern courtrooms, many other elements have been pared down to a bare minimum. The furnishings resemble those of the modern office, with blond wood often preferred over the sombre dark woods of the traditional courtroom. Such 'no fuss' courtrooms suggest a justice system that will operate in a brisk, business-like fashion unimpeded by antiquated rites or regulations.

Indeed, modern technologies of communication have led to the new scenario of a purely audiovisual courtroom. Video-link systems enable defendants, lawyers, witnesses and judges to interact with each other without gathering together in a room. This means that participants may be situated within very different physical and social environments, for example, within a prison or police station in the case of a defendant. It also means that the physical presence of televised participants is transformed into a flat image with accompanying sound. This can be an advantage for young or vulnerable witnesses who might find the experience of appearing in court overwhelming. However it also raises the question of whether the same respect will be felt and shown for electronic representations of witnesses and defendants – or judges – as for their embodied persons.

Televising court cases, in turn, means that justice may be seen – and heard – to be done by many more people. It also, however, gives rise to new perceptions of justice. The corporeal sensations of entering into and standing and sitting in the courtroom can be evoked by visual images but not fully conveyed. Similarly, the sense of contiguity with the community of people gathered inside the court is lost on the solitary spectator in front of a television at home. Certainly the intimacy and confidentiality of the courtroom are breached when its proceedings are broadcast to the world.

The other side of this much-debated issue involves how televising court cases affects what goes on inside the court. Is a greater emphasis placed on visual appearance by the actors in the proceedings? Do lawyers and judges take the television audience into account in what they say and do, with an eye to making a good impression on viewers? With the growing popularity of both virtual courts and televised trials the sensorial and social issues they raise will become ever more relevant.

The tactile rites of law

Sticks and stones

Ritual legal acts were particularly important in the predominantly oral societies of the past in which a dramatic corporeal action might carry more cultural
weight than a written text. This was the case in medieval Europe, where
'lawmaking, justice, orders, instructions, and military and fiscal procedures
were partially, indeed at times only sporadically, committed to writing prior to
the thirteenth century' (Bedos-Rezak 1996: 196).

Generally, the growing importance of writing in the late Middle Ages
and Renaissance contributed to a decrease in the importance of tactile signs as
markers of legal processes. This shift went hand-in-hand with a widening divide
between the increasingly literate upper classes and the mostly non-literate
working classes. Shakespeare commented on this sensory and social divide in his
historical drama, *Henry VI, Part 2*. In the play the nobility are accused by peasants of using their power to read and write to oppress the poor: 'thou has put
[poor men] in prison, and because they could not read thou hast hanged them'
(IV, vii). The peasants dream of burning written records and returning to an
oral and tactile way of life, but Shakespeare makes it clear that such dreams have
no future in a well-ordered state (see Classen 2012: 6–7).

For most of the Middle Ages, however, handclasps and kisses were deemed
to establish contractual relationships more powerfully than written contracts
(Clanchy 2012). They were understood to involve a direct bodily commitment by the participants and to carry a threat of dire corporeal consequences if
the contract were broken. A breach of an accord established through a ritual
handclasp could be punished by cutting off the hand of the offending party. A
good illustration of the moral and legal weight given to such tactile contracts
comes from the twelfth century when the matter of whether King Henry II
would seal a negotiated reconciliation with his exiled Archbishop Thomas á
Becket with a kiss was the subject of intense negotiation. In the end Becket
returned to England without the binding kiss only to be murdered by Henry's
knights shortly afterwards (Petkov 2003: 63–65, 172).

Another medieval legal rite consisted of grasping a *festuca* or stick to signify
the transfer of property or the acceptance of a judge's decision. This custom
was based on the necessity of physically touching, 'laying hands on', an object
(or person) over which one claimed possession in Roman law. If the object
was immovable, namely land, it was symbolized by a stick (Corbeill 2004: 21).
In medieval usage, court decisions were symbolically materialized in the form
of a stick so that those affected by them could physically attest to having made
them their own. After the action was taken, the *festuca* was often preserved as a
tangible memorial of the agreement. In the case of renouncing one's claims or
obligations, it would be ritually broken or cast away.

In criminal cases where the evidence was too scanty to allow for a clear
judgment and yet in which a verdict of guilt or innocence was considered

necessary, the matter might be ritually turned over to God. This occurred in the medieval trial by ordeal, which usually involved holding or walking over red-hot iron or picking a stone out of boiling water. If there was no resulting injury or if the injury showed signs of healing quickly, the innocence of the accused was assumed to have been established by a divine miracle. In other versions (of many) of the trial by ordeal, the accused were bound and thrown in water and presumed guilty if they floated (and pulled out if they sank), or obliged to eat sanctified bread and cheese and presumed guilty if they choked or showed other signs of distress (Bartlett 1988).

This practice was intended to make the body – with the supposed assistance of God – 'speak' of its guilt or innocence when the oral accounts presented by the accused and witnesses were unconvincing. As oral confessions were still preferred, however, judicial torture – aimed at extracting the guilty truth from recalcitrant prisoners – came to be a preferred method of solving the problem of lack of evidence, and trials by ordeal died out after the Middle Ages. Unlike the trial by ordeal, the trial by combat, in which two parties in a dispute determined the outcome through a sword fight, survived into modern times (although usually outside the legal system) in the form of the duel.

Judicial corporal punishments likewise often had (and still have in certain countries) important ritual elements, too complex in nature to consider more than very briefly here. In medieval law, corporal punishments were often matched to the crime: thus a thief might have his hand cut off and a slanderer his tongue. Such cases involved directly punishing the offending appendage as well as attempting to ensure that the crime could not be repeated. The latter aim, however, was secondary to that of marking the nature of the crime on the convict's body – for him to experience and everyone to see. This is evidenced by the fact that judicial mutilations sometimes preceded an execution. In one English case of 1631, for example, an accused who threw a stone at the chief justice after hearing his conviction, had his right hand cut off and affixed to the gibbet before he himself was hung (Pepys 1828: 353–54). This constituted a very tangible and visible display of the nature of the crime and the power of the law.

Judicial executions themselves were intended not just as punishments, but as public ceremonies to ritually manifest and annul the injury that the criminal had occasioned to the social body. Stoning as a form of execution was rare in the West, although many other methods for inflicting a painful and dramatic death on a condemned criminal were practiced at one time or another. With modern prison sentences, however, the emphasis shifted to 'correcting' deviant hands and bodies through laborious tasks, constant supervision, and group drills (see Foucault 1995; Classen 2012: 45, 62–63, 174).

Kissing the Bible

Among the tactile rituals still commonly performed within courtrooms today, none has generated as much controversy as the practice of touching the Bible when swearing an oath. The act of ritually touching an object when swearing has many antecedents. The ancient Israelites had the custom of swearing with a hand under the thigh of a patriarch (i.e., Gen 24: 2–9). This would seem to have been based on the reverence felt for the progenitor of an important line of descent. Objects employed in oath-taking in European societies ranged from sacred stones to weapons. The most binding form of touch in such practices was usually deemed to be a kiss, which was believed to carry something of the spirit of the kisser with it. The underlying concept was that the object sworn on, or the deity it represented, would punish perjurers.

Under the influence of Christianity, saintly relics and Bibles or missals gradually became the objects approved for touching during oath-taking (see, however, Gillespie 1997: 34). Relics were generally regarded as the more binding of the two, for saintly bones were perceived as more tangibly powerful – and more capable of exacting retribution if crossed than holy books (Classen 2012: 36).

However, due to the Protestant Reformation and the Catholic Counter-Reformation, and to the growing importance of texts, relics lost their legal role in the sixteenth and seventeenth centuries and the Bible became the usual object deemed appropriate for Christians to touch and kiss when taking an oath. (When a copy of the Bible or Gospels was not available, people might sometimes swear instead touching paper 'as if it were the Gospels' [Tyler 1835: 182].) The fact that witnesses wishing to give false testimony without incurring a divine penalty sometimes tried to avoid directly kissing the Bible by, for example, kissing the air or their thumb (which would be on top of the book when it was being held) indicates that the practice was no mere formality (Tyler 1835: 48).

At times exceptions were made for peoples of other religions, probably not out of deference to their differing beliefs, but with the realization that swearing on a Bible would have little hold over a non-Christian. Jews, for example, might be required to swear while holding a pen (for uncertain reasons), or on their phylacteries or sacred books. As European courts began to have more dealings with non-Westerners in the nineteenth century, and as a wider range of people was allowed to testify, the varieties of objects that might be touched in lieu of the Bible increased. An English article on the subject from 1830 noted that a Chinese man had taken an oath 'in the form of the Courts at China, by holding a saucer in his hand, which he dashed to pieces at the conclusion of the oath' (Templarius 1830: 599). English magistrates in India allowed oaths to be sworn on Hindu holy books or with a traditional swallow of Ganges water. Notably, while the ritual object could vary, a ritual touch was still essential. Touch conveyed, in a way mere words or looks or gestures could not, a sense of commitment.

For a number of Protestants, however, ritually touching an object, even one as important to Christians as the Bible, implied idolatry. No precedent for the practice could be found in the Bible itself – apart from the custom of putting a hand under the thigh of a patriarch, which did not recommend itself to the dissenters. Plenty of precedent for swearing oaths while touching sacred objects, on the other hand, could be found in the 'idol-worship' of the pagans. In consideration of such attitudes, witnesses were sometimes allowed to be sworn in without the offensive touching, making an appeal to Heaven in the form of a raised right hand instead. Hence in the seventeenth century the vice-chancellor of Oxford was permitted to be sworn in at court by reciting the oath, holding up his right hand and looking at, rather than touching, the Bible (Tyler 1835: 58). Sight, evidently, did not convey the sense of idolatrous homage implied by touch.

A nineteenth-century opponent of ritual Bible-touching wrote glowingly of oath-taking in Presbyterian Scotland: 'There is no *touching* of the book. There is no *kissing* of the book. Both judge and witness believe that the Holy Bible was given by God for a very different use, than that of having its boards kissed in the transaction of any civil business' ('On the nature' 1827: 346). In other words, the Bible was not to be valued as a material object, only for its immaterial contents.

In modern Western courtrooms, swearing an oath while placing a hand on the Bible is still customary in many places. Allowances, however, are usually made for alternative practices. These include permitting those who decline to swear at all to simply affirm the oath. However, the issue of whether one touches a Bible or not during oath-taking is still very much alive, judging by the discussion generated by the practice after both of Barack Obama's swearings-in as President of the United States (i.e., Franke-Ruta 2009).

The development of digital technology in the twentieth century has opened a potential new area for tactile rituals. With electronic voting machines, for example, votes can now be cast with the press of a button or the touch of a screen. In this regard, one state website in the United States advises voters that 'if you've ever used an ATM or even a microwave, you've used the same simple touch screen technology the new voting units employ' (Kemp n.d.). This is surely a novel way to think of participating in a democratic election: just one more machine to set in motion with a tap.

Thus far digital touch does not seem to have been attributed symbolic values or a ritual role. A layering of meanings onto what seem to be purely functional actions, however, may well yet happen. And, as the example of electronic voting indicates, digital touching *does* constitute an important new mode of establishing social order.

The senses as witnesses

A cartoon by Leo Cullum which appeared in the *New Yorker* shows an astute-looking dog sitting in the witness box and being asked 'And do you smell that man anywhere in the courtroom?' This cartoon raises interesting questions about the admissibility of non-visual and non-auditory evidence (as well as about the role of animal senses in the legal system), some of which we will consider here.

Among the kinds of evidence presented in a courtroom, that which has been – or can be – witnessed by the eyes has long been held to be the most authoritative. Auditory evidence follows behind, with that pertaining to the other senses lagging in the distance. The pervasiveness of cameras in contemporary society has widened the distance between sight and the other senses in this regard by vastly increasing the amount of visual evidence available in court cases. Not surprisingly, therefore, while a good number of books and articles have been written concerning visual evidence, discussions of other kinds of sensory evidence are scanty.

Given the importance attached to visual evidence, one would expect that those who were unable to see would be excluded from serving as jurors. This, as noted above, has customarily been the case. In 1891 when a new trial was granted by the Supreme Court of Indiana because of the poor eyesight of one of the jurors, the court declared:

> We think that the juror was not competent to sit, even in cases where the testimony consists entirely of the statements of the witnesses ... [S]urely no one who cannot see the expressions of [witnesses'] faces, nor observe deportment and demeanor, can justly weigh testimony.
>
> ('Notes of Recent Decisions' 1891: 293–94)

While in some countries pressure by disability rights groups has led to blind persons being permitted to sit on juries, this kind of reasoning is still often used today to argue against the practice. A related situation, which recently came before the Supreme Court of Canada, is whether a witness can testify wearing a niqab or veil (Makin 2012; see further Allen 2011: 74).

However, there is also an increasing consciousness of how *sight* might negatively affect jurors in their weighing of the evidence (as suggested by the classic image of Justice with a blindfold). A number of studies have shown, indeed, that such visual factors as the skin colour or the perceived attractiveness of the accused may play a role in whether defendants are judged guilty or innocent (Johnson 2000; Walker at al. 2009: ch. 6). (Presumably, it would also be possible to form a bias based on a person's manner of speech. However, due to the social importance placed on visual appearances, this is presumed to have less of a discriminatory effect.) While a (racially) colour-blind jury may be considered important for arriving at a fair verdict, however, blindness itself is still generally viewed as an impediment to the process.

As regards blind judges, a rare early example is that of the eighteenth-century English magistrate Sir John Fielding, who was one of the founders of the British police force. Other examples of blind judges do not seem to appear until the latter half of the twentieth century, when visual impairment, and disabilities generally, began to lose some of their social stigma (Maurer 1985; *Law Society Gazette* 1991; *New York Times* 2007). Interestingly, in one case from the 1980s a blind judge in Illinois was asked by a lawyer to disqualify himself on the grounds that he would not be able to see the defendant's expression in a videotaped confession. The implication was evidently that visual content was more important in video testimony than in the live testimony usually heard by the judge. The judge, Nicholas Pomaro, disagreed, saying that 'outer appearance doesn't make [someone] a truthful person and it doesn't make him a liar … It's what's inside that counts, and that's what I'm better able to get at' (Associated Press 1984).

Blind witnesses, in turn, are a popular trope in fiction and films, where they are shown using non-visual cues such as the sound of footsteps and the smell of cologne to identify criminals (Nelson 1994). Their ability to recall such non-visual sensations is often presented as quasi-supernatural, requiring 'faith' on the part of their supporters. In actual cases, however, courts have been reluctant to place much weight on evidence based on sounds (apart from speech) or smells, whether coming from a blind or sighted witness. For example, 'earwitness' testimony relying on voice identification is not held to be very trustworthy, except in cases where the witness was well-acquainted with the person's voice or where the voice had a distinctive feature. And while the US Supreme Court stated in 1948 that odours may be 'found to be evidence of the most persuasive character', they are rarely taken to be so (Bull and Clifford 1999; Gardner and Anderson 2010: 207).

One interesting eighteenth-century case in which olfactory – and gustatory – evidence *did* play a decisive role involved a murder by poisoning. In this case, Sir Theodosius Boughton, a young man of property, died shortly after taking a vial of medicine. Before giving him the medicine, his mother had noticed that it smelled of bitter almonds. When the stomach of the deceased was opened for examination the doctor perceived a biting acrid taste on his tongue, such as, according to his testimony, might be produced by the presence of toxic laurel water. It was noted that Sir Theodosius' brother-in-law, Captain John Donellan, who stood to gain control of the estate through his wife, had carefully cleaned the bottle of supposed medicine immediately after the young man died. He had also ordered that a still (which could have been used to prepare laurel water) be thoroughly cleaned. When a bottle of laurel water was produced in court, Sir Theodosius' mother recognized the smell as that she had smelled in her son's medicine vial. The evidence was all circumstantial and an important part of it came from the senses of smell and taste, but, rightly or wrongly, it was taken to be conclusive and Captain Donellan was convicted and hanged (Smith 1825: 250–65).

One use of olfactory evidence which has received attention in recent years is that testified to by dogs, as spoofed in Leo Cullum's cartoon. The superior olfactory abilities of dogs have long been employed to locate missing persons or corpses. However, their use in identifying criminals has been controversial. In 1996, for example, a young man was convicted of murder by a jury in California based largely on his identification by a bloodhound, who had smelled the victim's shirt and then tracked down the accused. The judge, however, overturned the verdict due to his lack of confidence in the accuracy of the dog's olfactory identification (Hansen 2000).

In other cases scent lineups have been used to identify criminals. These involve one or more trained dogs smelling a row of scent samples and signalling if one matches an odour they have previously smelled on the victim's clothing, or another article presumed to have been handled by the accused. While this 'dog-scent' evidence has led to convictions in some cases, the general opinion of courts is that it is insufficient as primary evidence (Ensminger 2012).

Allowing jurors themselves to see and handle evidence has long been held to be an effective courtroom technique as it helps to materialize the facts of the case. The highly-successful trial lawyer Melvin Belli wrote that 'jurors learn through all their senses ... let them see and feel and even taste or smell the evidence, then you will reach the jury' (Belli 1976: 91). During the 1941 case of a woman claiming compensation for a leg severed in a trolley accident, Belli had the jury pass around the woman's new artificial leg. 'Feel the warmth of life in the soft tissues of its flesh,' he instructed them, 'feel the pulse of the blood as it flows through the veins, feel the marvellous smooth articulation at the new joint and touch the rippling muscles of its calf' (Belli 1976: 108). Since they obviously would not be able to feel anything of the sort, the tactile experience brought home what the woman had lost in the accident. In another case from the United States involving an injured plaintiff, a jury was asked to touch the wounds on the woman's head to assess whether they had been filled in with hard bone or soft tissue (McAndrews *v.* Leonard 1926).

Occasionally tastes and odours have also been brought into the jury box. Jurors have been asked to determine the saltiness of a sample of well water, for example, and smell a rag from a fire for evidence of kerosene (Richardson 1974: 60). However, although one guide to winning trials enthusiastically advises lawyers: 'If you can find a way to bring in evidence that would require jurors to use their senses of smell or taste, go for it!' (Easton 1998: 21), the vast majority of the demonstrative evidence presented at trials is visual.

A final issue to be discussed here is the plain view doctrine. This doctrine allows police officers to seize evidence that is in plain sight without having a search warrant. One concern that has been raised about this doctrine is the extent to which it may apply to electronic evidence on computers. For example, if, when an officer is legally searching a suspect's computer files for evidence of drug-trafficking, files relating to other possibly criminal activities appear, should these be considered to be 'in plain view'? (Casey 2011: 235–36).

Another dimension of this doctrine is the extent to which 'plain view' includes 'plain touch', 'plain odour', 'plain hearing' and 'plain taste'. Most of the discussion of this issue has centred on 'plain touch' and 'plain odour', as the most commonly arising corollaries to 'plain view'. In one precedent-setting case in the United States in 1993 (Minnesota *v.* Dickerson), it was ruled (upholding the trial court decision) that a police officer could legally seize a suspicious object (in this case cocaine) he had felt while frisking a suspect for weapons.

To this court, there is no distinction as to which sensory perception the officer uses to conclude the material is contraband. An experienced officer may rely upon his sense of smell in DUI [driving under the influence] stops or in recognizing the smell of burning marijuana in an auto-mobile ... The sense of touch, grounded in experience and training, is as reliable as perceptions from the other senses. 'Plain feel', therefore, is no different than plain view.

(Minnesota *v*. Dickerson 1993)

The underlying question is whether objects or substances that cannot be seen and are therefore not in plain view, can be considered as being in plain view if they can be felt, smelt or otherwise sensed. Discussion of this perplexing question has amounted to almost a trial of the senses themselves. The Minnesota Supreme Court, for example, overturned the 1993 conviction based on 'plain feel' evidence, stating that touch is both less reliable and more intrusive than sight and therefore cannot be posited as its sensory equivalent. The US Supreme Court upheld this reversal. It also, however, to some extent vindicated touch, ruling that contraband seized during pat-downs could be used as evidence, but only if the officer had immediately recognized its probable nature by feel (Hess and Orthmann 2012: 289–90; see also Kentucky *v*. King 2011).

This hazy legal zone is even more contentious as regards smell. While touch has been said to be less reliable than sight, the sense of smell has been criticized in court as being less reliable than both sight and touch: 'When an officer sees or feels contraband, he knows it is present and he can tell who has possession of that contraband. The same is not true with the sense of smell' (cited in Sprow 2000: 301).

Crusaders for the equality of the senses in the plain view doctrine have argued that 'The sense of smell is at least as reliable as the sense of touch in determining whether contraband is present, and should therefore be accorded equal status to touch within the plain view doctrine' (Sprow 2000: 304). Even more provocatively, it has been stated that '[a]ny attempt to create a hierarchy of the senses [in the plain view doctrine] defies common sense and unjustifi-ably hinders effective law enforcement' (cited in Sprow 2000: 308–9)

The issue is further complicated when the senses that are picking up on evidence are not human. This is the case when dogs are used to sniff luggage or, more controversially, the exteriors of houses and vehicles, for the presence of illegal substances within (i.e., Florida V. Jardines 2013).

Electronic sensing and recording devices can similarly allow for the exterior monitoring of sensory signals that are not apparent to human senses. In one case (Kyllo *v*. United States 2001) a thermal-imaging device was used outside a house in which marijuana was suspected of being grown. The purpose was to determine the likelihood of the presence of heat-emitting, 'grow' lamps. The court affirmed that this use of thermal sensing was not an invasion of privacy. The heat escaping from the house could be said to have been in 'plain view', even though electronic sensors were used to detect it. This decision, however, was later overturned by the US Supreme Court in a 5–4 ruling (see also Katz *v*. United States 1967).

The extent to which either human or non-human sensory witnessing is considered permissible in the search for illegal objects depends a great deal on social perceptions of the importance of enhancing security compared to the importance of ensuring civil liberties. Thus we find that in public places where there is a heightened perception of security risk, notably airports, a broader range of search techniques – pat-downs, sniffer dogs, body scanners – are considered acceptable than in places deemed to be relatively safe. If security concerns increase, we can expect to see corresponding extensions of sensory surveillance of multiple kinds.

Regulating sensory boundaries

To consider all the ways in which the senses are regulated would require reviewing entire legal codes, for a vast number of laws are there to restrict the kinds of sensory – and in particular tactile – acts people are allowed to perform in society. In this section, however, we will narrow the topic down to the issue of what are considered to be sensorial nuisances. In particular we will examine situations in which odours and sounds – the most boundary-crossing sensory phenomena – have been considered offenses against the 'public sensorium'.

Auditory nuisances

To begin with sounds, concerns over auditory disturbances appear early in history. A piece of writing found amid the ruins of Pompeii concerns a request to a magistrate 'to prevent the people from making a noise disturbing the good folks who are asleep'. The first-century poet Martial, who felt as though the whole Roman army was marching through his bedroom at night, would have sympathized (Goldsmith 2012: 37).

Various attempts were made to control urban noise – particularly at night – by legislation over the centuries. Among the sounds notorious for disturbing the peace of the neighbourhood were the racket produced by noisy trades such as blacksmiths, the rattling of carts over cobblestones, the calls of street vendors, the singing of revellers and even the cries of women being hit by their husbands, as one gathers from a sixteenth-century prohibition on wife-beating after nine at night in London. Regulations, however, could do little to quell the rising tide of noise created by the increase in urban populations and traffic in the modern period (Goldsmith 2012: 45).

In the twentieth century, unwanted sounds continued to intrude on private life: 'People dare not enter a man's house or peep into it, yet he has no way of preventing them from filling his house and his office with nerve-racking noise' (Smilor 2004: 320). A growing intolerance led to the implementation of anti-noise ordinances in many Western cities. The nature of the unwanted noises had changed, however. While in nineteenth-century New York City complaints of noise had centred on pedlars, street musicians, animals and horse-drawn vehicles, by 1925 the dominant noises of New York were said to come from automobiles, subway trains, drills, and other mechanical sources (Thompson 2005: 190–91).

Thus far we have only dealt with sounds being considered nuisances because they were noisy. In some cases, however, the objectionable character attributed to a sound was due primarily to its cultural or symbolic associations. A classic example of this is the cultural clash between the Christian ringing of bells and the Islamic call to prayer. Both Christians and Muslims traditionally considered their own summoning sound to be central to devotional practice as well as endowed with the power to chase away evil spirits. Each was highly suspicious of the sounds employed by the other. Not surprisingly, in Islamic territories bell-ringing was usually prohibited and within Christian territories Muslim calls to prayer were likewise customarily banned (Corbin 1994: 101–4; Blanks and Frassetto 1999; Alibhai 2008: 28–30).

This auditory conflict was particularly intense in southern Spain, which was conquered by Muslims in the eighth century. There church bells were often destroyed by the conquerors or put to other, non-sonic, uses. The most notable occasion on which this occurred was in 997 when a Muslim army invaded the Christian pilgrimage city of Santiago de Compostela and brought back its bells to be turned into lamps and hung in the Great Mosque of Cordoba – thus transforming Christian sound into Islamic light. When Christians reconquered Cordoba in 1236 one of their most symbolically potent acts was to return these bells to Santiago to ring out once more (Alibhai 2008: 38–58; Constable 2011: 67).

Similar scenarios played out on other lands fought over by Christians and Muslims in subsequent centuries (see Baer 2011: 78), and also within popular representations. (When Don Quixote hears a puppeteer describe Muslims ringing bells in alarm at the escape of a Christian captive, he vociferously corrects him [*Don Quixote*, ch 26]). In contemporary society, this battle over the religious soundscape has once again become an issue with the rise in Muslim populations in Western countries. One line of argument holds that the Muslim call to prayer has as much right to be heard in public space as Christian church bells, while another rejects it as an auditory invasion (particularly when amplified). Thus far the issue has usually been decided by the individual municipalities in which it has arisen, rather than by nationwide policies (Langer et al. 2011; Weiner 2009).

In the battle over control of the Western soundscape, however, church bells themselves have sometimes been targeted. In the officially atheist Soviet Union the 'undesirable' religious significance of their peals led to their silencing. It is noise rather than religion, nonetheless, that is the focus of most modern complaints about church bells. Already in 1911 an Australian plaintiff gained an injunction to prevent a nearby church from ringing its bells before 9 a.m. on Sundays (Haddon *v.* Lynch 1911). Since then, a decline in church attendance, together with rising concerns over noise pollution, have led to a considerable increase in such complaints. Traditionalists argue that the sound of bells forms part of the fabric of Western life, but for those disturbed by them, they are noisy intrusions to be stopped or controlled by nuisance or environmental protection laws (Rivers 2010: 199–201).

Olfactory nuisances

As with noises, odours have a long history of being considered public nuisances. Premodern cities were often notoriously malodorous as a result of concentrations of waste products, foul-smelling industries such as tanneries, smoking fireplaces, and polluted rivers. In 1357, for example, King Edward III of England declared that

> When passing along the water of the Thames we have beheld dung and other filth accumulated in diverse places in the said City upon the bank of the river aforesaid and also perceived the fumes and other abominable stenches arriving therefrom.
>
> (cited in Classen 2005b: 293)

At the time, however, pervasive malodour seemed an inevitable corollary of crowded urban life.

The larger cities grew in subsequent centuries, the more such stenches increased. This was particularly worrisome because of the presumed connection between malodour and disease (a connection that led people to press perfumed handkerchiefs to their noses during times of plague). Attempts to alleviate the situation through increased regulation, however, were often blocked by objections that this would infringe on property rights. As one London sanitary reformer put it in 1854:

> When your orders are addressed to some owner of objectionable property which is a constant source of nuisance, or disease, or death; when you would force one person to refrain from tainting the general atmosphere with the results of an offensive occupation ... you will be reminded of the 'rights of property' and of 'an Englishman's inviolable claim to do as he will with his own'.
>
> (cited in Classen 2005b: 296)

Working-class neighbourhoods, with their dense populations and abysmal sanitation, were a particular focus of concerns about ill odours – concerns that at times made a virtual equation between 'working class' and 'stench'. Immigrant populations, living in crowded, unsanitary conditions, could also be a target of fears over olfactory (and social) pollution. In nineteenth-century San Francisco the Working Men's Party of California petitioned to have Chinatown – 'this laboratory of infection' – declared a nuisance: 'Filth ... is everywhere patent to the senses of sight and smell' ('Chinatown' 1880).

The extent of the problem, along with the outbreak of associated cholera epidemics, finally forced authorities in affected cities to take action. Networks of underground sewers were built, overcrowded tenements were outlawed, and zoning regulations removed noxious trades and garbage dumps from urban neighbourhoods. Factory smoke, however, continued to plague modern cities, as authorities were reluctant to compromise economic development for the sake of cleaner air. In the early twentieth-century, Western countries finally passed smoke abatement legislation (Brimblecombe 1999: 15–16).

What different people or cultures consider sources of malodour, however, can vary widely (see Classen et al. 1994; Henshaw 2013). While urban green spaces are valued today for their capacity to 'freshen' the air, for example, in ancient Jerusalem parks were prohibited out of concerns that the city would be annoyed by malodours from decaying vegetation and fertilizer (Sichel 1985: 30). In the modern world, not only have industrial and automobile emissions given rise to new malodours, fragrance itself, in the form of synthetic scents, is considered noxious by many suffering from environmental sensitivity (Fletcher 2005; Immen 2010). Even when they are not linked to health hazards, odours can legally be deemed a nuisance if they are shown to interfere with the enjoyment of life. Thus, even cooking smells from restaurants have come under attack as interfering with people's enjoyment of their homes and gardens. Despite such variations in what are deemed to be olfactory nuisances, however, many contemporary odour complaints are directed at the same sorts of sources – garbage dumps, manure pits, sewage – that have been upsetting people with their stenches for centuries.

When, as is often the case, odour complaints stem from agricultural activities, the problem is sometimes presented as a conflict between city-dwellers, who have artificial expectations for a deodorized environment, and farmers, who have not lost their connection with natural processes and odours (Classen 2005b: 295). Already in the nineteenth century Victor Hugo tried to counter city-dwellers' growing repugnance to waste by pointing out its agricultural uses:

> Those heaps of garbage at the corners of the stone blocks, these tumbrils of mire jolting through the streets at night, these horrid scavengers' carts, these fetid streams of subterranean slime which the pavement hides from you, do you know what all this is? It is the flowering meadow … it is perfumed hay, it is golden corn, it is bread on your table, it is warm blood in your veins, it is health, it is joy, it is life.

> (Hugo 1931: 1054)

However, while Hugo's words would certainly resonate today with advocates of organic composting, many current complaints concerning odours arise from a new phenomenon in the history of farming: concentrated animal feeding operations. In these increasingly prevalent operations high numbers of animals are packed into compact facilities with a resulting high concentration of waste and odours. When coupled with the spread of populations into agricultural areas, the result has been a barrage of complaints concerning malodour (i.e. Toombs 2012).

New sensitivities

In the contemporary world there has been a decline in the social and legal tolerance of public odours and noise. While we can locate the beginnings of this decline in the industrialized West, it has since occurred in other parts of the globe as well. In China, for example, where 'noise and smell nuisance have for a long time been morally acceptable', new sensitivities are resulting in more restrictive regulations (van Rooj 2006: 207).

This global trend towards increased control over sensory emissions can be said to result from a number of factors: the greater role of the state in public and private life, an emphasis on a separation of functions and of sensations in modernity, a scientific discourse of noise and odour pollution, a medical and popular discourse of nervous sensibility, and an increase in social and sensory 'refinement' brought about by public education and the growth of the middle class. Commercial interests in marketing odour and noise control technologies also play a role.

When a sensory phenomenon is deemed to constitute a nuisance, the customary solution has been to either remove or mitigate it. Thus, as we saw in the case of the cries of beaten wives disturbing the peace of London at night, a regulation was set in place to prevent it occurring after 9 p.m. Where the problem is one of traffic noise, the modern solution has been to put up sound barriers and build quieter cars. In the contemporary case of an olfactory nuisance arising from intensive animal farming, much effort is put into devising ways of diminishing the odour through ventilation systems, chemical treatment of manure, changes to the feed, and so on.

At times, however, such suppression of sensory phenomena may seem a way of avoiding dealing with underlying concerns. The question might be asked, as it eventually was, should wives be beaten? Or, should animals be kept in such crowded conditions? In such cases, what seems to be simply a sensory nuisance – that can be dealt with through increased regulation and technical remedies – may be found to signal a far deeper and more serious issue.

Trademarking the senses

In a Peruvian folk tale known as 'The Theft of Smell', a stingy baker takes his neighbour to court for 'stealing' the smells wafting from his bakery. The judge rules that the neighbour should pay the baker – with the sound of clinking coins. This amusing tale implies that there can be no property in such an ephemeral trait as odour.

This, indeed, has been the traditional position when it comes to trademarks. A trademark is a sign that serves to distinguish a product or service from others of its kind (without being intrinsic to the product, as would be the case with the aromas of baked goods). In such signs, it is recognized, there can be much value, and therefore property. However, trademarks have traditionally consisted of brand names, logos or phrases, with such potentially distinguishing marks as odours, colours and sounds being excluded.

As companies move to brand themselves and their products through multiple sensory channels, however, there is a push to enlarge the range of features considered distinctive marks and warranting a legal right to exclusive use. In certain cases this is intensified by the realization that, unlike patents, which expire after a limited period of time, trademark protection has no time limit. Hence even after other companies are legally allowed to manufacture copies of a product, the creator of the original can still maintain control over its distinctive trademarked feature.

Other factors influencing this shift include a recognition of the strong affective associations people may make with sensory signs such as colours, and the ability of these to capture attention at a greater distance than graphic signs. Globalization is also said to encourage the use of sensory trademarks, on the (questionable) grounds that they can transcend cultural differences (Firth 2008: 499).

A number of companies have now trademarked colours or colour combinations for their products, packaging and services. These include the pale blue used in Tiffany packaging, the purple of Nexium pills, and the dark brown of United Parcel Service vans. These colour associations are sometimes further promoted through advertising and slogans. UPS has used the tagline 'What can Brown do for you?' while Nexium is marketed as 'the purple pill' (see also Naeve 2011). Such branding does not prevent the same colours being used for unrelated products and services, only for those that compete for the same market.

The three-dimensional shape of a product or its container may also be trademarked, if it is deemed to act as a sign for the product and not simply have a functional role. This was done by Nestlé, for example, with the four-fingered shape of Kit Kat in 2002. Against the objections of its rival, Cadbury, Nestlé brought in reams of documents to demonstrate both the company's efforts to promote the look of the chocolate-covered biscuit and the product's popularity among consumers (apparently half the population of the UK ate at least one Kit Kat in 2002). Convinced by the evidence, the trademark registrar of the European Community decided that, while a four-fingered bar is not an inherently distinctive shape for chocolate, in the minds and mouths of European consumers it had come to mean 'Kit Kat' (Nieburg 2013). This decision noticeably played down the functionality – a customary impediment to the registration of three-dimensional shapes as trademarks – of the chocolate bar's form, which allows it to be broken into four easier-to-eat pieces.

Like colours and shapes, sounds can also be trademarked in certain jurisdictions. Often sound trademarks consist of a melody or jingle associated with a product in advertising. Such a melody, if catchy and distinctive, can be extremely effective in creating a memorable brand image. Not all sound marks are musical, however. A well-known example of this is the lion's roar accompanying the MGM logo in the company's films. In certain cases, sound marks are linked to the functioning of the product itself, as is the case with the distinctive MacIntosh computer startup chime – an F sharp major chord.

Occasionally consumers may assume that what has been designed to serve as a sound mark is a 'natural' (undesigned) consequence of the product's function. While the characteristic quiet hum of a Bentley engine, however, may seem a pleasant auditory byproduct of a smooth-functioning engine, it actually results from a design decision. 'From the very beginning acoustic engineers decided how the car should sound, and only then did they begin working to achieve this' (Lindstrom 2005: 76; Cleophas and Bijsterveld 2012). In order to attract a new market, Bentley has now brought out a car model with a noisier engine, whose 'growl' is intended to appeal to those looking for 'raw power' in a car (Madslein 2012).

No matter how carefully designed or unique to a particular make, however, engine sounds have proved difficult to trademark (Lindstrom 2005: 188). This is due in part to their close relation to engine function. It is also due to the fact that the trademarking of sounds generally has been hampered by the customary requirement of trademark registrars that a mark be represented visually. Thus only in 2012, for example, was MGM finally permitted to trademark its lion's roar in Canada (which has traditionally been very cautious about extending the boundaries of trademark protection [Lamb et al. 2011: 258]). This approval required the submission of a visual representation of the sound in the graphic form of a soundwave, a written description of the sound, and an electronic recording (Akkad 2012).

Other new sensory frontiers in trademarking include smells, tastes, gestures, movements, textures, and store layouts. Scent marks, for example, while facing even greater difficulties as regards their graphic representation than sound marks, have succeeded in obtaining legal recognition in a number of cases (Classen et al. 1994: 201; Maniatus 1996). In 1999 the first EU trademark for a smell was granted to a manufacturer of tennis balls, which scented its product with the aroma of 'fresh-cut grass'. Ironically, while engine sounds have been difficult to trademark, the Manhattan Oil company has procured a trademark in the United States for its use of fruit scents to aromatize engine lubricants (Ong 2008: 241). Although the aroma of baked goods cannot be transformed into a protected asset when used for such goods, therefore, it might well now be possible to receive trademark protection for its use on an unrelated product.

The spread of trademarking into new sensory domains has generated considerable controversy (see Elliot 2012). Should companies have the right to remove from the public sphere such broad sensations as colours – which seem given by nature rather than being the result of human artifice (as is the case with brand names and logos)? Although trademark protection in such cases may be said to be very limited in that it only covers the use of a sensory sign with particular kinds of goods, a company wishing to diversify could well desire to employ its trademark colour with an ever-increasing range of merchandise. The trademarked bright pink used by Mattel Inc. in the packaging of its dolls, for example, has been extended for use in dozens of other products marketed to girls, from bubble bath to computers. Arguably, therefore, Mattel Inc. is monopolizing bright pink.

When in 1996 British Sugar wished to protect its use of the word 'treat' for dessert toppings it was argued that this would enable 'big business to buy ordinary words of the English language as trademarks at comparatively little cost' (cited in Davis 2002: 342). Something similar can be said to be happening with sensations such as colours. They may possess an enormous wealth of cultural significance, but they are being purchased for exclusive commercial use at little cost.

Limiting what could be (partially) removed from the common stock of signifiers through trademarks was a prime concern of legislators in the nineteenth century, when modern trademark laws were established (Schecter 2008). In England, applications to trademark generic, descriptive or geographical names – 'Fruit Salt' for fruit drink powder, 'Perfection' for a make of soap and 'Yorkshire' for copper products – were highly contentious and usually turned down on the grounds that other manufacturers should have those terms available to them (Davis 2002).

The fact that a trademark can be protected indefinitely urged special caution regarding what it could entail. Thus, even if 'Yorkshire Copper' had no competitors in Yorkshire at the present time, it might conceivably in the future, it was argued, and these might also reasonably want to associate themselves with their place of operation (Davis 2002: 353).

The resources of language were, in the late nineteenth and early twentieth centuries, likened to common land that should be freely available to all. In 1889, for example, reference was made to the 'perpetual struggle' by merchants 'to enclose and to appropriate as private property certain little strips of the great open common of the English language' (cited by Davis 2002: 345). Using the same analogy in 1909, Sir Herbert Cozens-Hardy wrote that: 'Wealthy traders are habitually eager to enclose part of the great common of the English language and to exclude the general public of the present day and of the future from access to the enclosure' (cited in Davis 2002: 342).

In the mid-twentieth century a similar argument was used in England against the trademarking of colours. In one case in which a company claimed that its distinctive brown-coloured polishing cloth for eye-glasses had been copied by a competitor, the judge declared: 'It is to my mind quite impossible to say that the mere brown colour which anyone may use on buff cloth, which is common to the whole world, constitutes a get up [or trade dress] which nobody may take' (cited in Ladas 1975: 1020–21).

Interestingly, one of the arguments used against trademarking colours at this time was based on the assumption that consumers could readily distinguish similarly-coloured products by reading their labels. Thus, when two soda-water manufacturers went to court over similarly-coloured packaging, it was decided that, as the company names were clearly displayed on the labels, the similarity in colours was irrelevant. Lord Halsbury wrote on the case:

> ... if a person is so careless that he ... [buys the product] without reading what is written very plainly indeed upon the face of the label on which

the trader has placed his own name, then you certainly cannot say he is deceived, in fact he does not care which it is.

(cited in Ladas 1975: 1023)

In contemporary trademark legislation, however, such attitudes have been shelved. Lord Halsbury's argument is a relic of a verbocentric culture which is now being replaced by a culture of sensations. Trademark decisions themselves have changed from containing philosophical discourses of public rights and freedoms to involving pragmatic discussions of market behaviour: if a sign functions in the market as a trademark then it should be registrable as a trademark, whether it is a word, a logo, a colour, a sound or a scent (Davis 2002: 357, 362). Few concerns are raised about removing linguistic or sensory signs from the public domain, or about the hypothetical marketer of the future who might reasonably want to use a certain colour for a product only to find that that particular sensory territory had already been claimed. There are no longer any brakes on 'the progressive privatization of sensation' (Howes 2005b: 287–89.)

A recent instance of the spread of trademarking into new sensory domains and its potential consequences concerns the registration by Cadbury of the 'royal purple' used in its chocolate packaging. This led to a Christian fair-trade producer being obliged to change the purple colour of its Christmas chocolate packaging, a colour chosen for its traditional association with the pre-Christmas Advent season. In terms that suggest a corporate appropriation of religion, as well as of colour, the founder of The Meaningful Chocolate Company related: 'We have been legally advised that we were on dodgy ground because we were using "Advent purple" for our Christmas products and "Advent purple" now belongs to Cadbury'. A bishop of the Church of England, wading into the discussion, declared that the Church had been using purple as a symbolic colour long before the Cadbury company existed (BBC News 2012).

However, when it comes to marketing chocolate, the use of royal, or 'Advent purple' (Pantone 2685c) in England by someone other than Cadbury is now a 'theft of colour', or at least an illegal appropriation of some of the expectations and associations that supposedly go with that colour when applied to chocolate. The Meaningful Chocolate Company has had to relinquish a bit of its meaning and repackage its Christmas chocolates in red.

Surveying such recent decisions that take trademark protection into new areas of experience, it is hard not to come to the conclusion that in the twenty-first century what can be called the 'sensory common' is increasingly 'being enclosed and appropriated as private property'.

The senses in indigenous justice

Some of the most thought-provoking issues concerning law and the senses have arisen from the study of indigenous judicial traditions and their interaction with Western legal systems. Indeed, most of the topics considered in this chapter could also be fruitfully examined in relation to indigenous principles and practices of justice.

As regards the senses in the courtroom, for example, one could look at indigenous reworkings of the sensory space of the courtroom. In Australia, outdoor 'courtrooms' have been set up in the desert, with a picnic table transformed by a red cloth into a judge's bench, for hearing native land claims (Anker 2005: 113). In the courtrooms of the largely indigenous region of Zinacantan, Mexico, a defendant desiring resolution to a conflict will lay bottles of rum at the feet of the injured party. The latter signifies acceptance by touching the bottles. Successful hearings usually end with everyone involved partaking of rum (Collier 1973; see also Nader 1990).

In pre-Columbian Aztec culture, judges cast incense into the court fire for divine aid and inspiration. Those giving testimony swore to tell the truth by placing a finger on the earth and then putting it to their tongue. (The verb 'to swear', accordingly, meant 'to eat earth'.) The Aztecs, who venerated the earth and who held this oath sacred, were appalled at how lightly the Spanish appeared to take oaths sworn on their own god (Seus 1969).

Concerning the role of the senses in the presentation of evidence, one could explore the reception of indigenous oral traditions in Western courts of law and the responses of indigenous peoples. In one recent Australian case, aboriginal people making a land claim responded to the Western demand for visual evidence by creating a traditional painting of their territory and bringing it into court:

> When I go to court to tell my story, I must listen very carefully before I open my mouth. Maybe the [white people] will say 'We don't believe you' … That's why we made the painting, for evidence.
>
> (cited in Anker 2005: 92)

The painting was not simply a detached visual representation of their territory for the aboriginal claimants, however, but a tangible embodiment. Thus, when presenting their claim in court, they subverted Western notions of both evidence and art by standing on the painting and grounding themselves in their heritage (Anker 2005: 92, 100, 112).

One could also look at how indigenous witnesses and defendants have been perceived by Western courts. A noteworthy example of a difference in sensory practices that can lead to misperceptions in court is the Inuit custom of signifying respect by keeping one's eyes downcast. Since in the West downcast eyes are often understood to be an expression of shame or dishonesty, however, this practice can be taken to signify an unspoken declaration of untruthfulness or guilt, thus prejudicing a judge and jury against an Inuit defendant (Ross 2006: 4).

Research could also uncover many powerful examples of how sensory space has been contested by indigenous and colonizing nations (Hoffer 2005). In the colonial Americas, for example, the invading Europeans often tried to prohibit the playing of indigenous musical instruments in order to clear the air of 'heathen' sounds (see Stevenson 1968). When combatting the colonizers, the Amerindians, in turn, sometimes destroyed church bells (the sound of which, according to the Tarahumara in Mexico, spread disease [Graziano 1999: 92–93]). In one case that could hardly have lacked symbolic import, a Hopi shaman in Arizona transformed a fragment of a shattered church bell into a grinder for paint (which presumably would have been put to the service of the indigenous religion) (Mindeleff 1898: 609).

In terms of contemporary legal cases involving indigenous cultures and sensory conflicts, there are a few worthy of note. One concerns a nuisance suit brought by neighbours against a couple in Los Angeles who were building ceremonial fires 'that spewed flames, hot ashes, and nauseous and offensive smoke and odor in the air' in their backyard. The defendants, Hector and Xochitl Pacheco, claimed they were practicing a Native American sweat lodge ceremony, which involved burning medicinal herbs, and that this practice was protected by their constitutional right to free speech of a religious nature. They further argued that they had secured all the necessary permits and that the fire was no worse than that of a backyard barbecue. The trial court ruled, however, that there was no proof that an open fire was necessary to the ceremony and that 'the focus of [the Plaintiffs'] action is not to prevent Defendants from exercising their right to protected speech, but rather to stop "odor filled smoke and ash" from intruding into their property' (Bay 2007).

The field of trademarks and copyrights, in turn, becomes relevant when considering modes of protecting indigenous cultural and intellectual property. To return to the Australian aboriginal example of a painting depicting a territorial claim, each section of the painting was worked on by a painter with a claim to the land being represented so that there would be no infringement on another's territory. One artist explained:

> When I was a kid, if my father and my mother took me to someone else's country … we couldn't mention the name of that country because we come from another place, from different country. That is really the Aboriginal way of respecting copyright. It means that you can't steal the stories or songs or dances from other places. This law is still valid and it is the same when we paint. We can't paint someone else's country.
>
> (Wildburger 2013: 204)

Such indigenous notions of ownership or 'copyright' do not, however, translate into legal protection within the dominant culture. Thus Australian aborigines, like many other indigenous peoples, have been dismayed to find outsiders copying and even trademarking elements of their culture – from tribal names to traditional arts to native foods (i.e., Janke 2008; Howes 1996b).

If trademarking can be compared to an enclosure of land, in an indigenous context can such practices be seen as paralleling the appropriation of native lands by outsiders? To what extent can the sights and sounds, and even the smells and tastes, of indigenous cultures (which, in some cases, have become part of mainstream culture) be legally protected?

The only legal recourse, it would seem, would be for indigenous peoples themselves to resort to trademarking and turning aspects of their sensory and social identities into cultural industries. The Navajo nation, for example, which has trademarked its name for use on a range of products, was able to prevent a French company from using its own 'Navaho' trademark in the United States and has recently launched a lawsuit against Urban Outfitters for labelling a line of 'Native American style' clothing and other goods, including jewellery and liquor flasks, 'Navajo' (Fonseca 2012).

Finally, to conclude this chapter with the same topic on which it began, indigenous cultures offer a stimulating range of sensory models for social justice. The traditional Inuit singing duel, for example, provided an opportunity for two opponents (or their representatives) to air and often resolve their complaints in public assembly (Peterson 2003: 87–89). The multisensory 'potlatch' ceremony of Pacific Northwest Coast peoples served to maintain social order by affirming social hierarchies and alliances, distributing wealth, and resolving conflicts.

Potlatches, which brought together clan members and neighbouring peoples, were held by a host family or clan chief to mark important events. The ceremony, which varied from one tribe to another, involved speeches, dancing, singing, feasting, and the giving of gifts to guests. The various elements of the ceremony were intended to impress guests with the importance of the social histories and claims to titles and territories being presented; to obligate them through their acceptance of gifts to uphold those claims; and, to corporeally and socially bind people together through collective feasting. Masked dances were particularly important elements of the ceremony as they enacted ancestral histories and communal beliefs and thereby ensured an integration between ways of sensing and ways of life (Bracken 1997). The various strands of this ceremony are brought together in the following statement by a contemporary chief:

> My power is carried in my House's [clan's] histories, songs, dances and crests. It is recreated at the Feast when the histories are told, the songs and dances are performed, and the crests are displayed. With the wealth that comes from respectful use of the territory, the House feeds the name of the Chief in the Feast Hall. In this way, the law, the Chief, the territory, and the Feast become one.
>
> (Wa and Uukw 1989: 7)

From the late nineteenth to the mid-twentieth century, potlatches were outlawed in Canada on the grounds that they encouraged wasteful spending among indigenous peoples. Shortly after the potlatch was outlawed, one tribal chief confronted a visiting anthropologist about the issue:

> We want to know whether you have come to stop our dances and feasts ... Is this the white man's land? We are told it is the Queen's land; but no! It is mine! ... We will dance when our laws command us to dance, and we will feast when our hearts desire to feast ... It is a strict law that bids us dance. It is a strict law that bids us distribute our property among our friends and neighbors. It is a good law. Let the white man observe his law, we shall observe ours.
>
> (cited in Trosper 2009: 2)

Although the anti-potlatch law discouraged the ceremonial practice, it did not put an end to it and potlatches of various forms continue to be practiced today by the indigenous peoples of the region. After many years of being dismissed by the dominant legal system, furthermore, such sensory practices and oral traditions are finally gaining some credibility as legitimate ways of maintaining social order and establishing territorial titles (see Mills 1994, 2005; Howes 2005c: 15–21). Hence, while the incorporation of new electronic technologies point to one way in which the sensory dimensions of justice are changing in contemporary societies, such overtures – even if modest – to indigenous sensibilities point to another.

Part III

Marketing and Psychology

5 Sense appeal

The marketing of sensation

What is sensory marketing, and why is it interesting and also important? I define it as marketing that engages the consumer's senses and affects their behaviour. ... In the past, most firms ignored the sensory aspects of products, it was invisible in the no-nonsense era, hardly being mentioned if at all. ... Only recently, in the new millennium, are firms actively looking at the sensory aspects of products.

Aradhna Krishna, *Sensory Marketing* (2010)

Everywhere merchandise formed a decorative motif conveying an exceptional quality to the goods themselves. Silks cascaded from the walls of the silk gallery, ribbons were strung above the hall of ribbons, umbrellas were draped full blown in a parade of hues and designs, oriental rugs, rich and textural, hung from balconies for the spectators below ... [G]oods and decor blended one into another to dazzle the senses and to make of the store a great fair and fantasy land of colors, sensations, and dreams.

Michael B. Miller, *The Bon Marché: Bourgeois Culture and the Department Store, 1869–1920* (1981)

Contemporary advertising whispers, declares and shouts that products of all sorts can bring sensory fulfilment. Wrigley's 5 chewing gum claims to 'stimulate your senses'; Friskies cat food will 'feed the senses'; Salem cigarettes say they can 'stir the senses'; Yamaha declares that their new motorcycle will 'ignite your senses'. Products from coffee to fabric conditioner to bathroom fixtures claim to 'awaken' the senses. In an attempt to outdo its automotive competitors in 'sense appeal', Hyundai announced its 2006 Tucson model would not only 'excite all the senses', but also provide 'a "sixth sense" in the form of electronic stability control'. 'As senses go,' the promotional text assured readers, 'you can never have too many.' The latest automobile manufacturer to take this approach is Rolls-Royce, which has named one of its models 'Ghost Six Senses'. The advertising copy informs the reader that: 'The world of luxury is full of expressions that captivate the senses: a dazzling diamond necklace, a cloud of fragrance ... the pure sound of a Stradivarius or the caress of a cool silk on skin.' These, however, are said to 'excite one, or sometimes two, of the five senses', whereas the new Ghost Six Senses car is able to 'stimulate all your senses at once to awaken the elusive sixth sense'.

Judging by such ads, the primary role of many products on the market today would seem to be to provide consumers with multisensory experiences, rather than to perform any practical functions.

Such appeals to the senses do not end with advertising copy, but are carried over into product design, packaging, and retail environments. Aspects that were once thought of as simple sensory by-products of a commodity's structure or function – the crunch of a potato chip, the click of a camera lens, the smell of a new car – are increasingly deliberately designed to appeal to consumer sensibilities (see Postrel 2003; Zampini and Spence 2004). Packaging adds another sensory layer, with various companies promising to aid clients in 'packaging the senses'. And the more immersive the retail or service environment the more effective it is deemed to be. Thus the Rainforest Café themed restaurant chain, with its mist effects, waterfalls, simulated thunder and lightning, tropical plants and mechanical gorillas, is 'built around the five senses', according to its founder, Steven Schussler (Machak 1996).

Why all these invocations of the senses? Clearly, there is something stirring in the marketplace. A 1998 *Harvard Business Review* article entitled 'Welcome to the experience economy' theorized the shift, declaring that progressive companies no longer produce goods or supply services, but instead use services as the stage and goods as props for creating emotionally-compelling and memorable 'experiences'. The article states that: 'The more senses an experience engages, the more effective and memorable it can be.' The paragon example is the Disney theme park, and Rainforest Café is another, but Pine and Gilmore also give their theory a common sense ('under our noses all along') touch by observing that: 'Smart shoeshine operators augment the smell of polish with crisp snaps of the cloth, scents and sounds that don't make the shoes any shinier but do make the experience more engaging' (Pine and Gilmore 1998: 104).

Since the turn of the twenty-first century, this emphasis on providing engaging 'experiences' has led to what advertising guru and CEO Kevin Roberts calls 'the race to embrace the senses' in marketing (2005: 106). Three books with the same title, *Sensory Marketing*, appeared within months of each other in 2009–10. What is it about the senses that so appeals to marketers and advertisers? Why sensory marketing now? Does it have a history? How does cultural difference affect the sense appeal of commodities? These are among the questions we wish to explore in this chapter, which traces trends in sensory marketing and examines the discourse of experts on the subject, situating both within a larger cultural context.

Historicizing the trade in sensations

The elegant eighteenth century

One point that all the marketing experts insist on is the newness of the sensory turn. In *Sensory Marketing*, Swedish business professors Hultén, Brouwes and van Dijk speak of a 'new epoch' dawning in which the senses will be the prime focus of marketing (2009: 3). In her introduction to *Sensory Marketing: Research on the Sensuality of Products*, marketing professor Aradhna Krishna chides her fellow professionals for having 'missed the fact that products are sensual in nature' (2010: 1).

While the language and some of the techniques of sensory marketing might be new, however, the marketing of sensations is itself very old. In fact, some of the world's early forms of currency – salt in ancient Rome and other parts of the world, spices in the East, cocoa beans among the Aztecs, even gold and silver – gained their value precisely because they provided highly desirable and prestigious sensations. And although ancient and medieval markets and fairs would seem very limited in their range of goods to modern shoppers, at the time they were experienced as sites of sensory abundance, full of exciting sights, savours, scents, sounds and textures.

It is in the shops of the eighteenth century, however, that we can locate the beginnings of modern consumer culture and of the drive for commercial 'sense appeal'. Increasingly, during this century, customers would enter into a shop to make a purchase and not just buy from an open stall on the street. The invention of plate glass windows let more light into stores and made it possible to have eye-catching window displays. At the same time many more goods became available due to a dramatic increase in manufactured products and improved methods of transportation. The following eyewitness description of an eighteenth-century shopping street in London provides an idea of the cornucopia of sensations that tempted passers-by from carefully-crafted window displays.

> Behind the great glass windows absolutely everything one can think of is neatly, attractively displayed, in such abundance as to make one almost greedy. ...
>
> First one passes a watch-maker, then a silk or fan store, now a silver-smith's, a china or glass shop. The [wine shops] are particularly tempting ... Here crystal flasks of every shape and form are exhibited; each one has a light behind which makes all the different coloured spirits sparkle. Just as alluring are the confectioners and fruiterers where, behind the handsome glass windows pyramids of pineapples, figs, grapes, oranges and all manner of fruit are on show.
>
> (von La Roche 1933: 87; see also Kromm 2010)

The fact that much shopping was now conducted indoors rather than in open stalls or marketplaces meant that, rather than simply adding their own particular sights, sounds and smells to the urban sensory mix, shops began to create an alternative, interior counterpart to the cityscape. The increased sale of luxury goods in the eighteenth century in particular demanded a more luxurious setting in order to show such goods to advantage. Daniel Defoe wrote in his *Complete English Tradesman*: 'It is modern custom and wholly unknown to our ancestors ... to have tradesmen lay out two-thirds of their fortune in fitting up their shops ... in painting and gilding, fine shelves, shutters, boxes, glass doors ... and the like' (Defoe 1726: 312). Such attention to the interior decoration of shops was considered by many at the time to be highly frivolous, as well as somewhat dishonest, as it was calculated to artificially enhance the attractions of the goods being offered. However, modern shopkeepers realized that alluring settings and displays resulted in increased trade.

Shop decor created a material counterpart to the sales clerk's traditional patter, which verbally 'puffed up' and added allure to goods. Another way in which this was accomplished in the eighteenth century was through print advertising. Just as sales clerks, or for that matter street vendors and pedlars, would play up the sensory attractions of their merchandise, inviting customers to feel their 'supremely soft' linens or calling out that they had 'sweet fresh strawberries' for sale, so did print advertisements – although often in a more formal, literary fashion.

A striking example of this comes from alternative health practitioner James Graham's advertisement for the 'Celestial Bed' he rented out to couples wishing to conceive. This bed, he related in his promotional text, had mattresses of 'oat straw mingled with balm, rose leaves, lavender flowers and oriental spices', and sheets 'of the richest and softest silk', tinted 'pale green, rose colour, sky blue, white and purple' and 'sweetly perfumed'. It was further embellished with 'brilliant panes of looking glass', musical mechanisms to 'breathe forth celestial sounds', and 'a fine landscape of moving figures'. At the head of the bed, 'sparkling with electrical fire', was written the commandment 'Be Fruitful, Multiply and Replenish the Earth' (cited in Altick 1976: 82).

No one reading Graham's text can imagine that sensory marketing is all that new a phenomenon. Little wonder, in fact, that Dr Johnson declared that: 'The trade of advertising is now so near perfection that it is not easy to propose any improvement' (1837: 395). No doubt that renowned eighteenth-century writer and conversationalist would have thought today's ads, with their simple invocations to 'awaken' or 'stir' the senses, quite feeble, even when accompanied by the photographic images that his own day lacked.

The charm of the department store

As stores expanded their wares and the size of their premises in the nineteenth century they eventually became department stores, such as Le Bon Marché in Paris, Harrods in London, Macy's in New York and Eaton's in Toronto. Each department or division of a department store carried a different line of merchandise, from clothing to furniture to toys. This enabled customers to shop for many items under one roof, and at the same time it exposed them to many items they had not intended to buy but might be led to desire. In order to attract more customers to the store and keep them within the store once there, a range of services supplemented the merchandise on sale: restaurants, travel agencies, post offices, beauty salons, even art galleries and concert halls.

The boast of one department store that it contained a city within a store referred both to the variety of goods provided and to the variety of services. The implication was that virtually everything worth seeing, doing and buying in a city could be seen, done and bought within a store. 'Why not spend the day at Selfridges?' invited a prominent British department store (Rappaport 2000: 269 n89). Clearly the store was no longer simply a place one entered to make a purchase and then exited to return to city life outside. It had become a destination in itself.

Reaching its full development in the late nineteenth century, the department store came to appeal to the senses in a number of important ways (see Rappaport forthcoming). Like fairs and markets they massed together a wide range of colourful and stimulating goods. Unlike traditional markets, and like the elegant shops of the eighteenth-century, however, the department store was an enclosed setting that could be carefully manipulated to provide a maximum of sensory attractions and a minimum of discomforts. Always warm and dry, smooth and clean, free of traffic noise and bustle, the 'city within a store' presented a favourable contrast to the often cold, dirty and traffic-congested streets outside, with their uneven surfaces and puddles. Once inside, shoppers could forget about the hazards of the world outdoors and concentrate on the shopping experience.

The sensory ambience of department store interiors continued to be enhanced by new technological developments as the nineteenth century came to an end. When electric lighting was installed it was said to turn the store into 'a dazzling hall of light' (Lancaster 1995: 51). In the twentieth century, recorded music and air conditioning were added. While these elements are taken for granted by shoppers today, at the time they were seen by many to create an almost utopian atmosphere of sensory comfort. One mid-twentieth-century study of department stores declared:

> The customer certainly has the benefit of shopping under the most plea-sant conditions: air conditioning and brilliant lighting; the attractiveness of artistic interiors and window displays; the gentle fragrance arising from the perfume department and soft music from the radio sound system all help to provide a pleasurable setting.
>
> (Ferry 1960: 4)

Department stores were designed to be much more than a pleasant place in which to shop, however. They mimicked the most opulent and prestigious of settings – the palace – with grandiose façades, cavernous interiors and luxur-ious fittings: chandeliers, frescoed ceilings, ornate ironwork and stained glass. Within this modern palace of consumption, clerks played the role of polite, unobtrusive servants rather than pushy salesmen. Hence, there was less fear of being cornered by a clerk and having one's ears assaulted by an overbearing sales pitch. There was also no need to haggle over prices, a practice many found nerve-racking and that would have lowered the tone of the store, transforming it into a noisy street bazaar. It was said of Bon Marché by an experienced shopper in 1874:

> It is possible to visit this wonderful establishment without being hunted and screamed at by a pack of noisy shopmen, and wellnigh worried to death, as used to be the case in all the large shops of Paris a few years ago.
>
> (Hooper 1874: 466)

This retail novelty was made possible in part by a policy of fixed pricing, which reduced the need to speak with clerks to a minimum.

Another key characteristic of the department store was the open display of goods. Instead of being hidden away behind counters and in boxes, as in traditional stores, merchandise was placed out in the open on tables and shelves – even hung from ceilings and draped over railings. As regards the scene at the Bon Marché:

> Very gay and pretty do the sides of the staircases look, hung as they are with gay silks, shawls, rugs, and all sorts of bright-colored draperies, while overhead, long lines of [ribbons] are stretched from side to side making a brilliant and varied net-work, bright with all the colors of the rainbow.
>
> (Hooper 1874: 466)

The visual attractions of window dressing were in this way carried over into the store itself, which became all eye-catching exhibition.

Artfully arranged goods in attractive settings silently radiated their desirability to shoppers. Confident in the visual allure of its merchandise, one British store invited visitors with the following notice:

> A welcome to customers to walk around the store. Assistants are not allowed to speak to visitors. Walk around today, don't buy. There is time for that another day.
>
> (cited in Lancaster 1995: 30)

With so much on display, there was also much less need to ask to be shown the merchandise. It was now possible to enter a store and 'just look' without having to ask for anything, without a particular purchase in mind, and without being harangued by clerks. The new emphasis on visual ostentation meant that 'modern consumption is a matter not of basic items bought for definite needs, but of visual fascination and remarkable sights of things not found at home' (Bowlby 1985: 1). Marketing had always had a large element of sight-seeing in it; now sight-seeing was explicitly encouraged by store owners as a prelude to sales.

Allowing customers not only to look at, but also to touch goods without the mediation of a salesperson was another key novelty of the department store. While increasing the risk of theft and damage, promoting tactile encounters with merchandise built confidence in the quality of a product. Moreover, having held an item in their hands, customers were more likely to want permanent possession of it. Successful department store displays were not only eye-catching, they were also 'hand-catching'.

Department stores helped bridge the gap between picking up a product and purchasing it by facilitating impulse buying. To this end, small portable items or bargain goods were placed on the main floor near the entrances, where people casually strolling into the store might be tempted to walk out again with a purchase. Perfume counters were similarly often placed near entrances so that passers by might be led inside by their noses as well as by their eyes. Stores also strove to overcome customers' reluctance to part with money by allowing them to return unwanted purchases. Visitors could therefore shop with little forethought knowing that they might get their money back if they changed their minds. Store owners reasoned that, if goods were hard to put back once they were in the hand, they would be even harder to return once they were in the home.

Writing before the rise of the department store, Karl Marx held that the bourgeoisie were sensorially-deprived by the capitalist system due to its privileging of the accumulation of capital over sensual enjoyment.

> The less you eat, drink and read books; the less you go the theatre, the dance hall, the public-house; the less you … sing, paint, fence, etc., the more you *save* – the greater becomes your treasure which neither moths nor dust will devour – your *capital*.
>
> (Marx 1987 [1844]: 118–19)

Marx remained committed to theorizing the capitalist system as a mode of production and exchange throughout his work, and consequently failed to consider how it had already started to transform into a mode of presentation and consumption (see Howes 2005b: 283–84). He saw the abolition of private property (which was to be swept away by the communist revolution) as the only route to 'the *emancipation* of the senses' and sensual fulfilment (Marx 1987 [1844]: 139). As we have seen, however, there was another route, which involved capitalism catering to the senses, instead of curbing them. This was the technique used by the *grands magasins*, with their promises of sensory plenitude in return for a 'small' monetary outlay. Indeed, the relatively modest prices of the mass-produced merchandise for sale, along with the stores' self-presentation as a free spectacle (one of the 'wonders of the world' according to Bon Marché's advertising) enabled the middle classes to visit these 'pleasure palaces' without feeling they were violating the ethic of frugality.

The manipulation of desire

However, some held that the sensory attractions of these commercial establishments were too powerful, enticing shoppers – particularly women, with their imagined love of finery and impulsiveness – to make irrational purchases or even to steal the goods that lay so enticingly at hand. One nineteenth-century French psychiatrist who made a study of the subject wrote:

> These immense galleries ... enclose and expose ... the richest cloths, the most luxurious dress articles, the most seductive superfluities. Women of all sorts ... fascinated by so many rash provocations, dazzled by the abundance of trinkets and lace, find themselves overtaken by a sudden, unpremeditated, almost savage impulse.
>
> (cited in Miller 1981: 202)

The account of one female shoplifter confirmed this analysis:

> Once plunged into the sensuous atmosphere of the [store] ... I saw things as through a cloud, everything stimulated my desire and assumed, for me, an extraordinary attraction. I felt myself swept along towards them and grabbed hold of things without any outside and superior consideration intervening to hold me back.
>
> (cited in Miller 1981: 202)

This gives an idea of the impact the department store, full of beautiful and fashionable things to look at, touch and smell, had on the as-yet unjaded senses of those who visited them (see further Rappaport 2000; Classen 2012: 194–96).

To some extent the department store was intentionally designed to derange as well as delight the senses of its visitors. Planning a reorganization of Le Bon Marché that would oblige shoppers to take circuitous routes to different departments, the store's founder wrote:

> It would really be too much if, as they wander around in this organized disorder, lost, driven crazy, that they don't set foot in some departments where they had no intention of going, and if they don't succumb at the sight of things which grab them on the way.
>
> (cited by Bowlby 1985: 74)

This quote highlights the dystopian aspects of these seemingly utopian retail spaces. Salespeople might be discouraged from grabbing customers and leading them to merchandise, but store layout and the merchandise itself was intended to play the same manipulative role.

Aware that the sense of novelty was key to ongoing appeal, department stores frequently changed their displays. While maintaining a permanently balmy climate, the store varied its merchandise and decor in accordance with the changing seasons, the most dramatic instance of this being at Christmas. The slow shopping period after Christmas, in turn, might be enlivened by a 'white' sale of linens and other household items. For its white sale, the Bon Marché traditionally decorated its store all in white producing a dramatic contrast to the customarily colourful appearance of the interior.

Festive occasions such as Christmas also provided an opportunity for investing stores and their merchandise with the feelings of happiness and excitement those occasions evoked. During the Christmas season, the store interior was transformed into a fantasy world of toys, gifts and Christmas decorations presided over by the store's own Santa Claus. Carrying the campaign to be identified with festive joy to the streets, Christmas parades were often organized by department stores. The result for many was that department store extravaganzas became a cherished element of their holiday experiences.

Certain stores went even further and pursued active programmes of self-mythologization. This is particularly the case with the Bon Marché, which produced fairy tales and pictures about itself in which the store was associated with images of magic and wonder, such as flying carpets and Halley's comet. 'For the bourgeois child growing up in late-nineteenth-century France, the magical, the exotic, the fantastic, and the extraordinary … had also become the stuff of department stores' (Miller 1981: 176). This was a clever marketing trick, indeed, and one that relied on combining appeals to all of the senses with the evocation of a sense of wonder. 'Experience marketing' clearly is not just an invention of the late twentieth century, as marketing experts claim.

Catering to working-class sensibilities

Among the 'unpleasantries' of street life absent in the *grands magasins* were poor people. Shoppers at the Bon Marché or Harrods never had to brush against a sweaty factory worker, never had to hear the pleas of a street vendor or face the outstretched hand of a beggar. Department stores tended to exclude the working classes who couldn't afford their merchandise and who would have felt uncomfortable in the stores' grand interiors. Though the urban poor helped make many of the products for sale through their labour in factories, their income was insufficient to purchase them.

For vast numbers of poor people, therefore, there was little chance of enjoying the sensory pleasures paraded by the elegant new stores. Indeed, as social reformers attested, sensory deprivation and alienation were the norm for the working class. If the department store was a quasi-utopia for the senses, the factory was a dystopia in which, as Marx put it: 'Every organ of sense is injured in an equal degree by artificial elevation of temperature, by the dust-laden atmosphere, by the deafening noise, not to mention danger to life and limb among the thickly crowded machinery' (Marx 1954: 401).

Life at home in a crowded tenement was no more salutary for the poor, since there, living amid 'the *sewage* of civilization', the sensibilities of the worker were reduced to one, 'the need to *eat*'; and, there was nothing other than scabby potatoes and gin to satisfy this one sense. As for 'a musical ear, an eye for beauty of form – in short *senses* capable of human gratifications, senses confirming themselves as essential powers of *man*', such refined faculties were utterly lacking among the ill-fed and ill-used working class, according to Marx (1987 [1844]: 108–9, 117).

Although ever more people entered the middle class in the nineteenth century, enabling them to move from the pains of production to the pleasures of consumption (or at least between the two), there nonetheless remained vast numbers who could not buy even the relatively inexpensive trinkets in the *grands magasins*. In Theodore Dreiser's novel of 1889, *Sister Carrie*, his impoverished protagonist enters a department store in Chicago looking for work and is overwhelmed by attractions she cannot afford:

> Carrie passed along the busy aisles, much affected by the remarkable displays of trinkets, dress goods, stationary, and jewellery. Each separate counter was a show place of dazzling interest and attraction. She could not help feeling the claim of each trinket and valuable upon her personally. … The dainty slippers and stockings, the delicately frilled skirts and petticoats, the laces, ribbons, hair-combs, purses, all touched her with individual desire, and she felt keenly the fact that not any of these things were in the range of her purchase.
>
> (Dreiser 1971: 22)

In the late nineteenth century, however, a new kind of store sprang up to cater to the working and lower middle classes. This was the 'variety' or 'five and dime' store. While initially focusing on utilitarian housewares and hardware, variety stores came to offer a wide range of products, like department stores, but at less expensive prices. In keeping with their more accessible prices, the interiors of the variety stores lacked the palatial pretensions of department stores. They were more compact, without luxurious fittings, and without the fine restaurants, concert halls and art galleries that could be found in their upscale equivalents. The classic example of such variety stores was Woolworths, which originated in the United States in the late 1870s and went on to become a highly successful international retail chain.

The variety stores used the same novel merchandising methods as the department stores to attract customers:

> First, all the merchandise was to be sold at *one fixed price*. … Second, all merchandise was arranged *on the counters* so the purchaser could see and handle everything. This radical departure from the customary method of displaying goods was the greatest innovation of all. … The people were not accustomed to being invited to handle and see for themselves.
>
> (cited in Woolworth & Co. 1954: 9–10)

Woolworths and other variety stores allowed low-income families to participate in the sensory splendour of consumer society at prices they could afford. Along with common household articles, inexpensive but alluring knick-knacks, jewellery and perfumes were snapped up by customers who now had more disposable income due to the rising wages of the working class. Like the great stores, variety stores attempted to make 'every day a holiday' by creating a festive atmosphere and continually changing displays. Woolworths was colour-coded for important festivals: red for Christmas, green for St. Patrick's Day, yellow for Easter and so forth.

While not originally part of the variety store, candy soon came to add a key element to its attractions. Bought in bulk and sold at discount prices, cheap sweets were another way for cash-strapped families to enjoy luxurious sensations. As the founder of Woolworths put it: 'Who could possibly resist a chocolate treat for a few pennies?' Later on, luncheon counters, offering popular fare such as hot dogs, milkshakes, and a new drink called Coca-Cola, were added to stores as well. The variety of goods and services available in one place, the possibility of buying shoes and eating lunch in the same store, often amazed customers not familiar with the amenities of the great stores (Plunkett-Powell 1999).

If the sensations proffered by the variety store were less refined than those of the department store, they made up for it in boldness: 'It was as though the deprivations of the working classes required strong palliatives – the brightest colours, the sweetest flavours, the headiest perfumes, the chunkiest costume jewellery, the catchiest tunes thumped out on the store piano' (Classen 2012: 196). With the variety store, then, the sensory pleasures of consumer capitalism became available to lower-income families.

The potency of the sensory experiences they offered made variety stores highly memorable. The architectural writer Louise Huxtable recalled the Woolworths of the mid-twentieth century as consisting of a series of sensations:

> The store smelled of sweet candies and cosmetics and the burnt toast from the luncheonette counters ... they echoed to the sound of feet on hardwood floors, the ringing of old-fashioned cash registers. ... and there was the absolute saturation of the eye with every conceivable knick knack.
>
> (cited in Plunkett-Powell 1999: 74)

A nostalgic ode by Elizabeth Larrabee, in turn, celebrates 'The Smells of Woolworth's':

> Woolworth's was not an empire
> inherited by a debutante
> named Barbara
> It was a thousand distinct aromas:
>
> Lily of the Valley
> and Johnson's hard floor wax
> whammed your nostrils upon
> the in-swing of the glass door
>
> Hot chocolate sauce at the fountain,
> Over-ripe bananas disguised
> in strawberry smothered splits.

A stack of on sale percale
house dresses assaulted from the left
while freshly inked comic books
invaded your senses from racks
placed just right to extract
the one nickel from your pocket. ...

(cited in Plunkett-Powell 1999: 202 –
used by permission of Elizabeth Larrabee)

It must be taken into account that, just as Woolworths was not simply a com-mercial empire but a collection of aromas, the aromas of Woolworths were not simply smells but symbols of social values. These values decreed that sensory indulgences such as perfume and chocolate were but momentary respites from working life, and that back home the shopper would once again become a house-wife, polishing the floor with Johnson's Wax in her Woolworths house dress. Yet, as an ensemble of sensations – the glitter of Christmas ornaments, the rippling ribbons of candies, the gleaming housewares, the bright prints of fabrics, the tactile lure of new gadgets, the lurid colours of ketchup and mustard at the lunch counter, the heady scent of perfume, the chime of cash registers – the store pre-sented a potent fantasy of sensory and material abundance within the means of all.

Over the latter half of the twentieth century the excitement and novelty of both department and variety stores wore off. People looked elsewhere for their fantasies, and often shopped elsewhere – at specialty shops, at pharmacies with their expanded range of products, or at the new 'big box' discount stores springing up in the suburbs – for their goods (Golec 2010; Mack forth-coming). Many of the great chains founded in the nineteenth century, such as Woolworths, went out of business by the end of the twentieth, due to a combination of competition and overexpansion.

When current proponents of sensory marketing look back on the role of the senses in retailing, they tend to bypass this remarkable history of sensuous dis-play. The period prior to the mid-twentieth century is seen as 'prehistoric' as far as sensory marketing is concerned, while the mid-twentieth century itself is characterized as a 'no-nonsense era' during which marketers were unaware of the value of sense appeal and customers ignored product allure to focus on price and function (i.e., Krishna 2010: 3; Pine and Gilmore 1998). This characteriza-tion overlooks all the sensory excitement packed into a sparkling Christmas display at Harrods or the blissful sense of aromatic indulgence that could be purchased with one small blue bottle of Evening in Paris at Woolworths.

What marketers make of the senses

The new sensuous retail environment

In terms of retail environments, the senses arguably suffered a fall with the decline of traditional department and variety stores. Many contemporary department stores have traded at least part of their sensuous elegance for functional efficiency, along with dropping a number of their traditional departments, such as music, books, and fabrics. The refinements that often graced the first *grands magasins* – concert halls, roof-top gardens, art galleries – are also usually missing in today's stores. And though pharmacies, dollar stores, and big-box stores might be the successors to the old-time variety stores they convey little of their charm or atmosphere of sensory plenitude. It is difficult to imagine anyone penning an ode to the smells of Walmart.

No-frills, no-thrills big-box stores, like Walmart, can, in fact, be said to manifest an 'anti-aesthetics'. Shoppers rolling a cart down a non-descript warehouse aisle stacked high with merchandise can feel assured that not a cent of their purchase money is paying for 'wasteful' sensations. The plainness of the shop decor is taken to signify bargain prices, as well as a certain 'working-class' simplicity and honesty. However, many retailers have once again become interested in catering to the senses. A few years ago Walmart remodelled its big-box stores to make them 'more experiential'. They now have lower shelving, reduced clutter, 'fresh' colours, curved signage and are even aiming 'to create theater', through such things as allowing customers to see bakers at work and strategically deploying lighting (NBC News 2008).

One of the classic department stores, Harrods, recently hosted an exhibition on the senses with virtual reality illusions and 'soundscapes' and 'aromascapes' throughout the store. The garden furniture department was scented with the smell of grass, while the women's shoe department exhaled chocolate and vanilla. Even store receipts were aromatized (with lime and basil). The central attraction in the exhibition was the store lifts. These were themed for each of the five senses (which, in upscale 'Harrodspeak' became Listen, Stroke, Gaze, Inhale and Savour). The sound lift played a specially commissioned piece of music, while the sight lift had laser beams playing over Swarovski crystals. A sixth lift was themed as a cosmic wish lift – an elevator to one's dreams – with the implication that these could be fulfilled by the merchandise on one of Harrods floors (see Ogden-Barnes and Barclay 2011: 10–11).

Disney is often presented as a benchmark in the field of sensory retailing (i.e., Pine and Gilmore 1998; Lindstrom 2005: 122). Its theme parks offer kinaesthetic thrills aplenty immersed in a kitschy but seductive array of colours, sounds, savours and aromas – diffused by patented 'smellitzer' devices. The particular sensorial mix employed in a retail site, however, depends a great deal on the image a company is trying to create and on the particular services and products it is marketing. Theme park sensationalism will not do for a hotel marketing itself as an oasis of calm and comfort. Thus Westin Hotels, for example, chooses to offer a restful sensory atmosphere, with an aroma of white tea, soothing signature music, and a promise of 'ten layers of pure comfort' in its Westin 'Heavenly Bed'. This is the sensory ambience often cultivated by health resorts and spas. (For that matter, Disney World resort hotels offer 'Senses' spas to soothe the jangled nerves of theme park visitors.)

The lush, exotic sensations of Rainforest Cafés, in turn, tie in well with notions of coffee and flavourful foods coming from tropical countries. In the case of an electronics retailer, however, tropical would not be a sensory atmosphere to cultivate, as it might convey notions of low technology, clutter, and even organic decay. Apple stores are designed to attract customers through a futuristic sensory aesthetic abounding in glass and steel, with uncluttered walls and surfaces. This layout (which has now been trademarked) suggests that the devices being sold are similarly futuristic, uncluttered, and clear or straightforward. In order to counter any sensation of coldness that such a bare and glassy environment might evoke, Apple sales staff are trained to be warm but not pushy, and to encourage visitors to touch and interact with the products on display. Customers, indeed, are invited to think of the store as a play space. As a result, Apple stores serve as a sensory embodiment and promotion of the Apple brand as much as (if not more than) they serve as sites for retailing electronics (Lacroix 2010: 48–50).

A major reason for the sensory revolution in retailing is that physical stores are losing sales to online retailers. Playing up what their internet competitors lack – namely, multi-sensoriality – has become a way for stores to counter this trend. The idea is that a retail environment needs to be made as enticing as possible to give people a reason to tear themselves away from their screens and come and shop in person. The greatest challenge for online retailers, by contrast, is their sensorial limitations. When the products being sold are primarily directed at the senses of sight and/or hearing, such as books, music, and movies, then internet retailers, with their audiovisual capabilities do very well (and their success has, in fact, led to the closure of many stores dealing in those goods). When products, such as food and clothing, engage other senses, however, customers are more reluctant to buy (see, for example, Okonkwo 2010).

Retailer reputation, attractive images, sensuous text – and a promise of easy returns – go some way to compensate for the absence of first-hand encounters with products sold online. Sensory-enabling technologies such as three-dimensional rotation and virtual try-ons are another way to make online products seem more like in-hand products. With new developments in digital technologies, it may soon be possible for odour and feel to be communicated electronically as well. The creation of virtual shopping walls in public spaces with life-sized product images is a provocative new way of taking internet retailing out of the black box and giving it the illusion and public presence of real-world shopping. An example of this is a virtual supermarket that has been created on the wall of a subway in South Korea. The display shows shelves of food that can be scanned, purchased, and delivered to the shopper's home. Ironically, one contemporary phenomenon that works to the advantage of internet marketers is that of 'showrooming'. This involves customers examining products first-hand in a store and then ordering them through a competing online retailer. In such cases internet retailers benefit from 'borrowed' sense appeal.

Giving products sense appeal

In a 1930s book entitled *Consumer Engineering*, business professors Roy Sheldon and Egmont Arens argued that it was important to consider diverse sensory aspects when designing products. As regards the sense of touch they noted:

> Manufacturing an object that delights this sense is something that you do but don't talk about. [Yet, almost] everything which is bought is handled. After the eye, the hand is the first censor to pass on acceptance, and if the hand's judgment is unfavorable, the most attractive object will not gain the popularity it deserves. On the other hand, merchandise designed to be pleasing to the hand wins an approval that may never register in the mind, but which will determine additional purchases. ... *Make it snuggle in the palm.*
>
> (Sheldon and Arens 1932: 100–1)

Sheldon and Arens gave the example of a bar of soap, which, at the time, typically came in rectangular blocks that were not particularly easy or pleasing to grip, especially in the shower. Taking this previously underconsidered sensory dimension into account led to the creation of more tactually-pleasing hand-sized bars of soap.

Such 'sensory engineering' was not a new idea. It could be traced to the Arts and Crafts and Aesthetic movements of the nineteenth and early twentieth centuries, which placed an emphasis on creating sensorially-pleasing objects. These notions were carried over into the retail sector which, in essays with titles such as 'The Reign of the Artistic', called for the design of 'merchandise that appeals to the aesthetic senses' (Rappold and Forbes 1920: lx; see also Rappaport 2000: 158–59). Sheldon and Arens further noted that many traditional societies paid close attention to the sensorial qualities of their handicrafts, even suggesting that product designers might reconnect with their senses by studying tribal artefacts.

What was new in the twentieth century, particularly after World War II, was the broadened scope of the concept, its systematic study, and the incorporation of new sensory technologies. Sheldon and Arens were ahead of this curve when, already in 1932, they argued that 'sense appeal' was an important factor not only in the case of overtly sensuous products such as clothing and perfumes, but also of such utilitarian objects as soap and cameras. The sales of any product, even the most mundane, could be increased through sensory engineering. This recognition was the first step in a campaign that would culminate in the total commodification of the sensorium by the century's end. Figuring out precisely what directions product design should take was no longer held to be a matter of aesthetic intuition, but of the systematic investigation of precisely what shapes, textures, colours, scents and so on would appeal to the intended market. In a world where fragrances, flavours, sounds and colours can be synthetically produced there is no need to stick with the natural sensory characteristics of any product or material (see, for example, Classen et al. 1994: 192–200).

If an added fragrance might give added appeal to a product, however, which fragrance was it to be? The freshness of pine scent might make sense for use in an air freshener but not for a facial tissue, as it may evoke the prickliness of pine needles. Clear cola seemed like a refreshing concept, however in practice its transparency confused consumers who expected a dark colour to go along with a cola taste. Evidently, sensory qualities have to be considered in relation to each other when designing a product. And as consumer preferences could change, there was no once-and-for-all hitting on the perfect sensory mix for a product. Ongoing research and product tinkering was necessary to respond to (or to create) new sensory desires and stay ahead of the competition.

Certain sensory features of products are taken by consumers to reveal something about the nature or quality of the product, and this is used to advantage by designers. A crisp texture in food may be taken to indicate freshness, making crispness the subject of careful manipulation by snack food and cereal manufacturers. The smell of a product is often seen as revelatory of quality and ingredients. Hence in the 1920s and 1930s Fels-Naptha soap was advertised with the slogan: 'Real naptha. You can tell by the smell!' With artificial fragrances, however, it became possible to add a scent signal that had little to do with the actual contents of the product. An artificial lemon scent can be added to a detergent to signal freshness and cleaning power without any real lemon being present in the product.

'Sensory evaluation' is a big business, and a number of methodologies have been elaborated for the study of consumer sensory preferences. One recent one is kansei ('sensibility') engineering, developed in Japan. Kansei evaluates consumer responses to and associations with variations in sensory design. Another is the Italian-based Sensorial Quality Assessment Model, which similarly analyses user responses to product properties. Both of these approaches rely on the statistical analysis of their results in order to arrive at the 'ideal' design for a particular product. This form of sensory arithmetic, however, begs the question of whether product appeal can be manufactured by a simple adding up of pleasant sensations (Jordan 2004: 157–265).

A further element in product appeal concerns packaging. At the most basic level packaging presents the product it encases as protected, precious, and pure, untouched by any hands until it is opened by the purchaser. Packaging allows for the presentation of brand names and logos. It can also add a layer of sensuality, bringing vibrant colours to plain brown chocolate bars, sculptural forms to evanescent perfumes, and a glossy smoothness to the dullest product encased in clear plastic wrap.

The precise use that is made of product packaging depends partially on the associations a marketer wishes to convey. Promotional text and pictures would be considered rather vulgar and therefore inappropriate for the packaging of luxury goods, for example. No perfume box informs customers that it contains 'a burst of fragrance in every drop'. Generally, however, packaging text allows products to 'speak' to consumers, telling them how tasty/healthy/ entertaining/useful they are. Pictures, in turn, can depict products in use and evoke related sensations and emotions – an inflatable pool full of happy, splashing children, a coffee maker pouring out a perfect cup of steaming coffee, a salad bowl full of leafy, green lettuce and ripe, red tomato slices.

However, packaging also places a barrier between shoppers and products. Arguably, the increase in product packaging was a factor in the 'desensualization' of stores in the late-twentieth century by placing many products out of hand's reach. A toy store full of colourful boxes, for example, does not have the same sensory appeal as a toy store with rocking horses, plush toys, bins of tops and rows of dolls, just waiting, as it were, to be picked up and brought home. Whereas in traditional department and variety stores customers were invited to 'handle and see for themselves', often all that can be handled and seen in contemporary stores is the product packaging.

There is a fine line that contemporary marketers and retailers must walk between satisfying the consumer desire to handle a product directly before buying and taking into account the consumer disinclination to purchase a product that has been handled by others (see Morales 2010). One way of dealing with this dilemma is by having store models on display for customers to examine. Another way is to design packaging that both reveals and protects the product. This is the case with packaging that allows customers to touch the product inside through an opening or to set it working briefly by pressing an exposed button. One recent, and as yet little used, technique is to scent packaging using scratch and sniff technology. This offers customers a whiff of the product – food, shampoo, perfume – which lies concealed within its container. A recent instance of its use was in a promotional campaign for Froot Loops cereal, in which the cereal boxes were treated to emit the distinctive Froot Loops scent.

Advertising to the senses

How a product is presented can be just as important as how it is designed and produced. The most sensuous product will not have much chance to appeal if it is hidden in a back corner. Window displays exhibit products in an aesthetically pleasing context and entice passersby to enter the store and inquire further. Prominent counter display has the surest potential to induce customers to pick up and handle products, enabling the power of touch to work its 'magic'. Companies will accordingly pay a premium to have their merchandise presented at or near the check-out counter or within easy reach on a shelf, since 'product positioning' is key when it comes to pushing merchandise. Sales staff play a vital role as well, by drawing customers' attention to the desirability of the goods for sale. One early twentieth-century guide to retailing, for example, gave explicit instructions on how this might be done:

> Encourage your customer to touch the merchandise to note its quality, smoothness, fine texture, or whatnot. If it is an article that has an odor,

ask the customer to smell it and note its fragrance. If it is an article which can be tasted ask the customer to sample it and note its delicious flavor.

(Rappold and Forbes 1920: 69)

If two senses could be engaged at once, for example by encouraging a customer to touch silk and at the same time 'handling the silk in such a way as to appeal to her sense of hearing by producing a sound which denotes a rich quality of material' so much the better (Rappold and Forbes 1920: liii).

Beyond the retail environment come posters, banners, billboards, and the media proper – print media, such as newspapers, magazines, and catalogues; electronic media, such as radio and television; and, most recently, digital media – all of which have been pressed into service by advertisers.

As regards print media, over the course of the twentieth century advertising copy went from being primarily informative to largely suggestive – that is, it moved 'away from direct description of the qualities of the product to the use of more indirect associational imagery, in which meaning becomes elided and goods become associated with vague, but potent notions of lifestyle' (Featherstone 2001: 2264). The ratio of text to image also shifted to the point where visuals have come to occupy the whole page and the only text that remains often consists solely of the brand logo and some catchphrase. This diminution of product information was partly due to the legal consequences of making false claims about a product, which made it safer to suggest than state. It also had to do with the perceived need to make a quick impact on a public with ever-increasing demands on its attention. For this purpose pictures and short phrases work better than lengthy texts.

Whether relying more on text or on visuals, and whether appearing in traditional print media or on radio, television or the internet, advertising employs sense appeal in two basic ways: one is to present an item itself as appealing, the other is to claim that it will endow its users with sense appeal. A product, for example, can be said to feel silky itself or to make its user feel silky (or sometimes both). A variation on the second method is to play on anxieties by warning of the negative consequences of not using a product. Two early examples of this with relevance to the role of the senses in advertising are the promotion of Listerine as a 'cure' for 'halitosis' (bad breath) and of Lifebuoy as a preventive for 'BO' (body odour).

Originally sold as a general purpose antiseptic for home and hospital use, Listerine was repositioned as a mouthwash in the 1920s. The first ads targeted women, and were modelled after the advice to the lovelorn columns in the tabloids. One ad showed a young woman peering into a mirror, wondering at her failure to attract a husband even though she was quite pretty. 'What secret is your mirror holding back?' the ad asked. Malodour, being invisible, could not be seen in the mirror. Nor could one hear about it as it was not considered polite to talk to friends about their personal hygiene. Only the advertisement could warn of the devastating presence of the medical-sounding 'halitosis', and provide a treatment in the form of Listerine.

Listerine went on to tie its mouthwash, or rather the consequences of not using its mouthwash, to Depression fears of unemployment with a 1931 ad headlined 'Fired – and for a reason he never suspected'. Lifebuoy Soap followed suit with an ad that warned readers: 'Don't risk *your* job by offending with BO. Take no chances! ... When business is slack, employers become more critical. Sometimes very little may turn the scales against us' (Marchand 1985: 290). A recent example of an advertisement that conveys this threat of sensory repulsion if one does not use a product, rather than the promise of sensory appeal/gratification if one does, was an ad for a L'Oréal men's skin cream. It showed a man's face with the caption: 'He thinks he has great lines, she thinks he has wrinkles.'

In these ads a company presents itself in the role of a trusted advisor who warns people of the social rejection that awaits them due to their (often unrecognized) unattractiveness – bad smell, rough skin, unattractive looks – and offers the means for correcting it. Whereas in the early ads, however, these social rejections were presented along conventional gender lines as failing to attract a partner for women and losing employment for men, the L'Oréal ad, pitching a traditionally feminine product for men, attempts to foster a conventionally feminine anxiety in men: being insufficiently 'attractive' for romantic appeal.

The success of such an approach depends on the extent to which the disaster scenario presented responds to or creates real anxieties for which the advertised product seems the best palliative. In the case of Listerine the campaign was very effective: within a decade company profits went from $100,000 to over $4 million per year. This was without there being any change to the substance of Listerine, only to its new presentation as a mouthwash and its fear-mongering advertising (Classen et al. 1994: 182–86). This form of product advertising makes it clear that sensory design and promotion are not solely about 'giving the customer what he/she wants' – as they are often said to be. In many cases they are also about manipulating the customer through whatever means seem most effective to make a sale.

A more subtle advertising technique involving the senses uses lateral thinking to enhance the desirability of a product through related sensations. Examples of this include the 'The Loudest Taste on Earth' slogan of Doritos chips and the 'Taste the Rainbow' slogan of Skittles candy. Such ads have a synaesthetic appeal (a subject to be discussed in the following chapter) in that they evoke one sensation by means of another, suggesting a fantasy world of complete sensory satisfaction in which sights and sounds and colours can be tasted. The Ghost Six Senses Rolls-Royce advertising pursues a similar line of thought, claiming that the automobile will awaken a 'supernatural' sixth sense that will bring together sensations from all of the senses and provide a total sensory experience.

Rather than invoking too narrow an experience, this lateral form of sensory advertising aims to call up a constellation of sensuous associations around the product. This strategy, with its emphasis on sensory synergy, is in keeping with consumer research showing, as discussed above, that associated perceptions strongly influence one another. In the words of Kevin Roberts: 'Our senses work together and when they are stimulated at the same time the results are unforgettable. ... The only breakthroughs will only come with and/and. Taste *and* texture. Sight *and* sound. Taste *and* touch. Smell *and* taste' (K. Roberts 2005: 107).

Roberts himself takes pride in an ad campaign he helped devise for Brahma beer in Brazil. The brand's slogan, 'The Number 1', lacked sensuality, which the new ad campaign brought in by focusing on the sound of a beer can being opened, as expressed in the syllable 'Tss'. '"Tss" became the sound of good times, the sound of anticipation, and the sound of Brahma.' As a result of the 'Tss' campaign catching on, Brazilians could enter a bar and order a Brahma beer just by saying 'Tss'. The sound 'became an icon in its own right' (K. Roberts 2005: 211–12).

There are a number of promotional tactics that take advertising beyond the sensory limits of mass media. Customers, for example, are frequently enlisted as walking advertisements when they display brand logos on their clothing or use branded products such as canned drinks in public. The possibility of adding scent to print advertisements, in turn, has long intrigued. It suffered a brief setback in the 1990s when consumers complained of allergic reactions to scented ads in magazines. This was (partially) overcome by the encapsulation of aromatic oils requiring that the ad be rubbed to be smelt and it remains a popular practice for promoting sales of aromatic products (Nelson 2012: 51–53). In the inverse of the contemporary practice of pumping fragrances into retail environments, recently the restaurant chain Pizza Hut gave away bottles of Eau de Pizza Hut perfume, smelling of freshly-baked pizza dough, in order to attract customers. In a similar form of olfactory advertising, Westin sells the same white tea scent that it uses to aromatize its hotels.

Companies may also promote their products at public events such as sports games, in order to increase visibility and prestige, but also to link their brand with the dynamism of the event. The tobacco industry, for example, was heavily involved in the sponsorship of auto racing until bans on tobacco brand sponsorship were put in place in many countries in the late twentieth and early twenty-first centuries. Salem linked its 'Stir the Senses' advertising campaign with a concert tour by hip-hop artists in 2003. Promotional campaigns on the internet, in turn, can associate products with a range of multisensory practices. Following its 'Stir the Senses' campaign, Salem repositioned its cigarettes as soothing the senses (indicating the key role of advertising in promoting a particular sensory experience of a product). To the dismay of anti-tobacco agitators, Salem's website featured spa-like images, showing aromatic candles being sniffed and detailing massage techniques (Lewis and Wackowski 2006). The internet is still a new phenomenon and it is likely that such attempts to promote the sense appeal of products through virtual sensory immersion will increase in coming years.

The mind of the marketer

The contemporary interest in sensory marketing is grounded in the idea that the senses can be used to bypass reason and appeal directly to the emotions (Malefyt and Morais 2012: ch. 5). This view helps support the current emphasis on sensuous images over informative text in advertisements. While language makes us think, according to this approach, sensory evocations make us dream. And whereas thinking might lead to a rationalization of why one does *not* need a particular product, there is no arguing with dreams.

One can trace the roots of this approach to the rise of Behaviourism in the early twentieth century. Accounts of behavioural conditioning by psychologists encouraged marketers to think that they might make use of such conditioning for their own purposes (see, for example, Sheldon and Arens 1932: 97–100). If dogs could be conditioned to salivate for food at the ringing of a bell, then could not customers be conditioned to 'salivate' for a product at the sight of a logo? There hardly seemed to be any point in striving to convince potential customers through logical argument when they might be trained to respond reflexively to sensory cues. This approach presented people not as rational beings, but as creatures of habit and impulse who could be conditioned into certain consumer habits and impulses. While the influence of Behaviourism declined within psychology in the later twentieth century, the possibilities it opened up of sensory and emotional conditioning continued to hold a huge attraction for marketers.

While not precisely subliminal advertising, which aims to promote products by imbedding or briefly displaying images or words so that they will affect consumers subconsciously (Acland 2012), this approach to marketing still aims to tap into the sensorial unconscious. In *How Customers Think*, for example, Harvard Marketing Professor Gerald Zaltman writes that '95 percent of the decision-making process takes place below the conscious level' and that marketers must therefore aim their products and pitches at an emotional, rather than logical level (Zaltman 2003: 1). Brain imaging is presented as offering an important new tool, or at least validation, for this approach. As 'brain scans suggest that only a small portion of the brain's neural activity ultimately surfaces in language' (Zaltman 2003: 2), an alternative to linguistic advertising must be found. The alternative that presents itself is sensory stimuli: sights, sounds, smells, touches, tastes.

The 'experience economy' is one in which, as far as marketers are concerned, product information and the making of rational purchase decisions should be the last thing on consumers' minds – eclipsed (if not obliterated) by the impact of all the highly effective strategies of sensation management with which the 'experience designer' structures a given product or environment. In a similar vein, the 'lovemarks' marketing concept publicized by Kevin Roberts (2005) proposes that the future of brands lies in shedding their function as trademarks, which elicit confidence by indicating a trustworthy source, and coming to function as 'lovemarks' that, by mobilizing the emotions of the consumer, induce 'loyalty beyond reason'.

Smell, taste and touch, as the supposedly least rational – and therefore most susceptible to persuasion – of the senses, have been embraced by marketers. The fact that smell is described by scientists as conveying sensations directly to the brain with next to no intermediate processing (Herz 2010: 90) makes this sense of particular interest. The conclusion is that smell can reach deeper into the subconscious and memory than any other sense (Hultén et al. 2009: 5). If a fragrance is loaded up with associations, these will supposedly piggyback on the smell right to the primal depths of the brain. (This is sometimes called 'The Proust Effect', after Proust's description in *Remembrance of Things Past* of the host of memories called up by smells and tastes.) By associating products with distinctive odours, marketers hope to make them intensely and instantly memorable, increasing future sales. Hence the subtitle of the third in the recent spate of sensory marketing books: *Smells Like Profits* (Solomon 2010). Another reason for turning to the proximity senses in product design and marketing is that these will be perceived as countering an increasing feeling of alienation from our bodies in a computerized world. If we become detached from sensory immediacy through working with computers all day long, the ads assure us that we can come to our senses with the right chewing gum, cigarette, or bottle of shampoo.

One market area in which this shift to the 'lower' register of sensations is particularly noticeable is that of electronics. Traditionally, the names of companies making electrical devices often referred either to electricity or to the 'higher', more 'rational' senses of sight and hearing: Electrolux, Panasonic, General Electric, NuTone, Sunbeam. This brought out the high-tech capacities of their products. In a culture that is now pervaded by the remote sensations provided by modern technology, however, there is a growing trend to link the names of electronics companies and their products to the more intimate and sensuous pleasures of tastes and touches.

Steve Jobs started the trend by coming up with the name Apple for his company, in preference to other suggested names, such as Matrix Electronics, which would have been more in keeping with tradition. In terms of the youth market, it seemed more appealing to students to take an Apple computer to school, than a dull, no-nonsense sounding 'International Business Machine' – the company's main competitor. In 1999 Apple emphasized its 'taste-appeal' by launching the iMac line of personal computers in fruit colours: blueberry, strawberry, grape, lime, and tangerine.

Apple is no longer the only electronics company to have a friendly, fruity name with multisensory evocations. Research In Motion has renamed itself BlackBerry after its highly popular BlackBerry wireless device. Other high-tech companies have adopted low-tech brand names such as Sprint, Leap, and Fido.

Devices relying on distance sensing have themselves been reinvented as corporeally engaging. A forerunner in this regard was AT&t, which ran a successful ad campaign to boost long-distance telephone calls in the 1980s based on the slogan 'Reach out and touch someone'. This slogan encouraged customers to think of the disembodied act of communicating over the telephone as an intimate tactile encounter. In the twenty-first century a number of electronics manufacturers have played up and enhanced the tactile qualities of their devices, in several cases even using the 'low-brow' word 'touch' in the product name: HP TouchPad, Creative ZEN Touch, and, most famously, iPod Touch, or, simply, iTouch.

While the extent to which the sense of touch is actually engaged by these products is quite limited, highlighting their 'non-rational' tactility presents them as user-friendly and intuitive. Advertising for the iPod Touch, for example, declared that with the device: 'Everything you touch is easy, intuitive, and fun.' In this way, high-technology is invested with the hands-on ease-of-use and playfulness of a child's toy. Low-tech sensuality has obviously acquired a new importance in a high-tech world. Still, there are limits to the extent to which electronics companies wish to portray themselves and their products as 'tasty-feely'. Although they display an image of an apple on their front, Apple stores do not resemble fruit stands. Rather, as discussed above, they have the rectilinear glass, metal, and light hallmarks of high-tech style.

While the proximity senses are experiencing a marketing vogue as under-utilized avenues to consumer desire, some argue – along the lines of those nineteenth-century artists discussed in Chapter 2 who pursued the ideal of a total artwork – that it is necessary to engage all the senses to create totally-appealing products. In the view of Martin Lindstrom (2005), human beings come equipped with a 'five-track sensory recorder', and by our very nature 'we're at our most effective and receptive when operating on all five tracks'. Two 'tracks' are better than one, Lindstrom says, referring to the 'logo-fixated mind-set' of previous decades when the brand name and logo was often all that distinguished one company's products from another. The challenge facing companies now, however, is to break out of the 'two-track' or '2-D impasse' imposed by audiovisual media and move towards '5-D branding'. This is because: 'The more sensory touchpoints leveraged when building brands, the higher the number of sensory memories activated. The higher the number of sensory memories activated, the stronger the bonding between brand and consumer' (Lindstrom 2005: 69).

The ultimate goal behind all this sense-mongering, if we follow Lindstrom's reasoning through to its conclusion, is for brands to inspire the same 'irrational' fervour as religions. Religions 'touch us at a fundamental emotional level, which precludes any rational discussion' (Lindstrom 2005: 169). Religions are able to do this, he says, because they have mastered the 'Ten Rules of Sensory Branding', which include using sensory stimuli (incense, chants, candles, wine, etc.) and rituals to build a strong sense of community among their adherents. Follow the same rules, Lindstrom advises marketers, and your customers can be touched at the same level.

This is a highly revealing construction of the meaning of religions and of marketing, since it presumes that in both cases the attachment is an irrational, sense-based one. Underlying this construction is the long-standing Western opposition between the intellect or mind, on the one hand, and the body and senses on the other. (Although traditionally religion would have been ranged on the side of the mind.) It is ironic (and not a little pathetic) that, while contemporary branding appears to embrace the body and senses, it is actually more concerned with upholding and even strengthening the old mind/body split – that is, with separating the senses from the intellect. Any moral qualms about creating consumer religions or commodifying the senses ('iTouch gave ownership to [Apple] of that sense, the sense of "touch"' [Krishna 2010: 6]) seem slight or non-existent. These practices are just seen as admirable marketing moves.

The whole concept of the senses as 'direct links' to the brain, which animates so much of the discourse of sensory marketing experts is, however, fundamentally flawed. Marketers are certainly correct in their acknowledgement of the impact of sensory messages. However, when they see the senses as 'direct, provocative, immediate' (K. Roberts 2005:105), they fail to realize that they are adding a level of construction (and therefore mediation) to the senses with their marketing slogans and imagery. This is similarly the case when they depict the senses as primal: 'Our senses being primal, we react immediately and subconsciously to them, unlike to a brand name or an attribute, both of which are learned' (Krishna 2010: 4).

There is no recognition here of the fact that ways of sensing are themselves learned, as we have seen throughout this book, nor of the role sensations and imagery play in cognition. (If thinking were completely dependent on language we would never have any trouble putting our thoughts into words.) Nor do marketers recognize their own wishful thinking – their dream of a 'royal road' to consumers' hearts and wallets – in this construction. Rather, to their way of thinking, it is all a happy matter of biology and evolution (K. Roberts 2005: 108, see further Saad 2011). This itself, of course, is a form of advertising, whereby sensory marketing is presented as a straightforward, scientifically-based shortcut to profits.

Selling the senses across cultures

To discover that the senses of consumers are shaped by culture as well as by nature, it is only necessary to look across cultures. When we do this we can find the same product with the same sensory attributes eliciting different responses from consumers with the same sensory faculties but different sensory associations and preferences. Take the example of India, a country with an enormous market for consumer products but with consumer preferences and associations that sometimes differ widely from those of Westerners. Cadbury, for instance, had to withdraw its dark chocolate offerings from the Indian market because their bitterness was unappealing in a country that likes its sweets to be very sweet. In another example of cultural differences in sensory inclinations, whereas in the West televisions are usually marketed on the basis of their picture quality, in India, where having a 'big sound', is important, the electronics company Onida successfully promoted its televisions as offering superior audio capabilities (Kumar 2007).

Broader cultural associations also play an important role in marketing. Purity, which traditionally has very strong cultural and religious resonances in India is often emphasized in advertising, as conveyed by such slogans as 'Purity in Each Drop', 'for Every Mother Obsessed With Purity', 'Pure Banking, Nothing Else' and 'Purity-Sealed' (Cadbury chocolates). Tata brand salt, one of India's most trusted brands, gained its position through being marketed on the basis of its purity, a particularly apt association as salt has the symbolic significance of integrity in India (Shah and D'Souza 2009: 371). Another example of an advertising campaign with Indian cultural connotations is one that attributed 'smart eyes' to Ariel laundry detergent, which supposedly enabled it to perceive and remove stains. Such associations would resonate with traditional notions of the importance of ritual purity but also with the key Hindu concept of visionary sight.

It is clear from such examples that even such basic sensations as sweet and salty are mediated by culture and not simply straightforward sensory reactions. And while to some extent it is true that Western sensory values have travelled around the globe through the marketing of consumer goods, it is also the case that global consumers respond in their own ways to the sensory attributes of such products (Howes 1996a, 2003: ch. 8). The Hausa people of West Africa furnish a good example of this. The premium attached to 'brilliance' in the Hausa aesthetic order has made manufactured watches attractive substitutes for handcrafted silver bracelets, and shiny commercial enamel ware desirable replacements for traditional gourd containers. In this case, local sensory values support the adoption of certain consumer goods. However, the ways and contexts in which the Hausa use such goods – most importantly as display items in marriage ceremonies – differ from their Western usages (Arnould 1989).

The Hausa case is not unique. 'Preference formation' is always a cultural matter, based on local values and practices, and not simply a personal one. In Papua New Guinea Johnson's baby powder is bought for its pleasant fragrance and purificatory associations, but rather than being used on babies it is employed for ritual aspersions of corpses and mourners and for body decor (Howes 2003: 217–18). Certain Zimbabweans, in turn, use Lifebuoy soap not to wash their bodies but to add a much-valued sheen to their skin (Burke 1996). Lest such examples seem to be limited to tribal peoples who do not understand the 'correct' uses of the products they purchase, one can give the instance of North American teenagers enjoying the bright colours of Kool-Aid not in a drink, but as hair dye, or university students painting glow-in-the-dark designs on the walls of their rooms with Tide laundry detergent (which formerly contained phosphates) (see further Green 2000). Such striking illustrations of consumer-added values and uses underscore the importance of factoring local 'modes of consumption' into any account of sensory marketing.

When one explores cross-cultural reactions to sensory marketing there is also the phenomenon of local rejection of consumer commodities to take

into account. In Western craft movements, homemade products are often presented as having an authentic feel as opposed to the slick 'artificiality' of mass-
produced goods. Writing about the contemporary Arts and Crafts movement in
the United States, Frances Mascia-Lees (2011) describes participants as desiring
to cultivate their senses through craftwork as a contrast to the sensory distraction
which they experience in consumer culture. Japanese 'nativists', in turn, hold
that 'the process of *jikkan* – retrospection through traditional ways of sensing –
provides an antidote to immersion in the sensory world of consumer goods.
Thus the smell of incense at a shrine or the tactile and kinaesthetic sensations
of sitting on tatami [mats] ... can produce a reconnection with the eternal,
authentic Japanese culture and soul' (Tobin 1992: 34).

The rejection of Western consumer goods and their sensory values, however, is often centred on their 'foreignness' rather than on their perceived
undesirability per se. When Coca-Cola left India in the 1970s due to government pressure, it was replaced by a sweeter local cola, Thums Up, which
was promoted with the slogan 'Happy Days are Here Again'. (Thums Up was
later acquired by Coca-Cola and now has the more up-to-date sensory slogan
'Taste the Thunder'.) After the fall of the Berlin Wall and the entry of
Western brand-name goods in the German Democratic Republic or East
Germany, a demand emerged for products of the Communist era. These
products included the Trabant automobile, transistor radios, washing powder,
lemonade, and coffee. This desire for the consumer sensations of a vanished
past is known as *Ostalgie* – a word that combines the meanings of 'nostalgia'
and 'Eastern'.

> [The] very otherness of GDR products, manifest in their physicality that
> can be seen, felt, tasted, smelled, and heard, serves as the starting point of
> these journeys into the past. These products ... signify a group identity for
> their former consumers: since all former citizens of the GDR were – by
> necessity – also consumers of its goods, they can find an exclusive identity
> as former consumers and purchasers of these products since they all have
> once shared the specific knowledge about these products.
>
> (Blum 2001: 231)

This is a potent illustration of how it is not only the (presumed) superiority of
the sensations offered by a product, nor their capacity to excite or soothe,
which affect reception, but also the extent to which they provide a feeling of
cultural identity.

The above examples further bring out how consumption cannot be grasped
exclusively in terms of the reception or internalization of the 'messages' of
some hypothetical 'code' or 'system of objects' (to use Baudrillard's [1981,
1996] terminology). As anthropological research shows, there is no guarantee
that 'the intentions of the producer will be recognized, much less respected,
by the consumer from another culture' (Howes 1996a: 6; Foster 1996/97;
Coote et al. 2000). Consumption is an *active* process, where all sorts of

meanings and uses for products are generated that the designers and marketers of those products never imagined. Hence, even if a product has all its sensory touch points perfected, when it is inserted into the multisensory, dynamic context of everyday life it may end up having uses and values that differ considerably from those intended by the marketer.

Without taking away from these critiques of the marketing mentality, however, it is important to recognize that modern techniques of marketing and the products they promote, have become part of the cultural complex of values and practices shaping our senses and our lives. Many of the colours, smells, tastes, touches and sounds we encounter in our physical environments and call up in our mental worlds carry commercial associations. Already in the 1980s a study found that product aromas, such as baby powder and bubble gum, were more recognizable and memorable to most people than natural aromas, such as coffee and lemon. And they came with brand names attached: Johnson's baby powder, Bazooka bubble gum (Classen et al. 1994: 203). Marketers may be naive as regards the social nature of perception, and they may lack a sense of history, but it is the field of product design and marketing, more than any other, that is taking charge of fashioning the sensory imaginaries of the twenty-first century.

6 Synaesthesia unravelled

The union of the senses from a cultural perspective

It is an evidence of diseased and debilitated brain activity, if consciousness relinquishes the advantage of the differentiated perceptions of phenomena, and carelessly confounds the reports conveyed by the particular senses. ... It is a descent from the height of human perfection to the low level of the mollusc.

Max Nordau, *Degeneration* (1910 [1895])

We ... found that ... synaesthesia is a genuine perceptual phenomenon, not an effect based on memory associations or on vague metaphorical speech. ... [We] propose that [it is] caused by hyperconnectivity ... [that might in turn] be caused by a genetic mutation that causes defective pruning of connections between brain areas ...

V.S. Ramachandran and E.M. Hubbard,
'Synaesthesia – a window into perception, thought and language' (2001)

In one image the human brain ... consists of layers of innumerable hexagonal honeycombs. ... Each tiny hexagonal container holds honey of a different color, flavor, odor, or texture. ... A brain can be seen as a bouquet of flowers, a fluttering cluster of butterflies, a glistening swarm of tiny tropical fish, or a quivering mass of multicolored frogs.

Gerardo Reichel-Dolmatoff, 'Brain and mind in Desana shamanism' (1981)

Neuroscience enjoys tremendous authority at present. Due to this authority, as well as to interest generated by recent research in the field, terms such as 'neuroplasticity', 'mirror neurons' and 'hyperconnectivity' have transcended the scientific study of the nervous system and come to figure as sources of cultural capital (see Legrenzi and Umilta 2011). Part of this popular appeal undoubtedly rests on the attraction of the vividly coloured representations generated by the brain-imaging technologies employed to scan neural activity. As the brain is a rather sensorially-silent organ – unlike the heart or the stomach which we can feel and hear at work – such images seem to finally allow us sensory access to its mysterious processes.

Influenced by these developments, scholars in the social sciences and humanities increasingly employ the findings of neuroscience to help explain or 'validate' cultural theories and practices. This has particularly been the case within art history and within the study of the body and the senses in society (i.e., Bacci and Melcher 2011; Lende and Downey 2012). As a result, new subdisciplines such as 'neuroaesthetics' and 'neuroanthropology' have sprung up.

One fascinating topic that crosses the borders of neuroscience, the humanities, and the social sciences, just as it crosses the borders of the senses, is synaesthesia, the 'union of the senses'. From the standard neurological perspective, synaesthesia is a physiological condition in which certain perceptions trigger unrelated sensations, for example, a musical note may elicit a mental sensation of colour. Neurologists recognize that synaesthesia has been elaborated as an artistic practice and plays a role in language in the form of metaphor (as exemplified by such expressions as 'a sharp taste' or 'a loud colour'). However, they regard such cases as weak, compared to 'strong', 'brain-based' synaesthesia.

Traditionally synaesthesia was seen as a 'pathological' or 'abnormal' condition due to the seeming irrationality of the associations made between differing sensations (why should a particular musical note be green?). In recent years, this has changed somewhat. The stigmatization of synaesthesia has declined and many now see it as a 'gift' or sign of an artistic personality (van Campen 2010).

In this chapter, however, we are interested in synaesthesia as a cultural phenomenon, a phenomenon that has a vigorous history of social expression and reception and that extends beyond linguistic metaphors and artistic practices to inform a broad range of fields, from kinship relations to mathematics. From this perspective, viewing synaesthesia as either a 'pathology' or a 'gift' misses the key ways in which it is socially elaborated. Indeed, it is our contention that, far from being limited to genetic 'deviants', a predisposition for cross-modal connections is generally shared by humans (although it may be stronger in some individuals than in others). It is this commonality of the phenomenon that makes it useful for widespread cultural elaboration, as will be discussed below.

We intend to show that synaesthesia is too multifaceted and too culturally important to be left solely to neuroscientists to define. We also hope, on the one hand, to encourage neuroscientists interested in sensory integration to take more account of cultural factors, and, on the other, to stimulate historians, anthropologists and other scholars to look beyond, beside, and behind neurological models to explore the ways in which the senses – and sensory models – are shaped by culture.

The neuropsychological account of perception

According to the neuropsychological account of perception, sensing is a matter of 'information-processing'. It begins at the edge of the central nervous system and is conditioned by the properties of the receptor organs (Keeley 2002). In a nutshell, this account holds that:

> The events that culminate in perception begin with specialized receptor cells that convert a particular form of physical energy into bioelectric

currents. Different sensors are sensitive to different types of energy, so the properties of the receptor cells determine the modality of a sensory system. Ionic currents are the currency of neural information processing, and current flows that begin in the receptors are transmitted through complex networks of interconnected neurons and, in the end result in a pattern of brain activity we call perception.

(Hughes 2001: 7)

Within this framework, the senses are assumed to be structurally and functionally distinct: sight is concerned with colour (which is an effect of electromagnetic energy), hearing with sound (which is an effect of mechanical energy), taste with flavour (which is chemical in its constitution), and so forth. This modular conception of the sensorium is reflected in the analytic orientation of most of the extant research in the psychology of perception. Such research takes a 'sense-by-sense' approach to the study of perceptual processes (see for example Goldstein [2002] or any standard psychology textbook on sensation and perception). This approach is the outgrowth of the 'doctrine of specific nerve energies', which was first formulated by Johannes Müller in 1835 (Meulders 2010: 45).

While the 'one-sense-at-a-time' approach to the study of perception remains dominant in psychology, in recent years a more interactive, relational approach to the understanding of how the senses function has begun to take shape. This is a result of the growing body of evidence that points to the 'multisensory organization' of the brain. As Calvert, Spence and Stein write in the introduction to *The Handbook of Multisensory Processes*: 'even those experiences that at first may appear to be modality-specific are most likely to have been influenced by activity in other sensory modalities, despite our lack of awareness of such interactions' (Calvert et al. 2004: xi–xii). One laboratory example of such interaction would be the 'Stroop effect'. This is the finding that it takes longer to name the colour in which a colour term – such as 'blue' – is printed when that colour differs from the colour represented by the term – i.e., when the word 'blue' is printed in red (Mattingley and Rich 2004). Another example of such modulation would be the 'freezing phenomenon'. When subjects are shown a rapidly changing visual display, and an abrupt sound is played, the sound may seem to 'freeze' the display with which it is synchronized. As a result, the visual display will appear brighter or seem to last for a longer period than it does in real time (Vroomen and de Gelder 2004: 147). A third example is the 'McGurk effect'. A face on a video screen silently mouthing *ga* is synchronized with the sound of a voice uttering *ba*, and subjects 'hear' a third, in-between sound *da* (McGurk and MacDonald 1976).

Synaesthesia is another phenomenon that suggests that the senses may be more interconnected than is commonly supposed. What are deemed to be synaesthetic experiences do not, however, always cross the boundaries of the traditional fivefold sensorium. The most common type of synaesthesia, for example, is said to be colour-grapheme synaesthesia, in which letters or numbers are perceived as having particular colours. These are associations that take place within the visual domain (although the sound of a letter may also play a role). While some general tendencies have been recorded among (Western) synaesthetes, such as seeing the letter 'A' as red-coloured, associations tend to be highly subjective and variable (Ramachandran et al. 2004; L.E. Marks 2000; see further Baron-Cohen and Harrison 1997).

For the most part, neuropsychologists are only interested in the study of 'true' synaesthesia (also referred to as 'congenital synaesthesia' or 'constitutional synaesthesia') and they have designed procedures for screening out individuals for whom the cross-modal associations would appear to be merely 'conceptual' rather than 'perceptual', or merely 'metaphorical' rather than 'constitutional' (see Ramachandran et al. 2004: 867; Baron-Cohen and Harrison 1997). Thus, simply referring to a piece of music as 'soft' or a colour as 'loud' does not qualify as an expression of constitutional synaesthesia. Similarly, poetic synaesthesia holds no interest for the neuropsychologist, unless the poem or novel in question was written by a congenital synaesthete.

To determine if someone is a 'true' synaesthete, psychologists customarily use certain tests. One involves having a colour-grapheme synaesthete (the kind of synaesthete usually studied) match colours with letters and checking if these matches are consistent over a period of time. Another involves determining if such colour associations with letters are 'automatic'. A variation of the Stroop test may be used to see if a synaesthete can name a letter more quickly if its colour matches the one she or he associates with it. Brain-imaging has been used to investigate possible distinct features of the brains of synaesthetes, for example, to determine if the part of the brain deemed responsible for colour perception is activated when a colour-sound synaesthete hears a particular sound (Macpherson 2007: 73–75).

V.S. Ramachandran, the doyen of neuropsychology, has advanced a highly influential explanation of synaesthetic perceptions. He dismisses linguistic crossings of the senses as 'vague metaphorical speech', and instead affirms that 'true' synaesthesia has to do with the 'cross-activation of brain maps' (Ramachandran et al. 2004: 872; Hubbard and Ramachandran 2005). In the case of colour-grapheme synaesthesia – Ramachandran's chosen type – the areas corresponding to graphemes and colours are situated immediately next to each other in that part of the brain known as the fusiform gyrus. Ramachandran and his colleagues hold that, in view of this proximity, there is a strong likelihood of 'excess' cross-activation or 'hyperconnectivity' occurring. This is said to be due to 'defective pruning' as a result of a genetic mutation (see further Ramachandran 2011: ch. 3).

On the strength of this 'hyperconnectivity hypothesis' (limited though it be to grapheme-colour synaesthesia) it is argued that 'far from being a mere curiosity, synaesthesia deserves to be brought into mainstream neuroscience and cognitive psychology'. Indeed, precisely because it is increasingly possible for its (supposed) neural basis to be 'pinned down', it is claimed that synaesthesia 'may provide a crucial insight into some of the most elusive questions about the mind, such as the neural substrate (and evolution) of metaphor, language and thought itself (Ramachandran et al. 2004: 876, 881).

There is much to be said for the assignment of a genetic basis to synaesthetic tendencies, and for the supposition that synaesthesia may play an important role in cognition. However, such neurological accounts have the substantial drawback of failing to take social factors into account. They ignore the ways in which cross-sense linkages are fostered by culture and not simply experienced by individuals of a certain genetic type. To gain a fuller understanding of synaesthesia, and even of the social foundations of the interests of neurologists themselves, we need to explore the phenomenon in cultural context.

Synaesthesia as cultural practice

The anthropological-historical account of perception understands the sensorium to be a cultural as well as physiological formation. In brief, this account holds that:

> It is not only in clothing and appearance, in outward form and emotional make-up that [people] are the product of history. Even the way they see and hear is inseparable from the social life-process … The facts which our senses present to us are socially preformed in two ways: through the historical character of the object perceived and through the historical character of the perceiving organ.
>
> (Horkheimer quoted in Levin 1997: 63 n1)

This account of perception leads to a very different theorization of the phenomenon of synaesthesia. It begins with the social body, rather than with the individual body or brain.

To avoid confusion with 'congenital' or 'constitutional synaesthesia' as understood by neuroscientists, the types of cross-modal linkage which arise within social contexts could be called 'cultural synaesthesia'. While this distinction helps for purposes of exposition, however, it should be underlined that this chapter aims to explore interactions of biology and culture in the experience and expression of synaesthesia, rather than to uphold a notion of there being two distinct types of synaesthesia. Fortunately, the polysemy of the term 'constitutional' actually lends itself to supporting the anthropological-historical line of argument, for it can refer to the 'mode of organization' of a society, as well as to the mental character and to the physical makeup of an individual. It therefore spans the body, the psyche, and society. From the perspective advocated here, the constitution of society is seen as shaping the constitution of mind and body, and hence, of synaesthesia.

This is not to argue that all cases of synaesthesia are the product of culture, but rather that there is no strict division between the biological and the cultural in experiences of this multifaceted phenomenon. Even the idiosyncratic synaesthesia of the individual, as we shall see, can show the influence of the social and material environment in its formation.

Cultural synaesthesia and hallucinogenic visions: the Desana

The theory of cultural synaesthesia derives from the work of the Harvard-based scholar of comparative religion Lawrence Sullivan. In an article entitled 'Sound and senses' (1986), Sullivan presented a review of then current work in performance theory, hermeneutics and information theory in relation to sensory experience. His account culminated in the suggestion that: 'The symbolic experience of the unity of the senses enables a culture to entertain itself with the idea of the unity of meaning' (Sullivan 1986: 6). Sullivan went on to apply his model to the interpretation of the synaesthetic myths and socio-religious practices of a range of indigenous South American societies that make ritual use of the hallucinogenic *Banisteriopsis Caapi* plant (known locally as *yagé* or *ayahuasca*).

While the experience of cross-modal associations and transpositions commonly reported by persons under the influence of hallucinogens is a form of synaesthesia, it is not one that neuroscientists such as Ramachandran have shown much interest in studying. Indeed, it is dismissed by the latter as positively uninteresting because 'psychedelics-induced synaesthesia is far less organized than congenital synaesthesia', amounting to little more than 'sensory confusion' (Ramachandran et al. 2004: 868). This 'confusion' is taken as evidence that drug-induced synaesthesia does not involve the same neural mechanisms as congenital synaesthesia, since the latter appears to be quite precise in the sorts of intermodal associations (or cross-sense linkages) it evokes.

Drug-induced synaesthesia, however, may be employed in very precise ways for cultural purposes (as we saw in the chapter on medicine). Among the Desana of the Colombian rainforest, for example, the *Banisteriopsis Caapi* plant figures centrally in the myth of the origin of society:

> For [the Desana] ... the crying sounds of a mythic baby called Cajpi are also the tastes and visual images of the hallucinogenic drink made from his body (the magical plant, *Banisteriopsis Caapi*) 'for as soon as the little child cried aloud, all the people ... became intoxicated and saw all kinds of colours'. The divinity named Yepa Huaké commanded that the child be dismembered. A piece of his body was given to each social group. This distribution established not only the ranked hierarchy of groups in society today but also the different qualities of vision and modulations of sound that constitute each group's cultural existence as art, musical performance, and speech.
>
> (Sullivan 1986: 26)

There is a great deal of information about the Desana sensory and social order contained in this brief summary of the origin myth. Unravelling its strands will help us better understand this indigenous model of synaesthesia.

The myth may be interpreted as suggesting that in the beginning there was sound (the baby's cry). This sound embodied colours and temperatures, as well as smells and tastes. These sensations are meaningful to different senses now, but were indistinguishable from each other in the mythic world. That is, the sound of the baby's cry is understood to have contained the Desana 'sense ratio' (to borrow McLuhan's [1962] terminology) in embryo.

The division and distribution of the parts of the child's body modulated the original sound, just as it modulated society, partitioning the latter into ranked groups, each with its own style of singing, speaking, and use of colours, as well as other sensory media (odours, tastes). The division of sound, the division of the senses, and the division of society all arose together. Thus, the Desana social and symbolic universe is structured – or 'constituted' we might say (keeping in mind the polysemy of the term) – in accordance with a model derived from the interrelation of the senses under the influence of *yagé*.

According to the Desana theory of sensory correlations, colours emanate from the light of the Sun or Moon and then combine with heat to produce corresponding sets of odours and flavours. Purple, for example, is said to come from the Moon and is linked to a rotten smell and an acid flavour (see Classen et al. 1994: 121). As these different sensations represent different social categories and moral values, it is highly important for everyone to be aware of these cross-modal linkages. To combine sensations in the wrong order would be to ritually violate the Desana moral order, for example, by symbolically committing incest. Although it is inspired by hallucinogenic experience, in view of how carefully structured synaesthesia is among the Desana, it would plainly be wrong to simply dismiss it as 'sensory confusion' for failing to conform to the criteria laid down by the neuroscientists in their laboratories.

The Desana have their own theories of how the brain works, as described by the great Colombian ethnographer Gerardo Reichel-Dolmatoff. According to these indigenous theories of the brain, the left hemisphere is the seat of religious values and abstract principles. These include religious laws, shamanic spells, music, and the geometric patterns experienced during hallucinogenic visions. The right hemisphere, by contrast, deals with practical and biological matters. It is said to be concerned with the perception of sensory phenomena, including the figurative imagery of visions. The right hemisphere transforms the ideals of the left hemisphere into practical skill. The left hemisphere enables an individual to perceive the transcendent values encoded in the everyday sensations processed by the right hemisphere. (The Desana, however, do not categorize the hemispheres as left and right, but rather as 'one' and 'two', with the former considered superior.)

The two hemispheres are said to be connected by a process called 'to hear-to act', which refers to a form of inner communication. This internal listening gives rise to a state of awareness that is deemed to be the most important function of the brain. Such awareness, however, is said to require cultural guidance for its development. It is not, therefore, simply an automatic result of possessing a human brain, or purely congenital in nature. For the Desana, both thought and perception are shaped by culture.

The cerebral hemispheres are said to be divided into compartments, each of which contains a series of sensory qualities which are associated with particular traits, values and behaviours. 'Impulses' are said to be carried from one compartment to another by luminous 'threads'. No unisensorial image, such as one sees in fMRI or PET scans, however, would suffice to depict the Desana model of the brain, with its multisensory characteristics. In one Desana image, 'the brain is formed by a bundle of pencil-shaped hexagonal tourmaline crystals' containing 'a sequence of colors which, from bottom to top, express a range of sensibilities' and produce sound waves. Another image of the brain, cited at the head of this chapter, presents it as a humming beehive: 'Each tiny hexagonal container holds honey of a different color, flavor, odor, or texture, or it houses a different stage of insect larval development … ' (Reichel-Dolmatoff 1981: 83).

All of these different compartments of the brain are seen by the Desana as storage places for particular social values. Reichel-Dolmatoff records one occasion when an informant 'pointed rapidly to different areas on an outline of the brain he had drawn and said: "*Here it is prohibited to eat fish; here it is allowed; here one learns to dance* … "' (1981: 84). Significantly these cerebral models are not the domain of specialized individuals (medical experts or constitutional synaesthetes). Nor are they dependent on personal experience of drug-induced synaesthesia. Desana women, who do not customarily partake of hallucinogens, are nonetheless familiar with the trains of sensory and social associations. Thus, among the Desana, synaesthesia is above all a collective social phenomenon, not an idiosyncratic neurological condition, nor even a conceptual artistic device.

It is the task of the Desana shaman to enable people to make the appropriate connections between sensory phenomena and social values and thus trigger the correct behavioural responses. The shaman employs both the sensations experienced during visions and the sights, sounds and smells of daily life to, in the words of the Desana, 'make one see, and act accordingly', 'make one hear, and act accordingly', 'make one smell, and act accordingly' and 'make one dream, and act accordingly'. When the associations are properly engrained, they become automatic and involuntary, a mental 'presence'. Thus, according to the Desana: 'He who truly sees, does not need a personal memory' (Reichel-Dolmatoff 1981: 95). In other words, when sensory stimuli and mental imagery automatically evoke social concepts through continuous association, there is no need for individuals to 'artificially' learn such values through the task of memorization. The associations are collective and seemingly evident.

Coloured knots: numeracy and synaesthesia in the Andes

The orchestration of sensory associations by the Desana makes the colour-grapheme synaesthesia studied by neurologists seem very crude. As the Desana do not have a traditional mode of writing, however, they cannot furnish a counterpart to the synesthetic associations found in the West in relation to letters and numbers. We can find such a counterpart, however, in the cultural area to the southwest of the rainforest where the Desana live, among the traditions of the ancient Inca and present-day Andean peoples. Unlike the graphic signs for recording words and numbers that are used in the West, the Inca method for recording information, the *quipu*, was synaesthetic in its very nature. It consisted of a section of cord with coloured and knotted strings hanging from it. Although anthropologists do not entirely understand how the *quipus* were used by the Incas, we do know that that they were often employed to record numbers. This was done primarily by the use of different kinds of knots, the placement of those knots on the strings and by colour differences and combinations.

The Inca (and contemporary Andean) numerical system was similar to that used in the West in that it was based on multiples of ten. However the method of recording numbers was very different, involving colour, three-dimensional shape and tactility, as well as placement. What might the mental images of numbers have been like for Incas trained to 'read' the coloured knots of the *quipu*? Did the chromatic and tactile nature of the *quipu* signifiers make numbers easier to remember, to mentally 'grasp'? Whatever the answers to such questions, apparently associating numbers with colours was of social utility among the Incas, and not simply a neurological peculiarity.

It seems likely that *quipus* were also used to keep track of information of religious and political importance. In this case, knots and colours could signify different people, objects and actions. Possibly some of the more elaborate *quipus* represented spoken syllables. We don't know the extent to which conventions of representation were standardized for the *quipu*, but it is probable that there was a degree of variation among different localities and perhaps even among *quipu*-makers. Therefore, what one *quipu*-maker thought of as the colour, form and feel of a particular number might not have aligned with another *quipu*-maker's representation of it (Urton 1997, 2003).

The *quipu* lent itself to ritual uses as well, for by ordering and manipulating representations of peoples and things (or their numerical quantities) on its strings, a ritualist might hope to control the people and things themselves (see Salomon 2004). Keeping the particular code of one's own *quipus* a secret would have enhanced their value as objects of power. On a comparative note, there is ample evidence of the ritualistic and magical use of number symbols, written words and letters of the alphabet in European history – and of secret writing systems. However, whereas European writing is two-dimensional, the three-dimensional, material qualities of the *quipu* would have made the concepts – and therefore power – it encoded seem that much more concrete.

Whether a *quipu* was employed to record numbers, things or words, colour might have been used not just as a distinguishing mark, but as a way of adding an extra layer of meaning. This would have been in keeping with the extensive ceremonial use the Incas made of sensory symbolism (Classen 1993b; see also Stevenson 1968: 272). For example, colour might have been used to convey the relative certainty of the information recorded, i.e., whether it was based on eyewitness accounts or hearsay. This was indicated in the spoken language of the Incas, Quechua, and it seems possible that some such device as colour would have been used to convey a similar notion in *quipu* recordings. It might also have been used to suggest the contrasting values of the items being recorded (i.e., male and female) through, for example, an opposition of light and dark threads (Urton 2003).

Although Europeans did not manage to unravel the codes of the *quipus*, its synaesthetic qualities did not go unnoticed. In fact, the *quipu* helped to stimulate discussions about diverse sensory modes of communication. For example, the eighteenth-century writer and collector Horace Walpole reflected, after perusing a *quipu*, that he 'should as soon be able to hold a dialogue with a rainbow' as understand its signification. However, the idea of 'knotting verses' and 'construing by colour' appealed to him and he went on to consider how employing colour might add nuance to written language – 'a straw-colour U would be much more tender than one approaching to orange' – and how a *quipu*-like language, as a textile creation, might even be worn on the body (Walpole 1861: 489–90). Walpole's imaginative response indicates how even a partial knowledge of alternative sensory models and practices can help to open up new avenues of thought.

In the Andes today the Arabic numerals introduced by the Spanish are used to record numbers. Nonetheless, numbers still evoke collective trains of associations. The number 1, for example, is said to look like a hook or stick. It is associated with motherhood, with the thumb, and with the first ear to appear on a corn stalk, among other things. Spatially 1 is located at the top – at the head of the person counting – with the other numbers following behind and below the first number. As regards time, the first number in a sequence is linked with the past and the last number with the future. This layout is consistent with Andean notions of space/time that locate the future behind and below (Urton 1997; Classen 1993b). Single-digit numbers are often conceptualized in terms of their supposed birth order from the 'generating' number 1, giving them pseudo-familial relationships with each other. The most disliked number is 7. This number, which represents no 'proper' grouping in the Andes and cannot be evenly divided, is described as ugly, adulterous and devilish. Its name, *qanchis*, is said to resemble the discordant braying of a donkey. We lack information as to what, if any, colours are associated with different numbers, except in the case of 1 which is linked with the purple colour at the top of a rainbow (Urton 1997). (It is said to be dangerous to count the colours of the rainbow as this would involve separating hues that are merged in a synthetic unity.)

Some of these kinds of associations might be deemed 'metaphorical' (which, as will be recalled, is a dismissive term in the discourse of the neuroscientist). However, others – the spatial conceptualization of numbers, their perceived integration through family relationships, or the depiction of 7 as a nasty fellow – would have the kind of automatic perceptual 'reality' characteristic of the associations made by 'true' synaesthetes. What is called 'number form' synaesthesia by psychologists, in fact, consists of having a mental layout for numbers that positions them in space. 'Ordinal-linguistic' synaesthesia, in turn, consists of imagining numbers or letters as having social relationships or personalities. Thus, 5, for example, might be described as good-natured and generous, and the wife of 6 (Simner and Holenstein 2007).

If someone from an Andean community, making the traditional kinds of number associations described above, were to be examined by a psychologist interested in cross-modal perceptions no doubt she or he would be deemed a 'synaesthete'. The difference, however, would be that Andean cross-modal associations have been shaped by cultural conventions and therefore, can no longer be classified as neurological 'oddities'. In the West, where numbers are conceptualized as 'untainted' by social and sensory considerations, the kinds of associations made by synaesthetes can be seen as extraneous mental baggage. In traditional Andean communities, where numbers carry cultural as well as numerical values, to be without such 'baggage' would mean being disconnected from the web of social significance.

Ritual synaesthesia in ancient China

The range of cross-modal associations made by the Desana and present-day Andeans, while complex, are by no means unique. Many societies around the world have employed synaesthetic associations to express social values. In the ancient Chinese 'Theory of the Five Elements', each of the principal elements of Wood, Fire, Earth, Metal and Water corresponded to an odour, taste, colour, musical tone, season and direction. Thus, the element of Fire was associated with a smoky scent, a bitter taste, a red colour, the musical tone *chih*, the season of summer and the direction of south. The element of Water was associated with a rotten smell, a salt taste, the colour black, the musical tone *yu*, the winter season and the direction north (see Meade and Emch 2010: 436; Jütte 2005: 25–31).

At its most ritualistic – for example, in the ceremonial life of the emperor and his court – the application of such correspondences determined all aspects of daily life, including diet, perfume, colour of dress and the orientation of living space for each month of the year. One ritual prescription for the emperor's conduct in the first month of spring, for instance, states that:

> The Son of Heaven shall live in the apartment to the left of the Green Bright Hall. He shall ride in a belled chariot driven by dark green dragons [horses] and bearing green flags. He shall wear green clothes with green jade. He shall eat wheat and mutton.
>
> (cited by Henderson 2011 [1984]: 53)

Numerology played an important role in the Chinese system, with different numbers linked to specific trains of sensory values. Number 5, a key figure for establishing sets in Chinese cosmology, was linked with traits deemed to be pleasant and associated with the element of Earth, a yellow colour, a sweet taste, a fragrant smell and the musical note *gong*. The negatively perceived number 6, in contrast, was linked with the 'watery' qualities of black, salty, putrid and the musical note of *yu* (Wang 2000:122). Traditional Chinese medicine (with its elaborate calculus of flavours) also made use of these correspondences in its treatment regimens for diverse maladies (Farquhar 2002; Classen et al. 1994: 119–21).

While the cross-modal associations of ancient Chinese cosmology and court etiquette might appear purely symbolic, the fact that they were ritualized transformed them into lived experience or 'ways of sensing'. That is, while the associations were based on conceptual schemes, the *way* they were rendered sensible through being embedded in dress codes, perfume use, concerts, meals, architecture, and so forth made them *material* to the constitution of the bodies and psyches of the courtiers. Some of these linkages may seem more 'natural' than others, such as the correspondence between fire, a smoky scent and the colour red, but the point is that it would have been abnormal for a subject cognitively and perceptually trained in this system of categorization not to experience *all* these cross-modal associations as given in the order of things.

The attention paid to ritually reproducing the proper relations *between* sensations in ancient Chinese culture was of a piece with the importance attached to maintaining the proper relations between persons. Indeed, it remains the case that Confucianism (the ancient doctrine that in certain respects continues to provide the unwritten constitution of Chinese society) is distinguished by its 'refusal to conceptualize individuals in any way other than relational – as children, parents, lovers, youngsters, oldsters, employees, employers and on and on' (Glenn 2010: 337). In the words of one Chinese official:

> Heaven and Earth have their patterns, and people take these for their patterns ... [Among these patterns are] the five tastes, manifested in five colors and displayed in the five notes. When these are in excess, there ensue obscurity and confusion, and people lose their nature. That is why they were made to support that nature ... There were ruler and minister, high and low, in imitation of the righteousness of Earth. There were husband and wife, with the home and the world outside as their divided duties [the home being the female sphere]. There were father and son, elder and younger brother ...
>
> (cited by Wang 2000: 184)

The sensory and social patterns deemed to be 'set in the stars' (although in fact laboured over and systematized by diligent courtiers) constrained both rulers and subjects, with everyone expected to play his or her proper role in the cosmic dance. Each individual was a bundle of roles, a nexus of relationships. This makes it abundantly clear how sensory correspondences were mapped onto social relations. Thinking and living according to the established pattern of cross-modal connections provided a potent model for the maintenance of orderly and interdependent relationships within society.

Such a comprehensive set of sensory associations, like that of the Desana, would leave limited room for idiosyncratic synaesthetic perceptions. In a similar way the social coding of the letters of the alphabet with sounds in the West prevents the formation of idiosyncratic aural associations with letters in literate individuals. (It would take a good deal of mental effort for someone trained to read English to associate CAT with the sound 'reb', for example.)

It bears underlining that the associations made with concepts can be radically different across cultures. The Chinese saw the cardinal direction of south as red, for example, while the Maya saw it as yellow (Sharer 2006: 147). In the Andes the future is traditionally understood and felt to be located behind one's back (Classen 1993b); in the West the future is understood and felt to be located in front of one. While these associations are arbitrary, each will seem correct and almost self-evident to the people whose mental landscape it shapes.

Cultural synaesthesia in the West: historical examples

While the examples of cultural synaesthesia given above may seem exotic from a Western perspective, they are not without parallels in Western history. In premodernity, we can find many complex sensory and social associations being made. This is especially the case in Christian symbol and ritual, where blue was a customary colour of the Virgin Mary, incense was the olfactory counterpart of prayer, groupings of three represented the Trinity, and so on. Such commonly understood metaphors were supplemented by more esoteric systems of sensory, numerical and cosmological correspondences elaborated within alchemical and mystical contexts. These systems owed much to the schemes of planetary correspondences advanced in antiquity, which, in turn, had similarities with the Chinese cosmological orders discussed above. The prevalence of such associations meant that the world could be understood as a multisensory tapestry of material symbols.

The more concrete and sensuous a concept could be made, the more appealing and memorable and – for many – the truer it seemed. Thus saintliness that manifested itself in the form of a perceptible fragrance was taken for true saintliness by the mass of people, whereas saintliness that did not was suspect (see Classen 1998: ch. 3). Indeed, it seemed logical at the time for transcendent qualities and entities to have material expressions or counterparts. After all, God himself, according to Christian belief, had become incarnate – material and sensate – in the person of Jesus Christ.

One evidence of this desire for concrete experience is the emphasis on the tactile qualities of speech in medieval literature. For example, the following line from the fifteenth-century ballad 'The Tournament of Tottenham' conveys the rough-and-tumble feel of a wrestling match through its rolling r's: 'Among thes wery boyes he wrest and wrang./He threw tham down to the erth and thrust thaim amang' (cited in Anderson 1998: 205). The tactile qualities of words as felt in the mouth and throat gave an added sense of materiality and physical power to verbal accounts.

The alphabet was also drawn into these systems of correlations. Up until the end of the Middle Ages, and to a limited extent even today, the alphabet provided the figures for numbers – Roman numerals. Associations were also made between letters and musical notes, which survives today in the ABC-DEFG system of pitch names. In ancient Greece the alphabet similarly provided the figures for numbers. Furthermore, perceived connections between the seven vowels and the seven planets 'made these seven Greek letters part of a vast range of planetary "sympathies" used in astrology, alchemy and magic, including incenses, precious stones, metals, flowers, herbs, colors, musical notes, emotions, virtues and vices' (Barry 1999: 44). The following example of a ritual associating the Greek vowels with different directions and body positions may read like a fitness routine today, but at the time represented an integration of the body of the individual with the sacred power of the cosmos:

> Speaking to the rising sun, stretch out your right hand to the left and your left hand likewise to the left and say 'A'. To the North, putting forward only your right fist, say 'EE'. Then to the West, extending both hands in front of you, say 'HHH' [long e]. To the South holding both on your stomach, say 'IIII'. To the Earth, bending over and touching the ends of your toes, say 'OOOOO'.
>
> (cited in Barry 1999: 37)

Mystical and magical associations and uses were also made with the letters of the Hebrew alphabet (which were said to contain the names of God within their forms) and with the Latin alphabet in the Middle Ages (Yates 2011: 179, 189).

Most commonly in Western history we find sensory associations being made with letters of the alphabet for didactic purposes. Thus, in popular pictorial alphabets letters were depicted as objects: A as an open ladder, B as a bulging lute, C as a curved horn, and so on. This practice reminds us of the fact that the letters of the first alphabets were themselves pictorial in nature and not simply abstract signs for linguistic sounds. Hence in the Phoenician alphabet 'A' – aleph – was an ox, and 'B' – bet – was a house (making the underlying meaning of the word alphabet 'oxhouse'). It is interesting to speculate on the kind of synaesthesia this pictorialization of the alphabet might have induced. In another common sensory technique for teaching the alphabet, letters would be made from gingerbread, which a child could eat after naming them correctly, thus imbuing visual signs with taste and texture (a practice that also survives today in different forms, such as alphabet soup).

In order to fix the sounds that went with the letters of the alphabet in one's memory, it was recommended that each letter or letter combination be associated with an image whose name contained the correct sound. Hence, in

English, L could be associated with the image (and shape) of an elbow, a word that contained the 'L' sound. The written syllable 'AB', it was said, could be linked in the learner's mind with a picture of an abbot. Its reverse, 'BA', could be signified by an abbot standing upside down. Sounding out the letter combination 'BAL', it was then suggested, might be achieved through associating it with an image of an upside-down abbot chewing on an elbow. Lively and even grotesque images such as this were recommended as being highly memorable (Carruthers 2008: 170). While they might seem excessive to adult readers today, who have forgotten the many laborious hours they spent learning their ABCs as children, these systems reflect the considerable difficulties involved in mastering the written word.

Numerals might also be memorized using associated imagery. In his treatise on memorization, the medieval monk Hugh of St. Victor advised constructing a mental number line in imaginary space: 'Make this conception and this way of imagining ... practiced and habitual, so that you conceive of the limit and extent of all numbers visually, just as though [they were] placed in particular places' (cited in Carruthers 2008: 340). This today would be known as 'number-form synaesthesia'.

The memorization of texts similarly employed a range of mental sensory cues. 'It is of great value for fixing a memory image,' Hugh of St. Victor wrote, 'that when we read books, we strive to impress on our memory not only the number and order of verses or ideas, but at the same time the color, shape, position and placement of the letters' (cited in Carruthers 2008: 342). One can see from such texts that part of the reason for illuminating manuscripts with coloured letters and pictures in the Middle Ages would have been to make their contents easier to fix in the memory. In order to store large amounts of information the mental construction of a 'house of memory' was recommended. Each room of this house would be coloured differently and contain a sequence of ideas embodied in the form of striking figures who interact with each other so as to readily evoke the required train of thought (Carruthers 2008; Yates 2011).

In his treatise on the art of memorization Jacobus Publicius spoke of the memory as 'buried in a dark prison ... far from the senses'. Sensory associations, he argued, helped give the memory the vividness it lacked: 'simple and spatial intentions slip easily from the memory unless joined to a corporeal similitude'. With regards to the letters of the alphabet, he declared 'the combination of letters and material objects brings us a great, immeasurable, and almost divine advantage' (Yates 2011: 117–18; Carruthers and Ziolkowski 2004: 249).

The difference between such memorization techniques involving sensuous imagery and the sensory signs and correlations employed by the Church, or by synaesthetic cultures like that of the Desana, is that, as regards the former, it is largely left up to the individual to decide which colour or which figure to associate with an idea, letter, or number. This is because in the case of memorization the image employed is only a device to help recall a particular concept, and is not usually considered to carry any symbolic weight of its own. However, in both cases there is an underlying assumption that the ability to make synaesthetic mental connections is a general one and that, once made, the practice of calling up associations will become automatic.

Gaps, loops, and intersections: neurology and culture

There is evidently a considerable gap between the neurological approach to perception and the cultural approach presented above. In order to overcome this gap, the cross-cultural psychiatrist Laurence Kirmayer has proposed that there be greater recognition of the ways in which the organization of the mind 'is not confined to the brain but also includes loops through the body and the environment, most crucially, through a social world that is culturally constructed' (quoted in Howes 2011: 165–66). Neuropsychologists, with their focus on tracking neural impulses from receptor organ to brain and their examination of how different brain areas light up in MRI images, have not been very receptive to considering the impact of social factors, and thus of cultural variation, on neurology. As an example of this blindspot, consider the fact that in all the 900-plus pages of *The Handbook of Multisensory Processes*, there is but one reference to cross-cultural variation in the modulation of perception: it is noted that the McGurk effect is weaker in test subjects in Japan than in the United States (Bernstein et al. 2004: 207).

An obvious disadvantage arising from the disinclination to consider cultural differences in neurological studies of perception, is that it limits approaches to those that may be conceptualized within the researcher's own culture. There are no external paradigms or practices – no *quipu* – to spark new ways of thinking about the issue. There is also no possibility of qualifying universalizations of data with examples to the contrary from other cultures. For instance, as regards synaesthesia, it has been argued that there are 'strong anatomical constraints that permit certain types of cross-activation but not others' (Ramachandran et al. 2004: 877). One type of cross-activation that is presumed to be blocked is smell-hearing synaesthesia, according to neuropsychologists Richard Stevenson and Robert Boakes. 'Odors display taste properties,' they write, hence smell-taste synaesthesia is possible, 'but do not elicit auditory or visual sensations' (Stevenson and Boakes 2004: 73), which rules out smell-hearing synaesthesia. There can be no 'loud' smells, therefore (or, for that matter, 'blue' smells).

However, there are reports of coloured-smelling being a commonplace among the Pitjantjatjara people of the Australian Western Desert (see Young 2005) just as there are reports of smell-hearing synaesthesia being a common phenomenon in Melanesia. For example, in many languages of Papua New Guinea one speaks of 'hearing an odour'. This locution is even carried over in Tok Pisin (Pidgin English) as 'mi harim smel' – 'I hear a smell'. The experiential basis for this association could be that most communication takes place face-to-face (i.e., within olfactory range of the other) and odoriferous substances (e.g., anointing the body with aromatic oil, chewing ginger) are used to augment the power of a person's presence and words (Howes 2003: 74–76, 146–50).

This association between smell and hearing is not unique to Melanesia. For example, among the Dogon of Mali, it is understood that speech has 'material properties that are more than just sound'. Speech, in fact, has an 'odour'. Sound and odour, which are understood to have vibration as their common origin, are considered 'so near to one another that the Dogon speak of "hearing a smell"' (Calame-Griaule 1986: 39, 48 n69). Western culture is not without its parallels to such cases, for in Christian tradition there is the association of prayer with incense and of the name of Jesus with fragrance (partly based on the biblical text: 'Thy name is as ointment poured forth' [Song of Solomon 1:2–4]). While these last may be thought of as purely metaphorical, accounts show that, in medieval mystical practices, at least, people might actually experience these perceptual associations as real. These instances of audio-olfactory synaesthesia contradict the claim regarding the discreteness of olfactory and auditory sensations. Plainly it is not outside either neurological nor cultural possibility for auditory sensations to be given olfactory properties.

The notion that neurologists who study 'true' synaesthesia are somehow bypassing the cultural is, in any case, belied by the fact that what is taken to be the paradigmatic example of synaesthesia, colour-grapheme synaesthesia, is dependent on the very cultural process and product of writing (i.e., graphemes). And writing, let us keep in mind, has been an exceptional practice, rather than the norm, in the history of humanity. This is a fact which Ramachandran and his colleagues, focused on inner channels of communication rather than on the influence of external channels (or 'loops' in Kirmayer's terminology), such as writing, elide in their search for the biological basis of synaesthesia.

Synaesthesia in the expanded field

The role of learning in the formation of intermodal associations *has* been discussed by certain psychologists interested in synaesthesia. Lawrence Marks (1978), for example, has argued that the notion that blues and greens are 'cool' colours, while reds, oranges and browns are relatively 'warm' reflects associations that are acquired through social and perceptual experience. Marks bases his argument on his observation that 'preadolescent children do not reliably perceive or judge the colors orange and brown to be warmer than blue and green unless the children have been explicitly *taught* this scheme' (L.E. Marks 2000: 128, emphasis added). Marks has also noted that the letters of the alphabet that figure as the inducing stimuli in the case of colour-grapheme synaesthesia are not raw sense data, but rather are learned within a particular culture of literacy (2000: 125–27). Other examples of studies that point to the role of learning and perceptual experience in the formation of synaesthetic perceptions include Stevenson and Boakes' (2004) account of smell-taste synaesthesia, and the varieties of colour-sound synaesthesia discussed by Marks (2000) and van Campen (2010).

Marks and like-minded psychologists take a much broader view of synaesthesia than neuropsychologists such as Ramachandran. Marks, however, still uses the term 'strong synaesthesia' to refer to the congenital condition of interest to neurologists and 'weak synaesthesia' to refer to experientially-based and cultural instances of synaesthesia. 'Strong' synaesthesia is said to be characterized by traits such as automaticity, intensity, and consistency over time that are lacking from 'weak' synaesthesia (see Marks 1978: chs. 7–8; 2000). Yet these traits of 'strong' (or 'congenital') synaesthesia would equally well characterize the cultural – and, therefore, supposedly 'weak' – synaesthesia experienced by the Desana, who find that their shared sensory associations are so automatic, intense and consistent that, as will be recalled, they obviate the need for a 'personal memory'.

In fact, if cultural synaesthesia were not strong, it would be of limited social use. The nineteenth-century scholar of synaesthesia, Francis Galton, reported that synaesthetes were 'scandalized and almost angry at the heresy' of those whose sensory associations differed from their own, who saw 'A' as green, rather than red, for example (Anderson 1998: 197). It is precisely this characteristic of cross-modal associations to seem true and evident to those who hold them that gives them such potential importance as media of social values.

Thus, among, the Desana the colour purple automatically and seemingly naturally triggers images of putrid smells and of social and physical pollution. In the Andes, numbers automatically trigger thoughts of kinship relations. In Western social history (as was discussed in Chapter 3), a dark-coloured skin came to be associated with an unpleasant smell and with social undesirability. As George Orwell noted, these culturally-acquired perceptual associations are so engrained and come to seem so objectively true that they are highly difficult to overcome. It is this insistence and seeming truth of perceptual associations, once firmly made, that give the sensory values and correlations of a culture such psychological force. If such experiences of cultural synaesthesia are dependent on the presence of certain neural interconnections then these must not be as unusual as neurologists assume, or else cross-modal associations could not be as commonly and deeply held by members of a society as they are.

Not all cultural synaesthesia is necessarily intense. Where synaesthetic values are not strongly held, associations may be weak. In cases where no connection with an important social value is promoted, a cross-modal association may also be relatively weak, or more a matter of metaphor than of 'feeling', as in the case of poetic synaesthesia. Indeed, it may be that what is known as congenital synaesthesia is similarly not always intense and consistent. Where one synaesthete might be certain that 'A' is red, another might waver between two colours, or have only fleeting sensations of colour. By excluding individuals with the latter experiences from their studies, however, neurologists are able to claim that 'true' synaesthesia fits the criteria they have set for it, i.e., that it is intense and consistent.

Individuals with a particular propensity (which may well be congenital) to make cross-modal connections may come up with their own associations where culture does not dictate those to be made. For example, in the literate West, our culture tells us which sound to associate with each letter of the alphabet (and also which musical note in the case of the first seven letters) but not which colour. Individuals, disposed to extend the train of associations – or simply repulsed by the monochrome monotony of printed letters – may come up with their own connections. Individuals may also learn such colour associations. This has been documented in cases of 'Fisher-Price synaesthesia', where colour-grapheme associations were evidently based on exposure to commercially-produced sets of coloured letters (Witthoft and Winawer 2013). (It would be interesting, in this regard, to see if the colour-grapheme associations of young Western adults are more likely to reflect the bright colours of the alphabet blocks and toys of their childhood than those of older adults who grew up in a less colour-intense environment.)

Likely a combination of factors – exposure to coloured letters in print or as models, associations with the initial letters in colour terms ('B' is blue, because blue starts with 'B'), consideration of the appearance of a letter ('O' is white because it makes a white circle on white paper) – are at play in the construction of the coloured alphabets of most synaesthetes, and not simply random neurological impulses. As there are no collective norms for such associations, their nature and extent will vary widely. Only in certain cases, one example being where the meaning of a written word has strong sensory associations – 'fire' with redness or 'orange' with 'orangeness' – will there be more general agreement. This is a situation that the Desana, no doubt, or the ancient Chinese, would think a recipe for social chaos. To understand why this is not the case in contemporary culture we have to delve into the social history of the senses in the West.

The creation of the modern Western sensorium

What produces the perception of synaesthesia being an abnormal or idiosyncratic condition? Could there be a connection between individualism and sensory isolationism on the one hand (as exemplified by the modern West) and between the relational person and sensory interrelation or correspondence on the other (as seen in many traditional societies)? Whereas neurologists hold that congenital synaesthesia results from a lack of cerebral pruning, might not the decline of cultural synaesthesia in the West be the result of an abundance of social pruning?

The processes that led to the separating out of persons and senses in the West included, as described in previous chapters, the decline of feudal society, the growth of cities, the mechanization of society, and the heightened value given to analytic thinking. Another important factor is the enormous increase in literacy in modernity. Not only did writing provide a model for individualism in the transformation of an experientially organic whole – speech – into sequences of bits – letters, it also enabled information of social importance to be separated from the collective memory. One reason why modern

Westerners do not feel compelled to make more collective sensory associations, in fact, may be precisely because we rely on our collective knowledge being stored outside of human bodies and minds in written texts.

These processes and practices infiltrated society at different rates. Although writing, for example, was known from antiquity, texts were scarce and most people remained non-literate until the modern period. Speech, intermingled as it is with smells and sights, and even touches, made communicating a multisensory experience. Even among literate persons, the oral model held sway. The emphasis on techniques of memorization in the Middle Ages, for example, was the consequence of an age in which written manuscripts were not always at hand and in which oral exposition was highly valued. In fact, the medieval emphasis on associating letters and texts with material signs could be understood as part of a drive to re-embody the speech-world that had been disembodied and dismembered by writing. (This indeed raises the question of the extent to which the kinds of synaesthesia – colour-grapheme, number-form – of interest to neuropsychologists might arise as a response to the cognitive experience of writing, independently of any alleged genetic mutation.)

The notion of individual sensory faculties itself took time to become established across Western societies. In Old English, for example, we do not find the five-sense division to which we are so accustomed today. The word *smec*, for instance, stood for both smell and taste. In the medieval poem *Piers Ploughman* the five 'senses' are given as 'Sirs See-well, Hear-well, Say-well, Work-well-with-thine-hand, and Godfrey Go-well' (walking). The notion of the five senses being sight, hearing, smell, taste and touch was 'a learned Roman idea' and translating it posed difficulties for medieval English writers who tried to convey its sense in the words of a culture that had not articulated this particular division of experience (Anderson 2001: 117; see further Geurts 2002: 37–38 *passim*).

Even when the fivefold division of sensation became the norm, the Aristotelian notion of there being a governing and unifying 'common sense' (*sensus communis*) was long accepted. By the seventeenth century, however, 'the common sense' had disappeared, and the sensorium lost its wholeness (see Howes 2009: 15–20; also Heller-Roazen 2008; Gavrilyuk and Coakley 2012). While there would be some who countered this tendency – notably the French philosopher Charles Fourier, who conceptualized a whole utopian world based on synaesthetic associations (Classen 1998: 24–27) – in general, the consolidation of individualism and of the individuation of the senses proceeded apace in the eighteenth and nineteenth centuries.

During the nineteenth century, the period when the fully-formed modern individual finally emerged, the 'dissection' of the sensorium continued with the 'discovery' of the 'movement' sense of kinaesthesia, along with separate receptors for pain, pressure, temperature, balance, and so forth (Wade 2009; Howes 2009: 23) This was a period of extraordinary productivity as regards the invention of instruments and protocols for gauging sensory thresholds. These instruments included Lovibond's tintometer (for testing visual acuity),

Politzer's Hörmesser (for measuring auditory sensitivity), Zwaardemaker's olfactometer (for distinguishing smells), and the algometer (formerly a torture device) for measuring pain thresholds, to mention but a few (see Richards 1998). Inspired by Müller's 'doctrine of specific nerve energies' and Fechner's Law regarding the functional relation between sensation and stimulus, attention came to focus on the 'just noticeable difference' – that is, 'the magnitude of the stimulus needed to generate the very least noticeable sensation over and above the stimulus that is unnoticed by the human sensorium' (Crary 1990: 146). This delimitation of the bounds of each of the senses by experimental means was complemented by the identification of the 'areas' of each of the senses in the brain (Dias 2004). In this way, sensing came to be regarded as a psychophysical process, devoid of any particular moral or cultural import, and the mixing of the senses came to be viewed as an aberration.

A parallel development in modernity consisted in the rise of the notion of 'pure' science, a field that deals with underlying 'truths' and that supposedly exists and progresses 'untainted' by social or religious concerns and unaffected by cultural differences. We can find this expressed in the field of mathematics, for example, in the idea that numbers and numerical operations are abstract truths that are neither sensible, spatial, nor subjective, and that exist independently of the social world (see Urton 1997: 16–17). A similar, although less dogmatic, development occurred as regards the understanding of writing. The letters of the alphabet lost their old religious or mystical values, and associating letters with pictures and colours came to be considered childish. Print, with its stark, uniform, disconnected black letters, discouraged any such 'sentimentalism' at the same time as it removed any traces of personality – such as would be expressed by handwriting – from the page. Little wonder that in such circumstances ideas of letters and numbers having colours, personal traits or social relations came to be seen as abnormal.

While these developments were taking place, a countertrend was occurring in art. A broad range of artists, reacting against the scientific rationalism of the day, rediscovered the concept of sensory correlations and began to experiment with expressing a unity of sensation in their art (as discussed in Chapter 1). Almost a century after the coloured knots of the *quipu* inspired Horace Walpole to think about coloured vowels, the poet Arthur Rimbaud wrote a highly-influential poem, 'Voyelles', in which he described the vowels as having different colours: 'A black, E white, I red, U green, O blue … ' (Rimbaud might have been influenced in his choices by an alphabet of coloured letters popular during his childhood in which the vowels had almost the same colours, or by the colour symbolism of alchemy [Starkie 1968: 165].) This, along with writings and works by other artists which merged colours with sounds or sounds with odours, precipitated a flood of speculations on possible cross-modal correspondences.

Scientific thinkers generally saw these artists as indulging in fanciful at best and degenerate at worst tendencies. One acerbic spokesman for the latter view was the German physician Max Nordau, who considered the synaesthetic strivings of contemporary poets and artists 'symptoms of degeneracy and cultural decline, an aesthetic effort to valorize a reversal of the progressive specialization of the human senses to the most basic level of undifferentiated perception' (cited in Latham 2000: 9). Nordau, in fact, thought it quite likely that the artistic phenomenon of synaesthesia was symptomatic not only of mental illness but of 'diseased brain activity' (1910 [1895]: 142).

What troubled Nordau and like-minded thinkers about synaesthesia in the arts was the border transgressions and categorical mixings it suggested, both within the brain of the individual, who would no longer be able to think rationally, and within society, which, if it became 'contaminated' with such ideas, would dissolve into a similar confused morass (Latham 2000). However, as scientists were not, after all, insulated from social trends, the cultural interest in synaesthesia did stimulate research into the phenomenon in the late nineteenth century (Dann 1998: 26–34).

In the twentieth century, as society became ever more individualized and social life compartmentalized, and as mechanization and modern warfare fostered a sense of fragmentation, synaesthesia generally lost its interest. It seemed the product of soft, fuzzy thinking in an age that demanded clear minds and cold, hard facts. Synaesthesia could no longer be taken seriously. (The rise of Behaviourism, with its focus on observable behaviour over unobservable states of mind also contributed to the decline of interest in synaesthesia.) The influential psychologist and Nazi supporter, E.R. Jaensch went so far as to define the 'synaesthetic personality' as a weak and effeminate 'antitype' characterized by 'perceptual slovenliness'. Combining notions of sensory intermixtures with ethnic intermixtures, Jaensch held that this undesirable type was probably the result of 'mixed-race heredity' (Brown 2004: 39). Such negative attitudes evidently did not make synaesthesia a condition or practice to cultivate. Fortunately for the well-being of society (according to this view), it was decided that synaesthesia was a rare condition, most common among artists and other 'marginal' individuals. This psychological perspective coincided with a move towards visualism and abstraction in art (see Jones 2005) and a general dismissal of synaesthesia as a valid topic for consideration in the social sciences and humanities. One literary scholar, interested in onomatopoeia and other synaesthetic 'ideophones' recalls, for example, that until recently such an interest was thought to place one on the 'lunatic fringe' (Anderson 2001).

During most of the twentieth century, little work was carried out on synaesthesia. Once it stopped being a significant cultural manifestation it came to be regarded as unimportant to mainstream psychological research. What then accounts for the flowering of interest in synaesthesia at the turn of the twenty-first century? As noted previously, multisensory integration has recently gained ground as an organizing paradigm in neuroscience (Calvert et al. 2004). It has also trickled down to inform many popular accounts of how the sensorium functions (e.g., Brynie 2009: 185–89; Rosenblum 2010). There are even calls for synaesthesia to be brought 'into the mainstream of neuroscience and cognitive psychology' (Ramachandran et al. 2004: 881; see also

Cytowic 1993; Baron-Cohen and Harrison 1997). Furthermore, far from being thought a very rare condition, synaesthesia is now said by some researchers to be relatively common (Simner et al. 2006).

It is surely no coincidence that within contemporary society we find a parallel rise of interest in boundary-crossing social integrations and in cultural practices of synaesthesia. The former is stimulated by the World Wide Web, and by the global migration of peoples and interpenetration of cultures. As Clifford Geertz put it: '*Les milieux* are all *mixte*' (2000: 68). The new cultural fascination with sensory crossovers, in turn, finds expression in the recent explosion of personal and popular accounts of synaesthetic experiences (van Campen 2010; Seaberg 2011), in mixed-media art (Jones 2006; Schwartzman 2011), and, as we saw in the previous chapter, in synaesthesia trending in marketing. This last has given us fruit colours for computers (iMac), used music to intensify the flavour of coffee (Starbucks), and inundated us with such slogans as 'You've never seen a taste like this before' (Crystal Pepsi), 'The loudest taste on earth' (Doritos) and 'Listen and you'll see' (B&W loud-speakers). Marketers are also hard at work instilling a form of ordinal-linguistic synaesthesia in the public by designing products whose sensory aspects will lead them to be attributed personalities by consumers (see van Gorp and Adams 2012).

If neuroscientists and psychologists were to reflect on the links between scientific practice and the social trends we have been describing, and thereby recognize how their research interests (just as those of historians and anthropologists) take shape within a particular cultural context, then perhaps they might also see how synaesthesia can be shaped by culture as well as by biology. Perhaps they would even come to appreciate that science might not be the only or ultimate provider of insights about the nature of sensory experience. At that point a truly interdisciplinary and cross-cultural conversation can begin.

References

Acland, C. (2012) *Swift Viewing: The Popular Life of Subliminal Influence*, Durham, NC: Duke University Press.

Akkad, O.E. (2012) 'Canadian court clears way to trademark sounds', *The Globe and Mail*, March 28.

Alibhai, A.A.H. (2008) 'From sound to light: the changing symbolism of bells in Medieval Iberia in Christian and Muslim contexts', unpublished thesis, Southern Methodist University.

Allen, A. (2011) *Unpopular Privacy: Why Must We Hide?* Oxford: Oxford University Press.

Altick, R.D. (1976) *The Shows of London*, Cambridge, MA: Harvard College.

Anderson, B. (1991) *Imagined Communities: Reflection on the Origin and Spread of Nationalism*, revised edition, London: Verso.

Anderson, E.R. (1998) *A Grammar of Iconism*, Cranbury, NJ: Associated University Presses.

——(2001) 'Old English poets and their Latin sources: iconicity in Caedmon's Hymn and The Phoenix', in O. Fischer and M. Nanny (eds) *The Motivated Sign: Iconicity, Language and Literature*, Amsterdam: John Benjamins.

Anker, K. (2005) 'The truth in painting: cultural artefacts as proof of native title', *Law Text Culture*, 9: 91–123.

Arnold, K. (2003) 'Skulls, mummies and unicorns' horns: medicinal chemistry in early English museums', in R.G.W. Anderson, M.L. Caygill, A.G. MacGregor, and L. Syson (eds) *Enlightening the British: Knowledge, Discovery and the Museum in the Eighteenth Century*, London: British Museum Press.

——(2006) *Cabinets for the Curious: Looking Back at Early English Museums*, Aldershot: Ashgate.

Arnould, E. (1989) 'Toward a broadened theory of preference formation and the diffusion of innovations: cases from Zinder Province, Niger Republic', *Journal of Consumer Research*, 16: 239–66

Arudou, D. (2012) 'An introduction to Japanese society's attitudes towards race and skin color', in R.E. Hall (ed.) *The Melanin Millennium: Skin Color as 21st Century Discourse*, New York: Springer Dordrecht Heidelberg.

Associated Press (1984) 'Judge who is blind', *Associated Press*, June 24.

Bacci, F. and Melcher, D. (eds) (2011) *Art and the Senses*, Oxford: Oxford University Press.

Baer, M.D. (2011) *Honoured by the Glory of Islam: Conversion and Conquest in Ottoman Europe*, Oxford: Oxford University Press.

Barcan, R. (2011) *Complementary and Alternative Medicine: Bodies, Therapies, Senses*, Oxford: Berg.

Barnes, D.S. (forthcoming) 'The senses in medicine: seeing, hearing and smelling disease', in C. Classen (ed.) *A Cultural History of the Senses in the Age of Empire, 1800–1920*, London: Bloomsbury.

Baron-Cohen, S. and Harrison, J. (eds) (1997) *Synaesthesia: Classic and Contemporary Readings*, Oxford: Blackwells.

Barry, K. (1999) *The Greek Qabalah: Alphabetic Mysticism and Numerology in the Ancient World*, York Beach, ME: Samuel Weiser.

Bartlett, R. (1988) *Trials by Fire and Water: The Medieval Judicial Ordeal*, Oxford: Clarendon.

Bastien, J.W. (1985) *Mountain of the Condor: Metaphor and Ritual in an Andean Ayllu*, Prospect Heights, IL: Waveland Press.

Bateson, G. and Mead, M. (1942) *Balinese Character: A Photographic Analysis*, New York: New York Academy of Sciences.

Baudelaire, C. (1975) *Selected Poems*, trans. J. Richardson, Harmondsworth: Penguin.

Baudrillard, J. (1981) *For a Critique of the Political Economy of the Sign*, trans. C. Levin, Minneapolis, MN: University of Minnesota Press.

——(1996) *The System of Objects*, trans. J. Benedict, London: Verso.

Bay, T. (2007) 'Anti-SLAPP statute held not protective of freedom of religion', *Metropolitan News Enterprise*, April 26, www.metnews.com/articles/2007/cast042607.htm (accessed January 15, 2013).

BBC News (2012) 'Bishop of Chelmsford calls on Cadbury to "relax" on purple', *BBC News*, October 10, www.bbc.co.uk/news/england-essex-19895695 (accessed January 15, 2013).

Bedos-Rezak, B. (1996) 'Secular administration', in F.A.C. Mantello and A.G. Rigg (eds) *Medieval Latin*, Washington, DC: Catholic University of America Press.

Belli, M.M., with R.B. Kaiser (1976) *Melvin Belli: My Life on Trial*, New York: Morrow.

Bendix, R. and Brenneis, D. (eds) (2005) 'The senses', *Etnofoor*, 18(1) special issue.

Berg, J. W., Appelbaum, P.S., Lidz, C.W., and Parker, L.S. (2001) *Informed Consent: Legal Theory and Clinical Practice*, Oxford: Oxford University Press.

Berger, J. (1972) *Ways of Seeing*, London: BBC Books.

Bernstein, L., Auer, E. and Moore, J. (2004) 'Audiovisual speech binding', in G. Calvert, C. Spence, and B. Stein (eds) *The Handbook of Multisensory Processes*, Cambridge, MA: MIT Press.

Berry, J.W., Poortinga, Y.H., Breugelmans, S.M., Chasiotis, A. and Sam, D.L. (2011) *Cross-Cultural Psychology: Research and Applications*, 3rd edn, Cambridge: Cambridge University Press.

Blackman, L. (2012) *Immaterial Bodies: Affect, Embodiment, Mediation*, London: Sage.

Blanks, D.R. and Frassetto, M. (1999) *Western Views of Islam in Medieval and Early Modern Europe*, New York: St Martin's Press.

Bleakley, A., Farrow, R., Gould, D. and Marshall, R. (2003) 'Making sense of clinical reasoning: judgement and the evidence of the senses', *Medical Education*, 37(6): 544–52.

Blum, M. (2001) 'Remaking the East German past: Ostalgie, identity, and material culture', *Journal of Popular Culture*, 34(3): 229–53.

Boatwright, M.T. (2012) *Peoples of the Roman World*, Cambridge: Cambridge University Press.

Bogdashina, O. (2003) *Sensory Perceptual Issues in Autism and Asperger Syndrome: Different Sensory Experiences, Different Perceptual Worlds*, London: Jessica Kingsley.

Borell, M. (1993) 'Training the senses, training the mind', in W.F. Bynum and R. Porter (eds) *Companion Encyclopedia of the History of Medicine*, London: Routledge.

Bowlby, R. (1985) *Just Looking: Consumer Culture in Dreiser, Gissing and Zola*, New York: Methuen.

Bracken, C. (1997) *The Potlatch Papers: A Colonial Case History*, Chicago, IL: University of Chicago Press.

Bradstreet, C. (2010) 'A Trip to Japan in Sixteen Minutes: Sadakichi Hartmann's perfume concerts and the aesthetics of scent', in P. Di Bello and G. Koureas (eds) *Art History and the Senses: 1830 to the Present*, Farnham: Ashgate Publishing.

Brantlinger, P. (1988) *Rule of Darkness: British Literature and Imperialism*, Ithaca, NY: Cornell University Press.

Brigham, J. (2009) *Material Law: A Jurisprudence of What's Real*, Philadelphia, PA: Temple University Press.

Brimblecombe, P. (1999) 'History of air pollution', in J. Fenger, O. Hertel, and F. Palmgren (eds) *Urban Air Pollution – European Aspects*, Dordrecht: Kluwer Academic Publications.

Brown, R. (2004) 'The authoritarian personality and the organization of attitudes', in J.T. Jost and J. Sidanius (eds) *Political Psychology*, New York: Psychology Press.

Brynie, F.H. (2009) *Brain Sense: The Science of the Senses and How We Process the World Around Us*, New York: Amacom.

Buettner, E (2012) "Going for an Indian': South Asian restaurants and the limits of multiculturalism in Britain', in K. Ray and T. Srinivas (eds) *Curried Cultures: Globalization, Food and South Asia*, Berkeley, CA: University of California Press.

Bull, M. (2013) *Sound Studies*, London: Routledge.

Bull, M., Gilroy, P., Howes, D. and Kahn, D. (2006) 'Introducing Sensory Studies', *The Senses and Society*, 1(1): 5–7.

Bull, R. and Clifford, B. (1999) "Earwitness testimony", in A. Heaton-Armstrong, E. Shepherd and D. Wolcover (eds) *Analysing Witness Testimony: A Guide for Legal Practitioners & Other Professionals*, London: Blackstone Press.

Burke, J.G. (1974) 'Hermetism as a Renaissance world view', in R.S. Kinsman (ed.) *The Barker Vision of the Renaissance: Beyond the Fields of Reason*, Berkeley, CA: University of California Press.

Burke, T. (1996) *Lifebuoy Men, Lux Women: Commodification, Consumption, and Cleanliness in Modern Zimbabwe*, Durham, NC: Duke University Press.

Buruma, I. (2004) *Inventing Japan: 1853–1964*, Toronto: Random House.

Butler, S.R. (2007) *Contested Representations: Revisiting 'Into the Heart of Darkness'*, Peterborough, ON: Broadview Press.

Bylebyl, J. (1993) 'The manifest and hidden in the Renaissance clinic', in W.F. Bynum and R. Porter (eds) *Medicine and the Five Senses*, Cambridge: Cambridge University Press.

Calame-Griaule, G. (1986) *Words and the Dogon World*, trans. D. La Pin, Philadelphia, PA: Institute for the Study of Human Issues.

Calvert, G., Spence, C. and Stein, B. (eds) (2004) 'Introduction', in G. Calvert, C. Spence and B. Stein (eds) *The Handbook of Multisensory Processes*, Cambridge, MA: MIT Press.

Campo Baeza, A. (2009) 'El MA: Museo de la Memoria de Andalucia', *ON diseno* 303 (July).

Candlin, F. (2010) *Art, Museums and Touch*, Manchester: Manchester University Press.

Carrà, C. (1973) 'The painting of sounds, noises and smells', in U. Apollonio (ed.) *Futurist Manifestos*, London: Thames & Hudson

Carruthers, M. (2008) *The Book of Memory: A Study of Memory in Medieval Culture*, Cambridge: Cambridge University Press.

Carruthers, M. and Ziolkowski, J.M. (2004) *The Medieval Craft of Memory: An Anthology of Texts and Pictures*, Philadelphia, PA: University of Pennsylvania Press.

Caruso, G. (2005) *Onaya Shipibo-Conibo. Sistema médico tradicional y desafíos de la modernidad*, Quito: Ediciones Abya-Yala.

Casey, E. (2011) *Digital Evidence and Computer Crime: Forensic Science, Computers and the Internet*, Walton, MA: Academic Press.

Chatterjee, H.J. (2008) *Touch in Museums: Policy and Practice in Object Handling*, Oxford: Berg.

Chernoff, J.M. (1981) *African Rhythm and African Sensibility: Aesthetics and Social Action in African Musical Idioms*, Chicago, IL; University of Chicago Press.

Chidester, D. (2005) 'The American touch: tactile imagery in American religion and politics', in C. Classen (ed.) *The Book of Touch*, Oxford: Berg.

'Chinatown declared a nuisance' (1880) The Virtual Museum of the City of San Francisco, www.sfmuseum.org/hist2/nuisance.html (accessed January 15, 2013).

Churchill, W. (2005) *Kill the Indian, Save the Man: The Genocidal Impact of American Indian Residential Schools*, San Francisco, CA: City Lights.

Clanchy, M.T. (2012) *From Memory to Written Record: 1066–1307*, New York: John Wiley and Sons.

Classen, C. (1993a) *Worlds of Sense: Exploring the Senses in History and Across Cultures*, London: Routledge.

——(1993b) *Inca Cosmology and the Human Body*, Salt Lake City, UT: University of Utah Press.

——(1998) *The Color of Angels: Cosmology, Gender and the Aesthetic Imagination*, London: Routledge.

——(2001) 'The senses', in P. Stearns (ed.) *Encyclopedia of European Social History*, vol. 4, New York: Charles Scribner's Sons.

——(ed.) (2005a) *The Book of Touch*, Oxford: Berg.

——(2005b) 'The deodorized city: battling urban stench in the nineteenth century', in M. Zardini (ed.) *Sense of the City: An Alternate Approach to Urbanism*, Montreal: Canadian Centre for Architecture.

——(2005c) 'McLuhan in the rainforest: the sensory worlds of oral cultures', in D. Howes (ed.) *Empire of the Senses*, Oxford: Berg.

——(2012) *The Deepest Sense: A Cultural History of Touch*, Champaign, IL: University of Illinois Press.

——(general ed.) (forthcoming) *A Cultural History of the Senses*, 6 vols, London: Bloomsbury.

Classen, C. and Howes, D. (1996) 'Epilogue: the dynamics and ethics of cross-cultural consumption', in D. Howes (ed.) *Cross-cultural Consumption: Global Markets, Local Realities*, London: Routledge.

——(1998) 'Vital signs: the dynamics of folk medicine in Northwestern Argentina', in L. Phillips (ed.) *The Third Wave of Modernization in Latin America*. Wilmington, DE: Jaguar Books.

——(2006) 'The museum as sensescape: Western sensibilities and indigenous artifacts', in E. Edwards, C. Gosden and R. Phillips (eds) *Sensible Objects: Colonialism, Museums and Material Culture*, Oxford: Berg.

Classen, C., Howes, D. and Synnott, A. (1994) *Aroma: The Cultural History of Smell*, London, Routledge.

Cleophas, E. and Bijsterveld, K. (2012) 'Selling sound: testing, designing, and marketing sound in the European car industry', in T. Pinch and K. Bijsterveld (eds) *The Oxford Handbook of Sound Studies*, Oxford: Oxford University Press.

Clifford, T. (1984) *Tibetan Buddhist Medicine and Psychiatry*, New York: Samuel Wesier.

Cohen, W.A. (2009) *Embodied: Victorian Literature and the Senses*, Minneapolis, MN: University of Minnesota Press.

Collier, J.F. (1973) *Law and Social Change in Zinacantan*, Stanford, CA: Stanford University Press.

Collingham, E.M. (2006) *Curry: A Tale of Cooks and Conquerors*, New York: Oxford University Press.

Connerton, P. (1989) *How Societies Remember*, Cambridge: Cambridge University Press.

Connor, S. (2005) 'Michel Serres' five senses', in D. Howes (ed.) *Empire of the Senses*, Oxford: Berg.

Constable, O.R. (2011) 'Ringing bells in Hafsid Tunis: religious concessions to Christian *Fondacos* in the later thirteenth century', in R.E. Margariti, A. Sabra and P.M. Sijpesteijn (eds) *Histories of the Middle East: Studies in Middle Eastern Society, Economy and Law in Honor of A.L. Udovitch*, Leiden: Brill.

Coote, J., Morton, C. and Nicholson, J. (2000) *Transformations: The Art of Recycling*, Oxford: Pitt Rivers Museum.

Corbeill, A. (2004) *Nature Embodied: Gesture in Ancient Rome*, Princeton, NJ: Princeton University Press.

Corbin, A. (1986 [1982]) *The Foul and the Fragrant: Odor and the French Social Imagination*, trans. M. Kochan, R. Porter and C. Prendergast, Cambridge, MA: Harvard University Press.

——(1994) *Village Bells: Sound and Meaning in the 19th-century French Countryside*, trans. M. Tom, New York: Columbia University Press.

——(2005 [1990]) 'Charting the cultural history of the senses', in D. Howes (ed.) *Empire of the Senses*, Oxford: Berg.

Coulter, H. (1975) *Divided Legacy, Volume I: A History of the Schism in Medical Thought*, Washington: Wehawken.

Crary, J. (1990) *Techniques of the Observer: On Vision and Modernity in the Nineteenth Century*, Cambridge, MA: MIT Press.

Crowest, R. (1999) 'Multisensory interpretation and the visitor experience', unpublished thesis, University of Surrey.

Curtis, B.W. (2008) *Music Makes the Nation: Nationalist Composers and Nation Building in Nineteenth-Century Europe*, London: Cambria.

Cytowic, R. (1993) *The Man Who Tasted Shapes*, New York: G.P. Putnam's Sons

Daniels, I. (2010) *The Japanese House: Material Culture in the Modern Home*, Oxford: Berg.

Danius, S. (2002) *The Senses of Modernism: Technology, Perception, and Aesthetics*, Ithaca, NY: Cornell University Press.

Dann, K.T. (1998) *Bright Colors Falsely Seen: Synaesthesia and the Search for Transcendental Knowledge*, New Haven, CT: Yale University Press

Davis, J. (2002) 'European trade mark law and the enclosure of the common', *Intellectual Property Quarterly*, 4: 342–67.

Day, E.P. (1884) *Day's Collacon*, New York: International Printing and Publishing.

Day, J. (ed.) (2013) *Making Senses of the Past: Toward a Sensory Archaeology*, Carbondale, IL: Southern Illinois University.

Defoe, D. (1726) *The Complete English Tradesman*, London: Charles Rivington.

Degen, M. (2008) *Sensing Cities: Regenerating Public Life in Barcelona and Manchester*, London: Routledge.

Del Carmen, R.V. (2010) *Criminal Procedure: Law and Practice*, Belmont, CA: Wadsworth

Desjarlais, R.R. (1992) *Body and Emotion: The Aesthetics of Illness and Healing in the Nepal Himalayas*, Philadelphia, PA: University of Pennsylvania Press.

——(2003) *Sensory Biographies: Lives and Deaths Among Nepal's Yolmo Buddhists*, Berkeley, CA: University of California Press.

Dias, N. (2004) *La mesure des sens. Les anthropologues et le corps humain au XIXe siècle*, Paris: Aubier.

Dias, N. (2010) 'Exploring the senses and exploiting the land: railroads, bodies and measurement in nineteenth-century French colonies', in T. Bennett and P. Joyce (eds) *Material Powers: Cultural Studies, History and the Material Turn*, London: Routledge.

Di Bello, P. and Koureas, G. (eds) (2010) *Art, History and the Senses: 1830 to the Present*, Farnham, Surrey: Ashgate Publishing.

Dickens, C. (1850) *Oliver Twist; or, The Parish Boy's Progress*, Philadelphia: Lea & Blanchard.

——(1854) *Hard Times. For These Times*, London: Bradbury & Evans.

Dollard, J. (1937) *Caste and Class in a Southern Town*, New Haven, CT: Yale University Press.

Donahue, R. (1998) *Japanese Culture and Communication*, Lanham, MA: University Press of America.

Donden, Y. (2000) *Health Through Balance: An Introduction to Tibetan Medicine*, ed. and trans. J. Hopkins, Ithaca, NY: Snow Lion Publications.

Douzinas, C. and Nead, L. (eds) (1999) *Law and the Image: The Authority of Art and the Aesthetics of Law*, Chicago, IL: University of Chicago Press.

Downey, G. (2007) 'Seeing with a "sideways glance": visuomotor "knowing" and the plasticity of perception', in M. Harris (ed.) *Ways of Knowing: Anthropological Approaches to Crafting Experience and Knowledge*, Oxford: Berghahn Books.

Dreiser, T. (1971 [1889]) *Sister Carrie*, Cambridge, MA: R. Bentley.

Drewal, H.J. (2012) 'Creating Mami Wata: an interactive, sensory exhibition', *Museum Anthropology*, 35(1): 49–57.

Dudley, S. (ed.) (2009), *Museum Materialities: Objects, Engagements, Interpretations*, London: Routledge.

Easton, S.D. (1998) *How to Win Jury Trials: Building Credibility with Judges and Jurors*, Philadelphia, PA: American Law Institute.

Edensor, T. (2002) *National Identity, Popular Culture and Everyday Life*, Oxford: Berg.

Eleazar, E. (1999) 'With us ther was a Doctour of Phisic', in R.T. Lambin and L.C. Lambin (eds) *Chaucer's Pilgrims: An Historical Guide to the Pilgrims in* The Canterbury Tales, Westport, CT: Greenwood Press.

Elliot, C. (2012) 'Taste^{TM}: interrogating food, law and color', *The Senses & Society*, 7(3): 276–88.

Endacott, K. (1979) *Batek Negrito Religion*, Oxford: Clarendon Press.

Engels, F. (1971) *The Condition of the Working Class in England*, trans. W.O Henderson and W.H. Chaloner, Oxford: Blackwell.

Ensminger, J. (2012) *Police and Military Dogs: Criminal Detection, Forensic Evidence and Judicial Admissibility*, Boca Raton, FL: CRC Press.

Evans, K. (2010) *Common Sense Rules of Advocacy for Lawyers*, Alexandria, VA: The Capitol. Net.

Evelyn, J. (1955) *The Diary of John Evelyn*, Vol. II, ed. E.S. de Beer, Oxford: Clarendon Press.

Ewen, S. (1988) *All Consuming Images: The Politics of Style in Contemporary Culture*, New York: Basic Books.

Farquhar, J. (2002) *Appetites: Food and Sex in Post-Socialist China*, Durham, NC: Duke University Press.

Featherstone, M. (2001) 'Consumer culture', in *International Encyclopedia of the Social and Behavioral Sciences*, vol. 4: 2262–69, Amsterdam: Elsevier.

Feld, S. (1990 [1982]) *Sound and Sentiment: Birds, Weeping, Poetics and Song in Kaluli Expression*, 2nd edn, Philadelphia, PA: University of Pennsylvania Press.

Ferry, J.W. (1960) *A History of the Department Store*, New York: Macmillan.

Ficino, M. (2006) *Marsilio Ficino*, ed. A. Voss, Berkeley, CA: North Atlantic Books.

Finnegan, R. (2002) *Communicating: The Multiple Modes of Human Interconnection*, London: Routledge.

Firth, A. (2008) 'Signs, surfaces, shapes and structures – the protection of product design under trademark law', in G.B. Dinwoodie and M.D. Janis (eds) *Trademark Law and Theory: A Handbook of Contemporary Research*, Cheltenham: Edward Elgar Publishing.

Fishman, J.M. and Marvin, C. (2003) 'Portrayals of violence and group difference in newspaper photographs: nationalism and media', *Journal of Communications*, 53(1): 32–44.

Fletcher, C. (2005) 'Dystoposthesia: emplacing environmental sensitivities', in D. Howes (ed.) *Empire of the Senses: The Sensual Culture Reader*, Oxford: Berg.

Florida *v.* Jardines (2013) 133 S. Ct. 1409.

Fonseca, F. (2012) 'Navajo Nation sues Urban Outfitters over "Navajo" trademark', *USA Today*, February 29.

Ford, R. (1839) 'Oliver Twist; or the parish boy's progress', *The London Quarterly Review*, 63 (January–April).

Foster, R. (1996/97) 'Commercial mass media in Papua New Guinea: notes on agency, bodies, and commodity consumption', *Visual Anthropology Review*, 12(2): 1–17

Foucault, M. (1973) *The Birth of the Clinic: An Archaeology of Medical Perception*, trans. A.M. Sheridan Smith, London: Tavistock.

——(1995) *Discipline and Punish: The Birth of the Prison*, trans. A.M. Sheridan Smith, New York: Random House.

Four Seasons of the House of Cerutti, The (1984) trans. J. Spencer, New York: Facts on File Publications.

Fox, J. and Miller-Idriss, C. (2008) 'Everyday nationhood', *Ethnicities*, 8(4): 536–63.

Franke-Ruta, G. (2009) 'Obama isn't the first President to retake oath – or forgo Bible', *The Washington Post*, January 23.

Fuqua, J. (2012) *Prescription TV: Therapeutic Discourse in the Hospital and at Home*, Durham, NC: Duke University Press.

Gaiger, J. (2002) 'Introduction', in J.G. Herder, *Sculpture: Some Observations on Shape and Form from Pygmalion's Creative Dream*, ed. J. Gaiger, Chicago, IL: University of Chicago Press.

Garber, J.J. (2008) *Harmony in Healing: the Theoretical Basis of Ancient and Medieval Medicine*, New Brunswick, NJ: Transaction Publishers.

Gardner, T.J. and Anderson, T.M. (2010) *Criminal Evidence: Principles and Cases*, Belmont, CA: Wadsworth Cengage Learning.

Gavrilyuk, P. and Coakley, S. (eds) (2012) *The Spiritual Senses: Perceiving God in Western Christianity*, Cambridge: Cambridge University Press.

Gebhart-Sayer, A. (1985) 'The geometric designs of the Shipibo-Conibo in ritual context', *Journal of Latin American Lore*, 11(2): 143–75.

Geertz, C. (2000) 'The uses of diversity', in *Available Light: Anthropological Reflections on Philosophical Topics*, Princeton, NJ: Princeton University Press.

Gerstle, G. (2001) *American Crucible: Race and Nation in the Twentieth Century*, Princeton, NJ: Princeton University Press.

Geurts, K.L. (2002) *Culture and the Senses: Bodily ways of Knowing in an African Community*, Berkeley, CA: University of California Press.

Gibbon, J.M. (1938) *Canadian Mosaic: The Making of a Northern Nation*, Toronto: McClelland & Stewart.

Gibson, B. (2009) *Pocket A–Z of Criminal Justice*, Hook, UK: Waterside Press.

Gifford, P. (2004) *Ghana's New Christianity: Pentecostalism in a Globalising African Economy*, Bloomington, IN: Indiana University Press.

Gill, S.D. (1979) *Songs of Life: An Introduction to Navajo Religious Culture*, Leiden: E.J. Brill.
——(1982) *Native American Religions: An Introduction*, Belmont, CA: Wadsworth.
Gillespie, R. (1997) *Devoted People: Belief and Religion in Early Modern Ireland*, Manchester: Manchester University Press.
Glenn, H.P. (2010) *Legal Traditions of the World*, 4th edn, Toronto: Oxford University Press.
Goldman, R. and Papson, S. (1996) *Sign Wars: The Cluttered Landscape of Advertising*, New York: The Guilford Press.
Goldsmith, M. (2012) *Discord: The Story of Noise*, Oxford: Oxford University Press.
Goldstein, E.B. (2002) *Sensation and Perception*, 6th edn, Pacific Grove, CA: Wadsworth.
Goldwater, R.J. (1966) *Primitivism in Modern Art*, Cambridge, MA: Harvard University Press.
Golec, M.J. (2010) 'Design for display culture: domestic engineering to design research', in J. Kromm and S.B. Bakewell (eds) *A History of Visual Culture: Western Civilization from the 18th to the 21st Century*, Oxford: Berg.
Good, B.J. (1994) *Medicine, Rationality and Experience: An Anthropological Perspective*, Cambridge: Cambridge University Press.
Govinda, L.A. (1983) *Foundations of Tibetan Mysticism*, London: Rider.
Graham, H. (1999) *Complementary Therapies in Context: The Psychology of Healing*, London: Jessica Kingsley.
Graziano, F. (1999) *The Millennial New World*, Oxford: Oxford University Press.
Green, D.A. (2011) *The Aroma of Righteousness: Scent and Seduction in Rabbinic Life and Literature*, University Park, PA: Pennsylvania State University Press.
Green, J. (2000) *Clean Your Clothes with Cheez Whiz: And Hundreds of Off-Beat Uses for Dozens More Brand-Name Products*, Los Angeles: Renaissance Books.
Green, W.S. and Jordan, P.W. (eds) (2002) *Pleasure with Products: Beyond Usability*, London: Taylor & Francis.
Greenberg, C. (1989) *Art and Culture: Critical Essays*, Boston, MA: Beacon Press.
Gregor, M.J. (1983) 'Baumgarten's aesthetica', *Review of Metaphysics*, 37: 357–85.
Gregory, C. (2011) 'Skinship: touchability as a virtue in East-Central India', *Hau: Journal of Ethnographic Theory*, 1(1), www.haujournal.org/index.php/hau/article/view/16 (accessed January 15, 2013).
Griffiths, A. (2008) *Shivers Down Your Spine: Cinema. Museums, and the Immersive View*, New York: Colombia University Press.
Haddon *v.* Lynch (1911) VLR 5; Aff'd VLR 230.
Hahn, T. (2007) *Sensational Knowledge: Embodying Culture through Japanese Dance*, Middletown, CT: Wesleyan University Press.
Hansen, M. (2000) 'Smells fishy: some sniff that dog scent evidence stinks', *ABA Journal*, August.
Hart, M. (2002) *Patriotic Songs & Symbols*, Westminster, CA: Teacher Created Materials.
Hearn, L. (2006) *Out of the East: Reveries and Studies in New Japan*, New York: Cosimo.
Heller-Roazen, D. (2007) *The Inner Touch: Archaeology of a Sensation*, Cambridge, MA: Zone Books.
——(2008) 'Common sense: Greek, Arabic, Latin', in G. Nichols, A. Kablitz and A. Calhoun (eds) *Rethinking the Medieval Senses: Heritage, Fascinations, Frames*, Baltimore, MD: Johns Hopkins University Press.
Henderson, J. (2011 [1984]) *The Development and Decline of Chinese Cosmology*, New York: Columbia University Press.
Henry, R.D. and Taylor, J.D. (2005) *Spa: The Sensuous Experience*, Victoria, Australia: Images Publishing Group.

Henshaw, V. (2013) *Urban Smellscapes: A Guide to Understanding and Designing Olfactory Environments in the City*, New York: Routledge.

Herder, J.G. (2002) *Sculpture: Some Observations in Shape and Form from Pygmalion's Creative Dream*, ed. and trans. J. Gaiger, Chicago, IL: University of Chicago Press.

Hertel, R. (2005) *Making Sense: Sense Perception in the British Novel of the 1980s and 1990s*, Amsterdam: Rodopi.

Herz, R. S. (2010) 'The emotional, cognitive, and biological basis of olfaction: implications and considerations for scent marketing', in A. Krishna (ed.) *Sensory Marketing: Research on the Sensuality of Products*, New York: Routledge.

Herzfeld, M. (2001) *Anthropology: Theoretical Practice in Culture and Society*, Oxford: Blackwell.

Hess, K.M. and Orthmann, C.M.H. (2012) *Introduction to Law Enforcement and Criminal Justice*, Clifton Park, NY: Delmar/Cengage Learning.

Higgins, H. (2002) *Fluxus Experience*, Berkeley, CA: University of California Press.

Highmore, B. (2010) *Ordinary Lives: Studies in the Everyday*, London: Routledge.

Hinton, D, Howes, D. and Kirmayer, L. (2008) 'The medical anthropology of sensations', *Transcultural Psychiatry*, 45(2): 139–62.

Hjorth, L. (2011) *Games and Gaming: An Introduction to New Media*, Oxford: Berg.

Hoeniger, F.D. (1992) *Medicine and Shakespeare in the English Renaissance*, Newark, NJ: University of Delaware Press.

Hoffer, P.C. (2005) *Sensory Worlds in Early America*, Baltimore, MD: Johns Hopkins University Press.

Hooper, L.H. (1874) 'Parisian shops and shopping', *Appletons' Journal*, 11: 250–75.

Howes, D. (1988) 'On the odour of the soul: spatial representation and olfactory classification in Eastern Indonesia and Western Melanesia', *Bijdragen tot de Taal-, Land-en Volkenkunde*, 124: 84–133.

——(1990) '*We Are the World* and its counterparts: popular song as constitutional discourse', *International Journal of Politics, Culture and Society*, 3(3): 315–39, http://canadianicon.org/table-of-contents/we-the-people (accessed January 15, 2013).

——(ed.) (1991a) *The Varieties of Sensory Experience: A Sourcebook in the Anthropology of the Senses*, Toronto: University of Toronto Press.

——(1991b) 'Picturing the constitution', *The American Review of Canadian Studies*, 21(4): 383–408.

——(1996a) 'Introduction: commodities and cultural borders', in D. Howes (ed.) *Cross-Cultural Consumption: Global Markets, Local Realities*, London: Routledge.

——(1996b) 'Cultural appropriation and resistance in the American Southwest: decom-modifying "Indianness"', in D. Howes (ed.) *Cross-Cultural Consumption: Global Markets, Local Realities*, London: Routledge.

——(2003) *Sensual Relations: Engaging the Senses in Culture and Social Theory*, Ann Arbor, MI: University of Michigan Press.

——(ed.) (2005a) *Empire of the Senses: The Sensual Culture Reader*, Oxford: Berg.

——(2005b) 'Hyperaesthesia: the sensual logic of late capitalism', in D. Howes (ed.) *Empire of the Senses*, Oxford: Berg.

——(2005c) 'Introduction: culture in the domains of law', *Canadian Journal of Law and Society*, 20(1): 9–30.

——(2006) 'Charting the sensorial revolution', *The Senses and Society*, 1(1): 113–28.

——(2009) 'Introduction', in D. Howes (ed.) *The Sixth Sense Reader*, Oxford: Berg.

——(2011) 'Hearing scents, tasting sights: toward a cross-cultural multimodal theory of aesthetics', in F.E. Bacci and D. Melcher (eds) *Art and the Senses*, Oxford: Oxford University Press.

Howie, M. and Sawer, P. (2010) 'National Trust members clash over "Disneyfication" of properties', *The Telegraph*, October 30.

Hubbard, E. and Ramachandran, V.S. (2005) 'Neurocognitive mechanisms of synesthesia', *Neuron*, 48: 509–20.

Hughes, H.C. (2001), *Sensory Exotica: A World beyond Human Experience*, Cambridge, MA: MIT Press.

Hugo, V. (1931) *Les Miserables*, New York: Modern Library.

Hull, S.W. (1982) *Chaste, Silent and Obedient: English Books for Women, 1475–1640*, San Francisco, CA: Huntingdon Library.

Hultén, B., Broweus, N. and van Dijk, M. (2009) *Sensory Marketing*, New York: Palgrave Macmillan.

Huysmans, J.-K. (1998) *Against Nature*, trans. M. Mauldon, Oxford: Oxford University Press.

Igarashi, Y. (2000) *Bodies of Memory: Narratives of War in Postwar Japanese Culture, 1945–1970*, Princeton, NJ: Princeton University Press.

Immen, W. (2010) 'Scents and sensibility: the fragrant workplace', *The Globe and Mail*, April 9.

Jacob, J.I.H. (1987) *The Fabric of English Civil Law*, London: Stevens and Sons.

Janke, T. (2008) 'Indigenous cultural expression and intellectual property', in E. Johnston, M. Hinton and D. Rigney (eds) *Indigenous Australians and the Law*, London: Routledge.

Jay, M. (2003) *Refractions of Violence*, New York: Routledge.

Jenner, M.S.R. (2010) 'Tasting Lichfield, touching China: Sir John Floyer's senses', *The Historical Journal*, 53(3): 647–70.

Johnson, G.A. (2011) 'The art of touch in early modern Italy', in F.E. Bacci and D. Melcher (eds) *Art and the Senses*, Oxford: Oxford University Press.

Johnson, J.H. (1996) *Listening in Paris: A Cultural History*, Berkeley: University of California Press.

Johnson, S. (1837) *The Works of Samuel Johnson*, Vol. I, ed. A. Murphy, New York: George Dearborn.

Johnson, S.L. (2000) 'Black innocence and the white jury', in R. Delgado and J. Stefanic (eds) *Critical Race Theory: The Cutting Edge*, Philadelphia, PA: Temple University Press.

Jones, C.A. (2005) *Eyesight Alone: Clement Greenberg's Modernism*, Chicago, IL: University of Chicago Press.

——(2006) 'The mediated sensorium', in C.A. Jones (ed.) *Sensorium: Embodied Experience, Technology and Contemporary Art*, Cambridge, MA: MIT Press.

Jordan, P.W. (2004) *Designing Pleasurable Products: An Introduction to the New Human Factors*, London: Taylor & Francis.

Joyce, K.A. (2008) *Magnetic Appeal: MRI and the Myth of Transparency*, Ithaca, NY: Cornell University Press.

Jütte, R. (2005) *A History of the Senses: From Antiquity to Cyberspace*, trans. J. Lynn, Cambridge: Polity.

Kafka, F. (1977) *The Trial*, trans. W. and E. Muir, Philadelphia, PA: The Franklin Library.

Kahn, D. (1999) *Noise Water Meat: A History of Sound in the Arts*, Cambridge, MA: MIT Press.

Kant, I. (1911) *Critique of Aesthetic Judgment*, trans. J. C. Meredith, Oxford: Clarendon Press.

Katz, J. (1984) *The Silent World of Doctor and Patient*, New York: Free Press.

Katz *v.* United States (1967) 389 US 347.

Keeley, B. (2002) 'Making sense of the senses: individuating modalities in humans and other animals', *Journal of Philosophy*, 99(1): 5–28.

Kemp, B.P. (n.d.) 'Frequently asked questions', www.sos.georgia.gov/elections'electronic_voting/faqs.htm (accessed January 15, 2013).

Kemp, M. (1993) '"The mark of truth": looking and learning in some anatomical illustrations from the Renaissance and eighteenth century', in W.F. Bynum and R. Porter (eds) *Medicine and the Five Senses,* Cambridge: Cambridge University Press.

Kentucky *v.* King (2011) 302 S.W. 3d 649.

Kiernan, B. (2007) *Blood and Soil: A World History of Genocide and Extermination from Sparta to Darfur,* New Haven, CT: Yale University Press.

Kim, L.J. and Kim, G.S. (1998) 'Searching for and defining a Korean American identity in a multicultural society', in Y.I. Song and A. Moon (eds) *Korean Women: From Tradition to Modern Feminism,* Westport, CT: Praeger Publishers.

Kirmayer, L.J. (2003) 'Reflections on Embodiment', in J.M. Wilce (ed.) *Social and Cultural Lives of Immune Systems,* New York: Routledge.

Kirshenblatt-Gimblett, B. (1998) *Destination Culture: Tourism, Museums, and Heritage,* Berkeley, CA: University of California Press.

Kleege, G. (1999) *Sight Unseen,* New Haven, CT: Yale University Press.

Knellwolf King, C. (2008) *Faustus and the Promises of the New Science, c. 1580–1730,* Aldershot: Ashgate.

Knox, J. (1572) *The First Blast of the Trumpet Against the Monstrous Regiment of Women,* Edinburgh: n.p.

Kohl, J.G. (1843) *Russia and the Russians, in 1842,* Vol. I, Philadelphia, PA: Corey and Hart.

Koren, L. (2008) *Wabi-Sabi for Artists, Designers, Poets & Philosophers,* Point Reyes, CA: Imperfect Publishing.

Korsmeyer, C. (2002) *Making Sense of Taste: Food and Philosophy,* Ithaca, NY: Cornell University Press.

Krieger, D. (1979) *The Therapeutic Touch: How to Use Your Hands to Help or to Heal,* Englewood Cliffs, NJ: Prentice Hall.

Krishna, A. (2010) 'An introduction to sensory marketing', in A. Krishna (ed.) *Sensory Marketing: Research on the Sensuality of Products,* New York: Routledge.

Kromm, J. (2010) 'To the arcade: the world of the shop and the store', in J. Kromm and S.B. Bakewell (eds) *A History of Visual Culture: Western Civilization from the 18th to the 20th Century,* Oxford: Berg.

Kumar, S.R. (2007) *Marketing and Branding: The Indian Scenario,* New Delhi: Dorling Kindersley.

Kuriyama, S. (2002) *The Expressiveness of the Body and the Divergence of Greek and Chinese Medicine,* New York: Zone Books.

Kyllo *v.* United States (2001) 533 US 27.

Labruto, N. (2011) 'A play of senses: Displace (v 1.0) at the Hexagram-Concordia, Montreal QC', *Sensate Journal,* http://sensatejournal.com/2012/03/review-nicole-labruto-on-displace-v-1-0 (accessed January 15, 2013).

Lachmund, J. (1999) 'Making sense of sound: auscultation and lung sound codification in nineteenth-century French and German medicine', *Science, Technology and Human Values,* 24(4): 419–50.

Lacroix, J. (2010) *Belonging Experiences: Designing Engaged Brands,* Bloomington, IN: iUniverse.

Ladas, S.P. (1975) *Patents, Trademarks, and Related Rights,* Vol. II, Cambridge, MA: Harvard University Press.

Laderman, C. (1994) 'The embodiment of symbols and the acculturation of the anthropologist', in T. Csordas (ed.) *Embodiment and Experience,* Cambridge: Cambridge University Press.

Laderman, C. and Roseman, M. (eds) (1996) *The Performance of Healing*, New York: Routledge.

Lamb, C. (1886) *The Works of Charles Lamb*, Vol. II, New York: A.C. Armstrong.

Lamb, C.W. et al. (2011) *Marketing*, Scarborough, ON: Nelson Education.

Lamp, F.J. (2004) *See the Music, Hear the Dance: Rethinking African Art at the Baltimore Museum of Art*, New York: Prestel Publishing.

Lancaster, W. (1995) *The Department Store: A Social History*, Leicester: Leicester University Press.

Langer, R. et al. (2011) 'Ritual as a source of conflict', in R.L. Grimes et al. (eds) *Ritual, Media and Conflict*, Oxford: Oxford University Press.

Largey, G. and Watson, R. (2006) 'The sociology of odors', in J. Drobnick (ed.) *The Smell Culture Reader*, Oxford: Berg.

Latham, M. (2000) '"The private life of the senses": synesthesia, eidetic imagery and the denigration of Modern Art in National Socialist Germany', paper presented at the Uncommon Senses conference, Concordia University, Montreal, May.

Lauf, D.I. (1977) *Secret Doctrines of the Tibetan Books of the Dead*, trans. G. Parkes, Boulder, CO: Shambhala.

Law Society Gazette (1991) 'Breaking ground on the bench', *The Law Society Gazette*, February 20.

Lawrence, S.C. (1993) 'Educating the senses: students, teachers and medical rhetoric in eighteenth-century London', in W.F. Bynum and R. Porter (eds) *Medicine and the Five Senses*, Cambridge: Cambridge University Press.

Leahy, H.R. (2011) *Museum Bodies: The Politics and Practices of Visiting and Viewing*, Aldershot: Ashgate.

Lebrun, F. (1989) 'The two Reformations: communal devotion and personal piety', in R. Chartier (ed.) *A History of Private Life: Passions of the Renaissance*, trans. A. Goldhammer, Cambridge, MA: Harvard University Press.

Legrenzi, P. and Umilta, C. (2011) *Neuromania: On the Limits of Brain Science*, trans. F. Anderson, Oxford: Oxford University Press.

Lende, D.H. and Downey, G. (eds) (2012) *The Encultured Brain: An Introduction to Neuro-anthropology*, Cambridge, MA: MIT Press.

Levin, D.M. (1997) 'Introduction', in D.M. Levin (ed.) *Sites of Vision: The Discursive Construction of Sight in the History of Philosophy*, Cambridge, MA: MIT Press.

Lévi-Strauss, C. (1963) 'The effectiveness of symbols', in *Structural Anthropology*, trans. C. Jacobson, New York: Basic Books.

Lewis, M.J. and Wackowski, O. (2006) 'USA: Salem's new look website', *Tobacco Control*, 15(2): 81–82.

Lewis, R. and Lewis, S.L. (2009) *The Power of Art*, Belmont, CA: Thomson Wadsworth.

Lindemann, M. (2010) *Medicine and Society in Early Modern Europe*, Cambridge: Cambridge University Press.

Lindstrom, M. (2005) *BRAND sense: Build Powerful Brands through Touch, Taste, Smell, Sight, and Sound*, New York: Free Press.

Link, M.S. (1998) *The Pollen Path: A Collection of Navajo Myths*, Walnut, CA: Kiva Publishing.

Loeb, J. (2012) 'Shakespeare protesters storm British Museum Gallery over BP sponsorship', *Camden New Journal*, July 23.

Lombardi, L. (2009) *From Realism to Art Nouveau*, trans. A. Arnone, New York: Stirling.

MacDougall, R.C. (2012) *Digination: Identity, Organization, and Public Life in the Age of Small Digital Devices and Big Digital Domains*, Lanham, MD: Farleigh Dickinson University Press.

Machak, P. (1996) 'A trip to the Rainforest involves more than just dinner', *Chicago Tribune*, August 11.

Mack, A. (forthcoming) 'The senses in the marketplace', in D. Howes (ed.) *A Cultural History of the Senses in the Modern Age, 1920–2000*, London: Bloomsbury.

Macpherson, F. (2007) 'Synaesthesia, functionalism and phenomenology', in M. Marraffa, M. DeCaro and F. Ferretti (eds) *Philosophy and Psychology in Intersection*, Dordrecht: Springer.

Madslein, J. (2012) 'Bentley hopes engine choice will double sales', *BBC News*, www.bbc.co.uk/news/business-17773758 (accessed January 15, 2013).

Maffesoli, M. (1996) *The Time of the Tribes: The Decline of Individualism in Mass Society*, trans. D. Smith, London: Sage.

Makin, K. (2012) 'Wearing a full veil to testify: Supreme Court says sometimes yes, sometimes no', *The Globe and Mail*, December 20.

Malefyt, T. and Morais, R. (2012) *Advertising and Anthropology*, Oxford: Berg.

Manalansan, M.F. (2007) 'Cooking up the senses: a critical embodied approach to the study of food and Asian American television audiences', in M.T. Nguyen and T.L. Nguyen (eds) *Alien Encounters: Popular Culture in Asian America*, Durham, NC: Duke University Press.

Manderson, D. (2000) *Songs Without Music: Aesthetic Dimensions of Law and Justice*, Berkeley, CA: University of California Press.

Maniatus, S. (1996) 'Scents as trademarks: propertisation of scents and olfactory poverty', in L. Bently and L. Flynn (eds.) *Law and the Senses: Sensational Jurisprudence*, Chipping Norton: Pluto Press.

Marchand, R. (1985) *Advertising the American Dream: Making Way for Modernity, 1920–1940*, Berkeley, CA: University of California Press.

Marcus, J.R. (1972) *The Jew in the Medieval World: A Reader*, New York: Atheneum.

Marinetti, F.T. (1972) 'Tactilism', in R.W. Flint (ed.) *Marinetti: Selected Writings*, trans. R.W. Flint and A.A. Copotelli, New York: Farrar, Strauss and Giroux.

——(1989) *The Futurist Cookbook*, trans. S. Brill, San Francisco, CA: Bedford Arts.

Markham, G. (1986) *The English Housewife*, ed. M.R. Best, Montreal: McGill-Queens University Press.

Marks, L.E. (1978) *The Unity of the Senses*, New York: Academic Press.

——(2000) 'Synesthesia', in E. Cardena, S.J. Lynn and S.C. Krippner (eds) *Varieties of Anomalous Experience: Examining the Scientific Evidence*, Washington, DC: American Psychological Association.

Marks, L.U. (2000) *The Skin of the Film: Intercultural Cinema, Embodiment and the Senses*, Durham, NC: Duke University Press.

Martin, D. (2007) *Rebuilding Brand America: What We Must Do to Restore Our Reputation and Safeguard the Future of American Business Abroad*, New York: Amacom.

Martin, D.A. (2000) 'Introduction', in D.B. Klusmeyer and T.A. Aleinikoff (eds) *From Migrants to Citizens: Membership in a Changing World*, Washington, DC: Brookings Institution Press.

Marx, K. (1954) *Capital: A Critique of Political Economy*, Vol. 1, trans. S. Moore and E. Aveling, London: Lawrence & Wishart.

——(1987 [1844]) *Economic and Philosophic Manuscripts of 1844*, trans. M. Milligan, Buffalo, NY: Prometheus Books.

Mascia-Lees, F. (2011) 'Aesthetics: aesthetic embodiment and cultural capitalism', in F. Mascia-Lees (ed.) *A Companion to the Anthropology of the Body and Embodiment*, Oxford: Wiley-Blackwell.

Mattingley, J. and Rich, A. (2004) 'Behavioral and brain correlates of multisensory experience in synesthesia', in G. Calvert, C. Spence and B. Stein (eds) *The Handbook of Multisensory Processes*, Cambridge, MA: MIT Press.

Maurer, M. (1985) 'Too busy for equality', *Braille Monitor*, April–May.

McAndrews *v.* Leonard (1926) 136 A. 710 (Vt. 1926).

McCormack, N.Y. (2012) *Japan's Outcaste Abolition: The Struggle for National Inclusion and the Making of the Modern State*, Oxford: Routledge.

McGilvray, D.B. (1998) *Symbolic Heat: Gender, Health & Worship Among the Tamils of South India and Sri Lanka*, Middletown, NJ: Grantha.

McGurk, H. and MacDonald, J. (1976) 'Hearing lips and seeing voices', *Nature*, 264: 746–48.

McLuhan, M. (1962) *The Gutenberg Galaxy*, Toronto, ON: University of Toronto Press.

——(1994 [1964]) *Understanding Media: The Extensions of Man*, Cambridge, MA: MIT Press.

McLuhan, M. and Fiore, Q. (1967) *The Medium is the Massage: An Inventory of Effects*, Toronto: Bantam Books.

McNeil, D. (2011) 'Ex-minister blames his blood group for outburst after Fukushima disaster', *Independent*, July 6.

Meade, A. (1936) 'Training the senses in clinical observation', *The Trained Nurse and Hospital Review*, 97(6): 540–44.

Meade, M.S. and Emch, M. (2010) *Medical Geography*, New York: Guilford Press.

'Medical anthropophy in China' (1830) *The Asiatic Journal and Monthly Register*, 1: 254.

Meulders, M. (2010) *Helmholtz: From Enlightenment to Neuroscience*, Cambridge, MA: MIT Press.

Mighall, R. (1999) *A Geography of Victorian Gothic Fiction: Mapping History's Nightmares*, Oxford: Oxford University Press.

Miller, M.B. (1981) *The Bon Marché: Bourgeois Culture and the Department Store, 1869–1920*, Princeton, NJ: Princeton University Press.

Miller, S. (2002) *Visible Deeds of Music: Art and Music from Wagner to John Cage*, Hartford, CT: Yale University Press.

Mills, A. (1994) *Eagle Down Is Our Law: Witsuwit'en Law, Feasts, and Land Claims*, Vancouver: UBC Press.

——(ed.) (2005) *'Hang Onto These Words': Johnny David's* Delgamuukw *Evidence*, Toronto: University of Toronto Press.

Mindeleff, C. (1898) *Navaho Houses*, Washington, DC: US Government Printing Office.

Minnesota v. Dickerson (1993) 508 US 366.

Mintz, S.W. (1986) *Sweetness and Power: The Place of Sugar in Modern History*, New York: Penguin.

——(1996) *Tasting Food, Tasting Freedom: Excursions into Eating, Power and the Past*, Boston: Beacon

Morales, A. (2010) 'Understanding the role of incidental touch in consumer behaviour', in A. Krishna (ed.) *Sensory Marketing: Research on the Sensuality of Products*, New York: Routledge.

More, A.T. and Srivastava, R.K. (2010) 'Some aesthetic considerations for over-the-counter pharmaceutical products', *The International Journal of Biotechnology*, 11: 267–93.

Mulcahy, L. (2012) *Legal Architecture: Justice, Due Process and the Place of Law*, London: Routledge.

Murphy, P.T. (2012) *Shooting Victoria: Madness, Mayhem and the Rebirth of the British Monarchy*, New York: Pegasus Books.

Musée du quai Branly (2013) 'Collections', www.quaibranly.fr/en/collections (accessed January 15, 2013).

Mwakikagile, G. (2008) *African Immigrants in South Africa*, Pretoria, South Africa: New Africa Press.

Nader, L. (1990) *Harmony Ideology: Justice and Control in a Zapotec Mountain Village*, Stanford, CA: Stanford University Press.

Naeve, S.H. (2011) 'Heart pills are red, Viagra is blue – when does pill color become functional? an analysis of utilitarian and aesthetic functionality and their unintended side effects in the pharmaceutical industry', *Santa Clara Computer & High Technology Law Journal*, 27(2): 299–332.

NBC News (2008) 'Wal-Mart unveils new look for stores', *NBC News*, www.nbcnews.com/id/37443601/ns/business-retail/UUjHMeYm68.

Ndukaihe, V.E. (2006) *Achievement as Value in the Igbo/African Identity: The Ethics*, Berlin: Lit Verlag.

Nelson, J. (2012) *Airbrushed Nation: The Lure and Loathing of Women's Magazines*, Berkeley, CA: Seal Press.

Nelson, J.A. (ed.) (1994) *The Disabled, the Media, and the Information Age*, Westport, CT: Greenwood Press.

Nelson, M.R. and Hitchon, J.C. (1999) 'Loud tastes, colored fragrances, and scented sounds: how and when to mix the senses in persuasive communication', *Journal of Mass Communication Quarterly*, 76(2): 354–72.

Newhauser, R.G. (2010) 'Foreword: the senses in Medieval and Renaissance history', *The Senses & Society*, 5(1).

New York Times (2007) 'Richard Conway Casey, 74, blind Federal judge, dies', *The New York Times*, Obituaries, March 24.

Nichols, M.F. (2006) 'Plaster cast sculpture: a history of touch', *Archaeological Review from Cambridge*, 21: 114–30.

Nicolson, M. (1993) 'The introduction of percussion and stethoscopy to early nineteenth-century Edinburgh', in W.F. Bynum and R. Porter (eds) *Medicine and the Five Senses,* Cambridge: Cambridge University Press.

——(1997) 'The art of diagnosis: medicine and the five senses', in W.F. Bynum and R. Porter (eds) *Companion Encyclopedia of the History of Medicine*, London: Routledge.

Nieburg, O. (2013) 'Nestlé wins trademark case over Kit Kat shape after Cadbury row', www.confectionarynews.com/Regulation-Safety/Nestlé-wins-trademark-case-over-Kit-Kat-shape-after-Cadbury-row (accessed January 15, 2013).

Niehaus, I. (2001) 'Witchcraft in the New South Africa: from colonial superstition to post-colonial reality', in H. Moore and T. Sanders (eds) *Magical Interpretations, Mystical Realities: Modernity, Witchcraft and the Occult in Postcolonial Africa*, London: Routledge.

Nietzsche, F. (1989) *On the Genealogy of Morals and Ecce Homo*, trans. W. Kaufman, New York: Vintage Books.

Nordau, M. (1910 [1895]) *Degeneration*, New York: D. Appleton and Company.

Norton, R.E. (1990) *Herder's Aesthetics and the European Enlightenment*, Ithaca, NY: Cornell University Press.

'Notes of recent decisions' (1891) *The Central Law Journal*, 33: 293–94.

Nutton, V. (1993) 'Galen at the bedside: the methods of a medical detective', in W.F. Bynum and R. Porter (eds) *Medicine and the Five Senses,* Cambridge: Cambridge University Press.

Odin, S. (1996) *The Social Self in Zen and American Pragmatism*, Albany, NY: State University of New York Press.

Ogden-Barnes, S. and Barclay, D. (2011) *Store Sense: Reclaiming the Four Walls through Sensory Engagement*, Melbourne: Deakin University.

Ohnuki-Tierney, E. (2002) *Kamikaze, Cherry Blossoms and Nationalisms: The Militarization of Aesthetics in Japanese History*, Chicago, IL: University of Chicago Press.

Okonkwo, U. (2010) *Luxury Online: Styles, Strategies, System*, New York: Palgrave Macmillan.

'On the nature, obligation and form of a civil oath' (1827) *The Magazine of the Reformed Dutch Church*, Vol. I, February.

Ong, B. (2008) 'The trademark law provisions of bilateral free trade agreements', in G.B. Dinwoodie and M.D. Janis (eds) *Trademark Law and Theory: A Handbook of Contemporary Research*, Cheltenham: Edward Elgar Publishing.

Ong, W.J. (1982) *Orality and Literacy: The Technologizing of the Word*, London: Methuen.

——(1991) 'The shifting sensorium', in D. Howes (ed.) *The Varieties of Sensory Experience*, Toronto: University of Toronto Press.

Orbaugh, S. (2007) *Japanese Fiction of the Allied Occupation: Vision, Embodiment, Identity*, Leiden: Brill.

O'Rourke Boyle, M. (1998) *Senses of Touch: Human Dignity and Deformity from Michelangelo to Calvin*, Leiden: Brill.

Orwell, G. (1958 [1937]) *The Road to Wigan Pier*, Boston, MA: Houghton Mifflin Harcourt.

Ouzman, S. (2006) 'The beauty of letting go: fragmentary museums and archaeologies of archive', in E. Edwards, C. Gosden and R. Phillips (eds) *Sensible Objects: Colonialism, Museums and Material Culture*, Oxford: Berg.

Pagel, W. (1958) *Paracelsus: An Introduction to Philosophical Science in the Era of the Renaissance*, Basil: Karger.

——(1982) *Joan Baptista Van Helmont*, Cambridge: Cambridge University Press.

——(1984) *The Smiling Spleen: Paracelsianism in Storm and Stress*, Basel: Karger.

Panagia, D. (2009) *The Political Life of Sensation*, Durham, NC: Duke University Press.

Panayi, P. (2008) *Spicing Up Britian: The Multicultural History of British Food*, London: Reaktion.

Pandya, V. (1993) *Above the Forest: A Study of Andamanese Ethnoanemology, Cosmology, and the Power of Ritual*, Delhi: Oxford University Press.

Parezco, N. (1983) *Navajo Sandpainting: From Religious Act to Commercial Art*, Tucson, AZ: University of Arizona Press.

Paterson, M. (2009) 'Haptic geographies: ethnography, haptic knowledges and sensuous dispositions', *Progress in Human Geography*, 33(6): 766–88.

Peet, H.P. (1857) *On the Legal Rights and Responsibilities of the Deaf and Dumb*, Richmond, VA: n.p.

Pepys, S. (1828) *Memoirs: Comprising His Diary From 1659 to 1669*, Vol. 3, ed. R. Braybrooke, London: Henry Colburn.

Peterson, R. (2003) *Settlements, Kinship and Hunting Grounds in Traditional Greenland: A Comparative Study of Local Experiences from Upernavik and Ammassalik*, trans. J. Manley, Copenhagen: Danish Polar Center.

Petkov, K. (2003) *The Kiss of Peace: Ritual, Self, and Society in the High and Late Medieval West*, Leiden: Brill.

Pine, B.J. and Gilmore, J.H. (1998) 'Welcome to the experience economy', *Harvard Business Review*, 76(4): 97–105.

Pink, S. (2009) *Doing Sensory Ethnography*, London: Sage.

Plunkett-Powell, K. (1999) *Remembering Woolworth's: A Nostalgic History of the World's Most Famous Five-and-Dime*, New York: St. Martin's Press.

Pocock, D. (1993) 'The senses in focus', *Area* 25(1): 11–16.

Porter, J. (1965) *The Vertical Mosaic: An Analysis of Social Class and Power in Canada*, Toronto: University of Toronto Press.

Porter, R. (1993) 'The rise of physical examination', in W.F. Bynum and R. Porter (eds) *Medicine and the Five Senses*, Cambridge: Cambridge University Press.

Posset, F. (2004) 'The palate of the heart in St. Augustine and medieval spirituality', in F. Van Fleteren and J.C. Schnaubelt (eds) *Augustine: Biblical Exegete*, New York: Peter Lang.

Postrel, V. (2003) *The Substance of Style*, New York: HarperCollins.

Potter, N. (2011) 'London riots 2011: violence caught on surveillance cameras', http://abcnews.go.com/Technology/london-riots-violence-caught-surveillance-cameras/story?id=14273894 (accessed January 15, 2013).

Pratt, J.W. and Mason, A. (1981) *The Caring Touch*, London: HM+M Publishers.

Quiviger, F. (2010) *The Sensory World of Italian Renaissance Art*, London: Reaktion Books.

Raffield, P. (2004) *Images and Cultures of Law in Early Modern England: Justice and Political Power, 1558–1660*, Cambridge: Cambridge University Press.

Ramachandran, V.S. (2011) *The Tell-Tale Brain: A Neuroscientist's Quest for What Makes Us Human*, New York: W.W. Norton & Co.

Ramachandran, V.S. and Hubbard, E.M. (2001) 'Synaesthesia – a window into perception, thought and language', *Journal of Consciousness Studies*, 8(12): 3–34.

Ramachandran, V.S., Hubbard, E.M. and Butcher, P.A. (2004) 'Synesthesia, cross-activation, and the foundations of neuroepistemology', in G. Calvert, C. Spence and B.E. Stein (eds) *The Handbook of Multisensory Processes*, Cambridge, MA: MIT Press.

Rapalje, S. (1887) *A Treatise on the Law of Witness*, New York: Banks and Brothers.

Rappaport, E.D. (2000) *Shopping for Pleasure: Women and the Making of London's West End*, Princeton, NJ: Princeton University Press.

——(forthcoming) 'The senses in the marketplace: stimulation and distraction, gratification and control', in C. Classen (ed.) *A Cultural History of the Senses in the Age of Empire, 1800–1920*, London: Bloomsbury.

Rappold, O.S. and Forbes, J.F. (1920) *Retail Training Service: A Vocational Training for Retail Salespeople*, New York: Retail Training Corporation.

Rawls, J. (1999) *A Theory of Justice*, Oxford: Oxford University Press.

Rée, J. (1999) *I See a Voice: Deafness, Language and the Senses – A Philosophical History*, New York: H. Holt and Co.

Reed, D. (2004) 'The transformation into spirit through a "constellation of arts": a Dan mask (*Tanké Ge*)', in F.J. Lamp (ed.) *See the Music, Hear the Dance: Rethinking African Art at the Baltimore Museum of Art*, New York: Prestel.

Reichel-Dolmatoff, G. (1981) 'Brain and mind in Desana shamanism', *Journal of Latin American Lore*, 7(1): 73–98.

——(1985) *Basketry as Metaphor: Arts and Crafts of the Desana Indians of the Northwest Amazon*, Los Angeles, CA: Museum of Cultural History, University of California.

Reiser, S.J. (1993) 'Technology and the use of the senses in twentieth-century medicine', in W.F. Bynum and R. Porter (eds) *Medicine and the Five Senses*, Cambridge: Cambridge University Press.

Resnik, J. and Curtis, D. (2011) *Representing Justice: Invention, Controversy, and Rights in City-States and Democratic Courtrooms*, New Haven, CT: Yale University Press.

Ribner, J.P. (1999) 'Law and justice in England and France: the view from Victorian London', in C. Douzinas and L. Nead (eds) *Law and the Image: The Authority of Art and the Aesthetics of Law*, Chicago, IL: University of Chicago Press.

Richards, G. (1998) 'Getting a result: the expedition's psychological research 1898–1913', in A. Herland and S. Rouse (eds) *Cambridge and the Torres Strait: Centenary Essays on the 1898 Anthropological Expedition*, Cambridge: Cambridge University Press.

Richardson, J.R. (1974) *Modern Scientific Evidence: Civil and Criminal*, Cincinnati, OH: W.H. Anderson.

Ritter, F.R. (1879) 'George Sand and Frédéric Chopin: a study', *Dwight's Journal of Music*, March 1.

Rivers, J. (2010) *The Law of Organized Religions: Between Establishment and Secularism*, Oxford: Oxford University Press.

Robben, A. and Slukka, J. (eds) (2007) *Ethnographic Fieldwork: An Anthropological Reader*, Oxford: Blackwell Publishing.

Robbins, R.H. (2008) *Global Problems and the Culture of Capitalism*, 4th edn, Boston: Pearson Education.

Roberts, D. (2011) *The Total Work of Art in European Modernism*, Ithaca, NY: Cornell University Press.

Roberts, K. (2005) *Lovemarks: The Future Beyond Brands*, New York: PowerHouse Books.

Roberts, L. (2005) 'The death of the sensuous chemist: the "new" chemistry and the transformation of sensuous technology', in D. Howes (ed.) *Empire of the Senses*, Oxford: Berg.

Robertson, J. (2002) 'Blood talks: eugenic modernity and the creation of new Japanese', *History and Anthropology*, 13(3): 191–216.

——(2012) 'Hemato-nationalism: the past, present, and future of "Japanese blood"', *Medical Anthropology*, 31(2): 93–112.

Rodaway, P. (1994) *Sensuous Geographies: Body, Sense, and Place*, London: Routledge.

Roeder, G.H. (1994) 'Coming to our senses', *Journal of American History*, 81: 1112–22.

Romberg, R. (2009) *Healing Dramas: Divination and Magic in Modern Puerto Rico*, Austin, TX: University of Texas Press.

Roseman, M. (1991) *Healing Sounds from the Malaysian Rainforest: Temiar Music and Medicine*, Berkeley, CA: University of California Press.

Rosenblum, L.D. (2010) *See What I'm Saying: The Extraordinary Powers of Our Five Senses*, New York: W.W. Norton & Company.

Ross, R. (2006) *Dancing with a Ghost: Exploring Aboriginal Reality*, Toronto: Penguin.

Ryan, M. (1997) 'Efficacy of the Tibetan treatment for arthritis', *Social Sciences & Medicine*, 44(4): 535–39.

Saad, G. (2011) *The Consuming Instinct: What Juicy Burgers, Ferraris, Pornography and Gift-Giving Reveal About Human Nature*, Amherst, NY: Prometheus Books.

Salomon, F. (2004) *The Cord Keepers: Khipus and Cultural Life in a Peruvian Village*, Durham, NC: Duke University Press.

Salter, C. (2010) *Entangled: Technology and the Transformation of Performance*, Cambridge, MA: MIT Press.

——(2012) 'Displace v. 2.0', http://chrissalter.com (accessed January 15, 2013).

Samuels, G.B. (1999) *Enduring Roots: Encounters with Trees, History and the American Landscape*, New Brunswick, NJ: Rutgers University Press.

Sandelowski, M. (2000) *Devices and Desires: Gender, Technology and American Nursing*, Chapel Hill, NC: University of North Carolina Press.

Schecter, F.L. (2008) *The Historical Foundation of the Law Relating to Trademarks*, Clark, NJ: The Lawbook Exchange Ltd.

Schott, G.D. (2004) 'The sick Dürer: a Renaissance prototype pain map', *British Medical Journal*, 329(7480): 1492.

Schott, R.M. (1988) *Cognition & Eros: A Critique of the Kantian Paradigm*, Boston, MA: Beacon Press.

Schrader, L. (1975) *Sensacion y sinesthesi*, Madrid: Editorial Gredos.

Schrempf, M.F. (2007) 'Bon lineage doctors and the local transmission of knowing medical practice in Nagchu', in M.F. Schrempf (ed.) *Sounding Tibetan Medicine: Anthropological and Historical Perspectives*, Leiden: Brill.

Schwartzman, M. (2011) *See Yourself Sensing: Redefining Human Perception*, London: Black Dog Publishing.

Seaberg, M. (2011) *Tasting the Universe: People Who See Colors in Words and Rainbows in Symphonies*, Pompton Plains, NJ: Career Press.

Selim, S. (2004) *The Novel and the Rural Imaginary in Egypt, 1880–1985*, London: Routledge.

Sen, S. (2005) 'The imperial touch: schooling male bodies in India, part II', in C. Classen (ed.) *The Book of Touch*, Oxford: Berg.

Serres, M. (1985) *Les cinq sens: philosophie des corps mêlés*, Paris: Grasset

——(2008) *The Five Senses: A Philosophy of Mingled Bodies*, trans. M. Sankey and P. Cowley, London: Continuum

Seus, J.M. (1969) 'Aztec law', *American Bar Association Journal*, 55: 736–39.

Shaw, J.E. and Welch, E.S. (2011) *The Making and Marketing of Medicaments in Renaissance Florence*, Amsterdam: Rotopi.

Shah, K. and D'Souza, A. (2009) *Advertising and Promotion*, New Delhi: Tata McGraw-Hill.

Sharer, R.J. (2006) *The Ancient Maya*, Stanford, CA: Stanford University Press.

Sheldon, R. and Arens, E. (1932) *Consumer Engineering: A New Technique for Prosperity*, New York: Harper.

Shimojo, S. and Shams, L. (2001) 'Sensory modalities are not separate modalities: plasticity and interactions', *Current Opinion in Neurobiology*, 11: 505–9.

Sichel, M. (1985) 'Air pollution – smoke and odor damage', in *The Jewish Law Annual*, Vol. 5, Leiden: Brill.

Silverman, R.A. (2004) 'The olfactory', in F.J. Lamp (ed.) *See the Music, Hear the Dance: Rethinking African Art at the Baltimore Museum of Art*, New York: Prestel.

Simner, J. and Holenstein, E. (2007) 'Ordinal linguistic personification as a variant of synaesthesia', *Journal of Cognitive Neuroscience*, 19(4).

Simner, J. et al. (2006) 'Synaesthesia: the prevalence of atypical cross-modal experiences', *Perception*, 35(8): 1024–33.

Skeates, R. (2010) *An Archaeology of the Senses: Prehistoric Malta*, Oxford: Oxford University Press.

Smilor, R.W. (2004) 'American noise, 1899–1930', in M.M. Smith (ed.) *Hearing History: A Reader*, Atlanta, GA: University of Georgia Press.

Smith, A.D. (1998) *Nationalism and Modernism: A Critical Survey of Recent Theories of Nations and Nationalism*, London: Routledge.

Smith, J.G. (1825) *An Analysis of Medical Evidence*, London: Thomas and George Underwood.

Smith, M.M. (2006) *How Race is Made: Slavery, Segregation, and the Senses*, Chapel Hill, NC: University of North Carolina Press.

——(2007) *Sensing the Past: Seeing, Hearing, Smelling, Tasting, and Touching History*, Berkeley: University of California Press.

——(2008) 'Getting in touch with slavery and freedom', *Journal of American History*, 95: 381–91

——(2012) 'Transcending, othering, detecting: smell, premodernity, modernity', *Postmedieval: A Journal of Medieval Cultural Studies*, 3(4): 380–90.

Solomon, M. (2010) *Sensory Marketing: Smells Like Profits*, Upper Saddle River, NJ: FT Press.

Sprow, M.A. (2000) 'Wake up and smell the contraband: why courts that do not find probable cause based on odor alone are wrong', *William and Mary Law Review* 42(1): 289–318.

Starkie, E. (1968) *Arthur Rimbaud*, New York: New Directions.

Sternberg, E.M. (2009) *Healing Spaces: The Science of Place and Well-being*, Cambridge, MA: Harvard University Press.

Stevenson, R.J. and Boakes, R. (2004) 'Sweet and sour smells: learned synaesthesia between the senses of taste and smell', in G. Calvert, C. Spence and B.E. Stein (eds) *The Handbook of Multisensory Processes*, Cambridge, MA: MIT Press.

Stevenson, R.M. (1968) *Music in Aztec and Inca Territory*, Berkeley, CA: University of California Press.

Stoller, P. (1989) *The Taste of Ethnographic Things: The Senses in Anthropology*, Philadelphia, PA: University of Pennsylvania Press.

——(1997) *Sensuous Scholarship*, Philadelphia, PA: University of Pennsylvania Press.

Stronach, B. (1995) *Beyond the Rising Sun: Nationalism in Contemporary Japan*, Westport, CT: Praeger Publishers.

Sturken, M. and Cartwright, L. (2009) *Practices of Looking: An Introduction to Visual Culture*. Oxford: Oxford University Press.

Suhartono, H. (2011) 'Singaporeans' culinary anti-immigration protest: curry', Reuters, 11 April.

Sullivan, L.E. (1986) 'Sound and senses: toward a hermeneutics of performance', *History of Religions*, 26(1) 1–33.

Synnott, A. (1993) *The Body Social: Symbolism, Self and Society*, London: Routledge

Templarius (1830) 'Forms of oath among various nations', *The Gentleman's Magazine and Historical Chronicle*, 23(2).

Tester, S.J. (1987) *A History of Western Astrology*, Woodbridge: Boydell Press.

Thomas, K. (2005) 'Magical healing: the King's touch', in C. Classen (ed.) *The Book of Touch*, Oxford: Berg.

Thompson, E. (2005) 'Sound of the city', in M. Zardini (ed.) *Sense of the City: An Alternative Approach to Urbanism*, Montreal: Canadian Centre for Architecture.

Thornbury, W. (1881) *Old and New London: The City Ancient and Modern*, London: Cassell, Petter, Galpin & Co.

Thorndike, L. (1934) *A History of Magic and Experimental Science*, 3 vols, New York: Columbia University Press.

Tickner, L. (1988) *The Spectacle of Women: Imagery of the Suffrage Campaign 1907–14*, Chicago, IL: University of Chicago Press.

Tobin, J.J. (1992) 'Introduction: domesticating the West', in J.J. Tobin (ed.) *Re-made in Japan: Everyday Life and Consumer Taste in a Changing Society*, New Haven, CT: Yale University Press.

Toombs, M. (2012) *Odour Control on Livestock and Poultry Farms*, Toronto: Ontario Ministry of Agriculture and Food.

Tristan, F. (1993) *Flora Tristan: Utopian Feminist, Her Travel Diaries & Personal Crusade*, ed. and trans. D. and P. Beik, Bloomington, IN: Indiana University Press.

——(2003) *Peregrinaciones de una paria*, Lima: Fond. Editorial UNMSM.

Trnka, S., Dureau, C. and Park, J. (eds) (2013) *Senses and Citizenships: Embodying Political Life*, London: Routledge.

Trosper, R. (2009) *Resilience, Reciprocity and Ecological Economics: Northwest Coast Sustainability*, Oxford: Routledge.

Twain, Mark. (2003) *Mark Twain's San Francisco*, ed. B. Taper, Berkeley, CA: Heyday Books.

Tyler, J.E. (1835) *Oaths: Their Origin, Nature and History*, London: John W. Parker.

Urton, G. (1997) *The Social Life of Numbers: A Quechua Ontology of Numbers and Philosophy of Arithmetic*, with the collaboration of Primitivo Nina Llanos, Austin: University of Texas Press.

——(2003) *Signs of the Inca Khipu: Binary Coding in Andean Knotted String Records*, Austin, TX: University of Texas Press.

Vallas, L. (1967) *The Theories of Claude Debussy*, trans. M. O'Brien, New York: Dover Publications.

van Campen, C. (2010) *The Hidden Sense: Synaesthesia in Art and Science*, Cambridge, MA: MIT Press.

van Gorp, T. and Adams, E. (2012) *Design for Emotion*, Waltham, MA: Morgan Kaufmann.

van Loon, J. (2008) *Media Technology: Critical Perspectives*, Maidenhead: Open University Press.

van Rooj, B. (2006) *Regulating Land and Pollution in China: Lawmaking, Compliance, and Enforcement: Theory and Cases*, Leiden: Leiden University Press.

Vannini, P., Waskul, D. and Gottschalk, S. (2011) *The Senses in Self, Society, and Culture: A Sociology of the Senses*, London: Routledge.

von La Roche, S. (1933) *Sophie in London, 1786: Being the Diary of Sophie v. La Roche*, London: J. Cape.

von Tschudi, J.J. (1847) *Travels in Peru*, London: David Bogue.

Vroomen, J. and de Gelder, B. (2004) 'Perceptual effects of cross-modal stimulation', in G. Calvert, C. Spence and B. Stein (eds) *The Handbook of Multisensory Processes*, Cambridge, MA: MIT Press.

Wa, G. and Uukw, D. (1989) *The Spirit in the Land: The Opening Statement of the Gitksan and Wet'suwet'en Hereditary Chiefs in the Supreme Court of British Columbia May 11, 1987*, Gabriola, BC: Reflections Press.

Wade, N. (2009) 'The search for a sixth sense: the cases for vestibular, muscle and temperature senses', in D. Howes (ed.) *The Sixth Sense Reader*, Oxford: Berg.

Walker, S., Spohn, C. and Delone, M. (2009) *The Color of Justice: Race, Ethnicity, and Crime in America*, Belmont, CA: Wadsworth Cengage Learning.

Walpole, H. (1861) *The Letters of Horace Walpole, Earl of Oxford*, Vol. VII, ed. P. Cunningham, London: Henry G. Bohn.

Wang, A. (2000) *Cosmology and Political Order in Early China*, Cambridge: Cambridge University Press.

Wear, A. (2000) *Knowledge and Practice in English Medicine, 1550–1680*, Cambridge: Cambridge University Press.

——(2003) 'Puritan perceptions of illness in seventeenth-century England', in R. Porter (ed.) *Patients and Practitioners: Lay Perceptions of medicine in Pre-Industrial England*, Cambridge: Cambridge University Press.

Weber, E. (1976) *Peasants into Frenchmen: The Modernization of Rural France, 1870–1914*, Stanford, CA: Stanford University Press.

Weiner, I. (2009) 'Religion out loud: religious sound, public space, and American pluralism', unpublished thesis, University of North Carolina at Chapel Hill.

Weiner, M. (1997) 'The invention of identity in pre-war Japan', in F. Dikotter (ed.) *The Construction of Racial Identities in China and Japan*, Honolulu, HI: University of Hawaii Press.

Weinberg, S. (1994) *Dreams of a Final Theory: The Scientist's Search for the Ultimate Laws of Nature*, New York: Vintage.

Wenk, A. B. (1976) *Claude Débussy and the Poets*, Berkeley, CA: University of California Press.

Weygand, Z. (2009) *The Blind in French Society: From the Middle Ages to the Century of Louis Braille*, trans. E.-J. Cohen, Stanford, CA: Stanford University Press.

Wildburger, E. (2013) 'Indigenous Australian art in practice and theory', *Coolabah*, 10: 202–12.

Williams, F.E. (1923) *The Collection of Curios and the Preservation of Native Culture*, Port Moresby, Papua New Guinea: E.G. Baker.

Williams, G. (1975) *The Ages of Agony: The Art of Healing 1700–1800*, London: Constable.

Wilson, A.H. (1993) *The Meaning of International Experience for Schools*, Westport, CT: Praeger.

Wiseman, B. (2010) 'Sensing others', *The Senses & Society*, 5(2): 250–53.

Witherspoon, G. (1977) *Language and Art in the Navajo Universe*, Ann Arbor, MI: University of Michigan Press.

Witthoft, N. and Winawer, J. (2013) 'Learning, memory and synesthesia', *Psychological Science*, 24(3): 258–65.

Wober, M. (1991 [1967]) 'The sensotype hypothesis', in D. Howes (ed.) *The Varieties of Sensory Experience*, Toronto: University of Toronto Press.

Wollheim, R. (1991) 'What the spectator sees', in N. Bryson, M.A. Holly and K. Moxey (eds) *Visual Theory: Painting and Interpretation*, London: Polity Press.

Wood, W.M. (1849) *Wandering Sketches of People and Things in South America*, Philadelphia, PA: Carey and Hart.

Woolworth & Co. (1954) *Woolworth's First 75 Years: The Story of Everyone's Store*, New York: Rudge and Sons.

Wootton, D. (2006) *Bad Medicine: Doctors Doing Harm since Hippocrates*, Oxford: Oxford University Press.

Work, A. (2011) 'Child support judge to get a larger room', *The Times Record News*, www.timesrecordnews.come/news/2011/apr/05/courthouse-renovations-child-support-judgeto-get (accessed January 15, 2013).

Yates, F. (2011) *The Art of Memory*, London: Pimilco.

Young, D. (2005) 'The smell of green-ness: cultural synaesthesia in the Western Desert (Australia)', *Etnofoor* 18(1): 61–77.

Yu, N. (2009) *The Chinese Heart in a Cognitive Perspective: Culture, Body, and Language*, Berlin: Mouton de Gruyter.

Zaltman, G. (2003) *How Customers Think: Essential Insights into the Mind of the Market*, Cambridge, MA: Harvard Business Review Press.

Zampini, M. and Spence, C. (2004) 'The role of auditory cues in modulating the perceived crispness and staleness of potato chips', *Journal of Sensory Science*, 19: 347–63.

Zardini, M. (ed.) (2005) *Sense of the City: An Alternate Approach to Urbanism*, Montreal: Canadian Centre for Architecture.

Index